For Doris

The Individuality of
PORTUGAL

The Individuality of
PORTUGAL

A Study in Historical-Political Geography

BY DAN STANISLAWSKI

University of Texas Press, Austin

Requests for permission to reproduce material from this work
should be sent to:
  Permissions
  University of Texas Press
  P.O. Box 7819
  Austin, TX 78713-7819
  http://utpress.utexas.edu/index.php/rp-form

Library of Congress Catalog Number 59-8119

ISBN 978-1-4773-0507-2, paperback
ISBN 978-1-4773-0508-9, library e-book
ISBN 978-1-4773-0509-6, individual e-book

*Originally published with the assistance of a grant from the Ford Foundation under its
Program for the Support of Publications in the Humanities and Social Sciences*

Acknowledgments

I AM GRATEFUL to the John Simon Guggenheim Memorial Foundation and to the Social Science Research Council for the material aid given to me for the field work that preceded the writing of this book.

Many individuals have been generous in reading parts or all of the manuscript: Carl O. Sauer, John B. Leighly, and Raymond I. Storie of the University of California at Berkeley; Jan O. M. Broek of the University of Minnesota; Billie Lee Turner of the University of Texas; and Júlio Caro Baroja of the Museo del Pueblo Español, Madrid, Spain. None of them, however, should be penalized for their generosity by blame for any errors in my conclusions, or other deficiencies.

Very special gratitude goes to my wife for the great help that she has given me through all stages of inquiry and the preparation of the book.

I am indebted to the Instituto do Vinho do Porto for the photograph of the Douro River canyon that is used.

To the dozens of other Portuguese and Spaniards who so generously helped me I offer my thanks. The list is too long to print.

D. S.

Contents

Photographs

Figures

The Individuality of
PORTUGAL

Figure 1. Iberia

IBERIA - PLACE NAMES

Introduction

N THE PRESENT state of world affairs, it is not uncommon for cynical representatives of great powers to
sketch boundaries of new small states on flat maps,
ignoring the peoples involved, their wishes, or their
habitual associations. Perhaps the average person, thinking of
Western Europe, is apt to assume that in a world of quick and
radical change most small states have been established in this
way. It is often overlooked that there are durable states, with
persistent boundaries that represent more than mere colored
outlines in an atlas, whose frontiers mark the limits, not only
of an area of land, but of a population that has long been associated with that territory. The habits and values of such people
have been established in relation to the land upon which they
have lived, to the climate affecting it, and to the soils and
vegetation that respond to a complex of factors belonging to
that specific territory. Economy, transport, and human associations of all sorts become involved with the specific milieu and
are to some extent limited by it.

The populations of neighboring states, which have developed

under variant physical and historical conditions, have become associated with their land through an individual set of cultural practices which, though useful where they have evolved, may not be fitting elsewhere. In short, culture has roots, not only in men's minds, but in the land upon which it develops. Once having taken shape, a culture complex thrives best in its own type of surroundings. When peoples migrate, taking with them their attitudes and values, they choose areas for settlement that broadly meet their habitual needs, areas that are physically reminiscent of that from which they came.

However, culture is not a static thing. It is always changing. Although in a conservative area the trend and degree of change may be imperceptible to any one generation, it is rapid and obvious with migration. No matter how diligently a human group may seek lands which are precisely the same as those from which it came, success can be only partial. No piece of land is exactly the same as a second, any more than one man is the exact duplicate of another. Migrants make adjustments in their new environment, and in so doing create new values and attitudes. Thus the new territory is the birthplace of a new culture group, related to that of the older territory, yet with its own distinct characteristics.

This book is concerned with Portugal, but Portugal is a small part of a semi-isolated peninsula which seems to be, and is, in many respects, a natural unit. Yet a Portuguese is not a Spaniard. No Portuguese would say otherwise, and probably few foreigners who know both nations would disagree. Spaniards, however, may take exception to such a statement, for the belief is traditional in Spain that the unitary quality of the peninsula is the important fact and that differences are negligible. Spaniards point to physical areas common to both Spain and to Portugal and to the mutually shared historical experiences under the Romans, the Visigoths, and the Moslems. In view of these facts, they say it is culturally contradictory, economically disadvantageous, and politically inexpedient that one small section be divorced from the rest of the peninsula. The Portuguese reply to the Spanish contention is apt to be something like this—"Of course we are part of the peninsula, and we obviously share common peninsular traits with Spaniards, but the peninsula is not homogeneous. Our part of it is unique, and our habits and attitudes are distinct. We make up an independent unit with good reason."

As a part of the peninsula, Portugal has shared with Spain both physical areas and cultural experiences, the latter especially in prehistory and in early historical times. These cultural experiences are profoundly important to both nations, and the evidence of their importance is still to be found on both sides of the political border. In an attempt to describe the unique personality of the Portuguese state it will be necessary to describe, as a part of that personality, the introduction and development of many of the cultural qualities that belong also to Spain. But Portugal is unique, and in stating this one has also said that Spain is unique. Each one may be distinct either by its own unique experiences or by the lack of the experiences of the other. The problem of Portuguese individuality must be attacked not only through a study of Portugal, but also in seeking the fundamental bases of individuality and uniqueness in Spain as well. In limited fashion, but sufficiently to establish Iberian differences, it is hoped, the physical and historical conditions of Spain will be treated. For example, one chapter of this book is devoted largely to Greek trade along the coasts of the area of present Spain, and in it hardly a word is said about Portugal. This is necessary, for a unique Spain is part of the evolution of a disparate Portugal. That Portugal took almost no part in Greek trade is as important to its distinction as is the earlier "castro" or hilltop fort culture that was mostly Portuguese and Spanish only in minor degree.

The question must be answered, however, as to how Portugal came to a sense of its own distinct character, and then, conscious of its individuality, was able to establish its independence from the other four-fifths of the peninsula. Is Portugal clearly different from Spain physically? If so, what has been the effect of this difference upon the development of culture regions? Or are those Portuguese authors correct who claim that their country is a unit only because of the accidents of history, or the inspiration and determination of individual leaders?

The problem would be far simpler if the Portuguese, in almost complete unanimity as to their individuality, did not differ so widely as to its genesis. Divergent opinions are almost as numerous as the individuals expressing them. In the middle of the nineteenth century, the great Portuguese historian, Alexandre Herculano, maintained with vigor that credit should be given to Portuguese nobles and kings, whose personal decisions led to the political independence of Portugal.[1] His conclusion was commonly accepted throughout the latter nineteenth century, and indeed has strong support today. Professor Aristides de Amorim Girão, the eminent geographer at the University of Coimbra, says flatly that the strong arms of the early Portuguese are to receive credit, and that the physical nature of the area has had little or nothing to do with the case.[2]

Other scholars in late years have supported quite another point of view. Many believe that there are important physical differences which, although not compulsive, have contributed substantially to the Portuguese individuality finally reflected in independence. Hermann Lautensach, the German geographer, who has worked long and productively in Portugal, conceives of Portugal as being distinct geomorphologically, in the complex of its vegetation, in climate, in population distribution, and in other factors essentially based upon a unique physical nature. He would make no claims for an environmental determinism, but points to what he believes to be an especial physical constitution in Portugal that was the foundation upon which a discrete culture area developed.[3]

[1] Alexandre Herculano, *História de Portugal* (7th ed.), I, 36–40.

[2] A. de Amorim Girão, *Condicões geográficas e históricas da autonomia política de Portugal,* pp. 19–20, 30; "Imposibilidade de sustentar pela geografia a separação política entre Portugal e Espanha," *Biblos,* V (1929), 304–314; "Origines de l'état Portugais," *Revue Géographique des Pyrénées et du Sud-Ouest,* XI, Nos. 3–4 (1940), 155–158.

[3] Anyone concerned with the geography of Portugal should, at the outset, express gratitude to Hermann Lautensach for his many excellent

It is not a simple problem to compare and assess the opposing contentions and to try to reach a reasonable conclusion as to merits and deficiencies. Many things are involved—more, obviously, than can be properly handled by one author, and many more than can be satisfactorily treated in one book. So I shall make no attempt to fit within the accustomed categories "historical geography" or "political geography." Especially in the case of political geography I shall not attempt to consider many of the materials that are conventionally used, since they are not, in my opinion, pertinent to the subject of the book—Portuguese individuality.

The Portuguese state is the logical expression of a unique culture area which had evolved early in history and took clearly defined form before the sixteenth century. For this reason, economic and historical development prior to that time will be given the most attention. The materials used will be those which seem to have the greatest bearing upon the problem and which offer most aid to its understanding.

This study will maintain the point of view that there was a culture area in the northwest of the peninsula distinct from that of the interior, and that although a human decision was the immediate cause of Portuguese political independence, such a decision would have been fruitless had there not been

publications. With reference to the ideas expressed in this introduction see the following: "Geopolitisches von der Spanisch-Portugiesischen Grenze," *Zeitschrift für Geopolitik*, V (1928), 371–374 (in this article he forswears any complete dependence of the political unit upon "natural" factors; see especially p. 372); "Die Iberische Halbinsel als Schauplatz der geschichtlichen Bewegung," *Zeitschrift der Gesellschaft für Erdkunde zu Berlin*, Nos. 3–4 (June, 1948), pp. 101–123, especially p. 120; "Lebensraumfragen der Iberischen Völker," *Lebensraumfragen Europäischer Völker*, I, *Europa*, 493–536, especially p. 509; "Der politische Dualismus der Iberischen Halbinsel," *Zeitschrift für Geopolitik*, VI, No. 2 (1929), 782–788. In many of his articles, Lautensach specifically disavows a crude environmentalism. However, it is impossible for a reader not to infer from his selection and treatment of materials his belief in the fundamental importance of physical factors. This attitude is even more obvious in his "A Individualidade geográfica de Portugal no conjunto da Península Ibérica," *Boletim da Sociedade de Geografia de Lisboa*, XLIX (1931), 362–409.

8

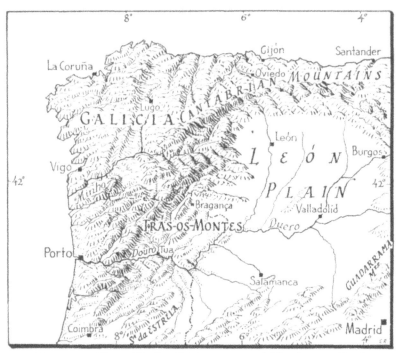

Figure 2. "Rain-Shadow" Mountains of Northwest Iberia

persistent historical and cultural differences between the northwest periphery and the great interior tableland, the *meseta*.
It was in the northwest, where physical differences between
the *meseta* and the Atlantic border are the most obvious, that
the culture hearth and the political state of Portugal were first
established. (Fig. 2.) To understand the development of Portuguese individuality this fact must always be kept in mind. The
south is a later appendage, and the thesis that physical differences are basic to present political differences cannot be maintained for this region, as political factors may have had greater
importance there.

Although the association of physical areas with culture
regions will be made, there will be no attempt to support the
view that the physical area inspired or compelled culture
growth. All of Iberia has been affected by numerous migratory

groups. It will be the contention of this book that, insofar as we know, these migratory groups have selected areas suitable to their values, experience, and habits of use and wont. In short, selection has been made in terms of environmental suitability to technological equipment and habitual preferences.

Central Europeans migrating into the Iberian peninsula have made their greatest mark upon the rainy northern and northwestern regions of Iberia, areas similar to those from which they came. Mediterranean migrants from either Europe or Africa who moved into Iberia concentrated in the lands fringing the sea. This fact gives a large degree of physical unity—and considerable cultural unity—to its bordering shores. However, in Iberia there is a great body of land lying between the green north and northwest and that southern fringing area which can be called Mediterranean. This great central tableland, the *meseta*, is a blend of Europe and Africa. The concept that "Africa ends at the Pyrenees" is not without merit, but to avoid distortion one might also add that Europe ends at the Sierra Morena, just to the north of the Guadalquivir River. The *meseta* is a world in itself. Its climate is unique in Europe. The blend of European with African cultures has created a culture both complex and unique. Perhaps it is the mixture of Central European and Mediterranean (both European and African Mediterranean) cultures in the *meseta* that has made it—bleak, harsh, and sparsely populated as it is—the center of control of Iberia through much of the time since the breakdown of Rome.

Cultural differences between Mediterranean Iberia (the south and northeast) and Central European Iberia (the north and northwest) reach beyond historical or archaeological evidence. But insofar as we have knowledge, they seem to have always been equated in their distribution with the major physical differences within the peninsula. As the association of physical areas with culture groups will be stressed, it should be well to outline, at the outset, those traits of the physical landscape that have bearing upon the subject, such as topography, climate, soils, and vegetation. In dealing with them it should be remembered that Portugal is the subject of primary interest—especially northwest Portugal where the state took form—and that other areas are considered only when they have bearing upon the major concern. Later chapters dealing with historical development will also treat the northwest as the center of attention.

CHAPTER 1

Landforms of Northwest
and West Iberia

T HE HIGHLAND rim extending continuously from the eastern Pyrenees across northern Spain and southward into northern Portugal has a distinct physical character and, through its effect upon climate, creates a distinct character for the *meseta*. The surface form of the great central tableland is relatively simple and for the purposes of this study need not concern us. The landforms of the northwest, however, especially those in the north of present Portugal, must be considered in some detail, for this area is pertinent to our problem.

THE MINHO PROVINCE

The most important fact of North Portuguese landform is its seaward slope. This orientation is most obvious in the province of the Minho, where mountains to the east (the Peneda, Gerez, Cabreira, Alvão, Marão, and Montemuro) form an amphitheater facing the Atlantic Ocean (Fig. 3. See Fig. 1 for additional place names). Such heights allow northwest

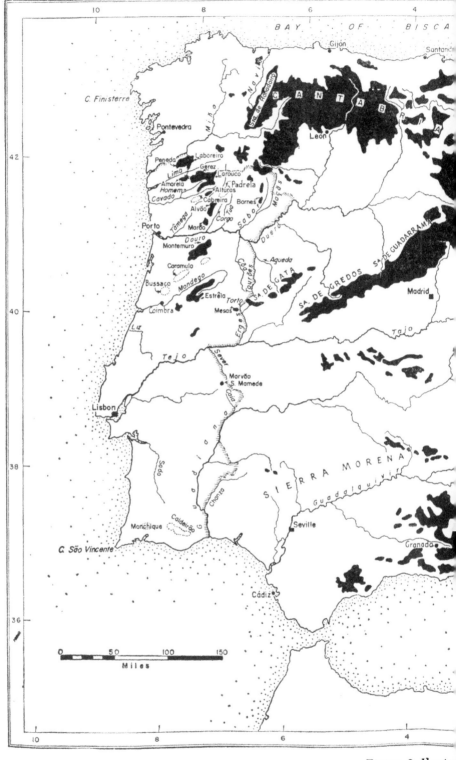

Figure 3. Iberia

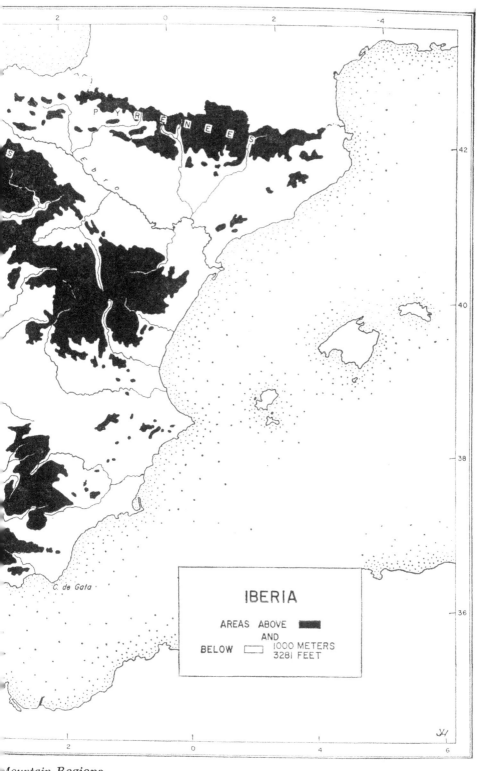

IBERIA

AREAS ABOVE ▬
AND
BELOW ☐ 1000 METERS
3281 FEET

Mountain Regions

Portugal to turn its back upon the *meseta* of Spain. Due not only to their elevation but also to their geologic and tectonic history, they represent an area of limited usefulness and sparse population. Here events of nearly three hundred million years ago cast their shadow upon present human affairs. The general area is one of Hercynian folding, which resulted not only in the metamorphosis of existing rocks but also in great intrusions of granite.[1] Late Tertiary re-elevation and subsequent erosion resulted in the complete exposure of the ancient crystallines and granites along a line making a gentle arc, convex toward the sea, from near La Coruña, running south-southeastward through the areas of Vila Real and Guarda in Portugal and into Spain near Alcántara. It is also a zone of shatter breaks marked by lines of thermal springs, especially in the granites.

In this part of Iberia, geology has no relation to the political boundary. A granite massif extends from the west border of Asturias through Galicia and thence southward through the province of the Minho. South of the Douro River it is buried along the coast by later (post-Paleozoic) sediments, but inland it continues as a surface feature almost to the city of Coimbra. This massif in Galicia forms an amorphous mass, but its projections extending into Portugal take clear form as crests roughly parallel to each other, running in a south-southwest direction (Peneda, Gerez, Alturas, Alvão). The Minhotos call these collectively *as Montanhas* (the Mountains), one of the subdivisions that they make of their province. Paralleling these ridges, the rivers run in their deeply trenched valleys, the Lima, the

---

[1] In this chapter I have used material from the following works of Hermann Lautensach: 1. "A Individualidade geográfica de Portugal no conjunto da Península Ibérica," *Boletim da Sociedade de Geografia de Lisboa*, XLIX (1931); "Portugal: Auf Grund eigener Reisen und der Literatur." 1. "Das Land als Ganzes," *Petermann's Mitteilungen*, No. 213 (Gotha, 1932); 2. "Die portugiesischen Landschaften," *ibid.*, No. 230 (Gotha, 1937).

I have made use also of materials from Orlando Ribeiro, *Portugal;* from A. de Amorim Girão, *Geografia de Portugal;* from Pierre Birot, *Le Portugal;* and from Mariano Feio, *A Evolução do relevo do baixo Alentejo e Algarve.*

Lima River in Portugal, Not Far from the Spanish Border

Cávado, the Homem, and the Tâmega. A typical phenomenon of the Minho Province is that of a broad, flat valley floor lying sharply against steep bordering slopes. The form and the parallelism of the valleys suggest tectonic derivation—and the horsts of Marão and Padrela at the eastern edge seem to confirm it—but the genesis is largely of another sort. The forms are simply the result of the typical erosional development of granite in northwest Portugal. Here, either along fault lines or in rejuvenated valleys the process of river erosion widens the floor without reducing the angle of slopes, which recede parallel to their earlier position.[2]

Seaward from the granite crests is an area of low valleys, called *o Centro* (the Center), irregular in shape and size and partially enclosed by granite spurs. It is a fertile area of dense settlement and the core of Portuguese nationality. The Coast is the third division which a Minhoto makes of his province. It is an emergent coast, with a narrow beach sloping gradually upward to the slight eminences just a few miles inland, against which the waves of the Pliocene sea washed.

TRÁS-OS-MONTES PROVINCE

The Minho shares with its eastern neighboring province the mountains described above. These heights form the physical division—topographic and climatic, with all that this implies in human terms—between the green Minho Province and its eastern neighbor, the aptly named province of Trás-os-Montes.[3] The latter, lying in the lee of the mountains, in the northeast of Portugal, is bordered on two sides by Spain and physically is an extension of the Spanish *meseta*. However, it has characteristics peculiarly its own. Unlike the Spanish peneplane with its low relief and Tertiary cover, the high, partly dissected

[2] Orlando Ribeiro, *Portugal*, pp. 19–23, 31.

[3] That is, "on the other side of the mountains." The name properly implies the history of the province with regard to the earlier establishment of the Minho as a political center and the later adherence of Trás-os-Montes.

Tua River in Trás-os-Montes

The Duero River at Zamora

plateau on the Portuguese side of the border is constituted largely by Pre-Cambrian materials, and is deeply incised by its rivers, which have carved canyons up to sixteen hundred feet deep into the ancient crystalline rocks. In addition to this difference in the effect of the rivers, there is the feature of unreduced remnants of former elevations, which project high above the peneplane surface on the Portuguese side of the border.

RIVERS AND THEIR EFFECT UPON HUMAN AFFAIRS

The Spanish Duero flows lazily westward to beyond Zamora; and its tributaries, also leisurely streams, come into it from the east-southeast or from the northwest. At Paradela, where it becomes international (the Douro, in Portugal),[4] it suddenly bends to the southwest, cutting violently into the old plateau surface, dropping over sixteen hundred feet during the next seventy-six miles. To the west of the canyon, the right bank

---

[4] For the international streams both the Portuguese and the Spanish names will be given in the first reference. In subsequent references the spelling will be suited to the area under discussion.

e Duero (Douro) River Where It Is the Boundary between Portugal and Spain

Bragança and the High Plains of Trás-os-Montes

tributaries in Trás-os-Montes roughly parallel the international stream, and are separated from each other by northeast-southwest trending crests. This change in direction and degree of slope of mountains and rivers is a phenomenon of the zone of northeast Portugal that borders León.

Because of the position of the highland areas, most of the streams of Portugal north of the Douro are purely Portuguese streams. There is an important Spanish section of the Minho River (Miño, in Spain), which has its sources in the northern mountains of Galicia. The Lima (Limia, in Spain) River runs for approximately half of its course in southern Galicia and enters Portugal through the sharply cut canyon between the *serras* of Peneda and Amarela. The Tâmega also has a portion of its course in Galicia, in the region of the town of Verín. This stretch, however, is but a few miles long and is separated from the rest of Galicia by relatively high country. Aside from these three streams, all others have their sources either within Portugal or on the south slope of the mountains along the frontier. The valleys of the streams are narrow and of limited, if any, usefulness near their headwaters, but they widen downstream.

The fact that all of the Trás-os-Montes streams cut deep canyons into the old plateau surface is not only of physiographic but also of economic and political significance, for these valley bottoms, where they are wide enough for use, with advantageous climatic conditions, are ribbons of fertility in an otherwise meagre territory. Their topographic gradient is also their economic and political gradient. Routes to the west are open, whereas all are blocked to the east and north, either by high mountains or by narrow canyons, where the turbulent streams make navigation impossible and where cultivable land is absent (e.g., the Douro between Paradela and Barca d'Alva, and the international Maçás, in Spain, the Manzanas). The economic current, by reason of these facts, is westward, away from the Spanish border and toward the Portuguese lowland.

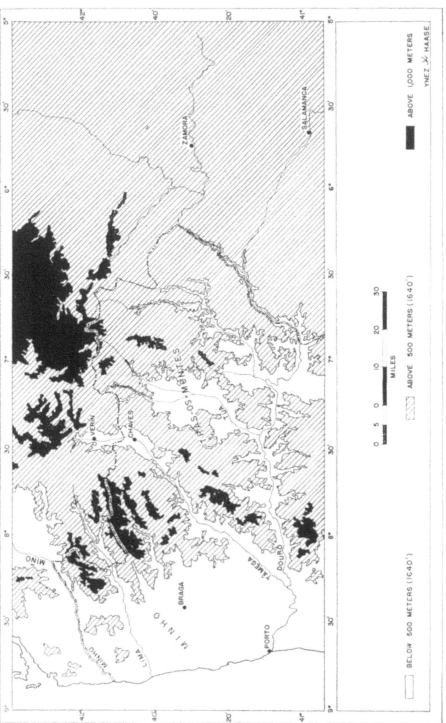

Figure 4. Northern Portugal and Adjacent Regions of Spain

THE EXTENSION OF NORTHERN ROCKS AND FORMS
INTO MIDDLE PORTUGAL; UPPER BEIRA

The rocks and landforms of the Minho extend southward
beyond the Douro River to a point north of the city of Coimbra,
where the granite Caramulo, whose northeast-southwest strike
is that of its counterparts in the northern province, marks their
termination. This brings the rocks and landforms of the Mountains of the Minho Province well into the drainage of the
Mondego River of Middle Portugal. However, not only the
Mountains of the Minho extend south of the Douro River; the
Center of the Minho also is extended recognizably as the low
mountain-girt valleys of the Beiras; and a short stretch of coast
to the south of the Douro River is a southern extension of the
Coast of the Minho.

Most of Middle Portugal is included in the Beira provinces,
so named (Beira means border) because the lands south of the
Douro River were frontiers during the period of reconquest
and resettlement (ninth to twelfth centuries) which stemmed
from the early Portuguese nucleus in the Minho. Likewise, they
form the frontier of Trás-os-Montes, and here also one can
recognize a southern companion-piece to the northern province. The heart of Upper Beira (that part of the Beiras lying
to the northwest of the great dividing range, the Serra da
Estrêla) is an elevated plain, partly dissected by the streams
of the Mondego system. Although the carving of the streams
has been vigorous, it has not destroyed the essential unity of
interfluvial surfaces. Like Trás-os-Montes, this high plain is an
extension of the *meseta* of Old Castile. Also, like its northern
neighbor, it differs from the Spanish area in the form of its
stream valleys.

The Agueda River, a left-bank tributary of the Duero, takes
its northwesterly course through the high plateau of Old Castile in leisurely fashion, comparable to that of the Spanish
Duero. At the frontier it has cut an even steeper gradient than
the Duero into the ancient rocks before the two streams meet
above Barca d'Alva. (In fifteen miles the Agueda drops nearly

eight hundred feet for an average decline of approximately fifty-two feet per mile compared with twenty-one feet per mile for the international Duero.) The valley of the Côa River, another left-bank tributary of the Douro River, is called *terra quente* (hot country) by the Portuguese, a term used to describe such low, protected valleys which are favored by climatic conditions so different from those of the high plateau directly above them. The term is applied equally to the valley of the Sabor River in Trás-os-Montes, due north of the Côa, and to several others in each province. Most streams of the Beira meet the Douro in an acute angle as do those from the north. The exceptions on either side of the master-stream seem to be those directed by tectonics. For example, the Côa and its northern companion-piece, the Vilariça, tributary of the Sabor, flow almost due north and south respectively along fault lines. The high plain of the Beiras extends westward until it ends at the Bussaco Mountains, north-northeast of the city of Coimbra. On the northwest it is bounded by the mountains of Caramulo, Montemuro, and their extensions. On the southeast its boundary is the great fault line along which the Serra da Estrêla was raised.

Transmontane Beira

The northeastern section of Upper Beira, sometimes termed Transmontane Beira, is like Trás-os-Montes not only in that it is distant from the ocean, but also in that the effect of oceanic influence is diminished because of the mountain masses west of it. The area includes the drainage of the Côa River. Farther south, this Portuguese extension of the Spanish *meseta* continues through the so-called Guarda Gate, lying to the east of the city of Guarda, a high, bleak plateau surface, averaging almost three thousand feet in elevation, between the Serra da Estrêla on the west and the Sierra de Gata and its Portuguese relative, the Serra das Mesas, on the east. The Guarda Gate, like its Spanish companions, the Gates of Béjar and Avila, connects, without major topographic obstacle, the ancient erosion surface of the north *meseta* with that of the south.

LOWER BEIRA

About fifteen miles south of the latitude of the city of Guarda is the water parting between the affluents of the Douro River at the north and those of the Tejo River (Tajo, in Spain; Tagus, commonly on American and English maps) at the south. This divide is approximately at the northern boundary of the province of Lower Beira, most of which lies between the levels of sixteen hundred feet and seven hundred feet elevation. From its highest elevations, Lower Beira slopes southward to the Tejo River. As Upper Beira (or its eastern section known as Transmontane Beira) is a continuation of the plateau of Old Castile, Lower Beira is an extension into Portugal of Spanish New Castile; both provinces are transitional in character. Upper Beira reflects the traits of its nearest neighbors, the Minho and Trás-os-Montes, and Lower Beira shows strong affinities toward the Alentejo, into which it imperceptibly merges on the south. Castelo Branco of the Lower Beira is in many respects suggestive of an Alentejo city, and the countryside is similarly reminiscent.

THE SERRA DA ESTRÊLA

Between the Mondego and the Transmontane Beira extensions of the ancient plateau, the great horst of the Serra da Estrêla has been thrust. This greatest Portuguese range has an average width of about thirty miles and a length of seventy-five miles. Here is found the highest point of the country (6,532 feet). This range, like the Serra das Mesas and the Spanish sierras of Gata, Gredos, and Guadarrama, was elevated along great fault lines in Middle Tertiary time. As the great so-called dividing ranges of Spain separate Old and New Castile, so does the Serra da Estrêla make an effective barrier between the northern and southern parts of Portugal. Only along the littoral on the west, or by the Guarda Gate on the east, is contact between them conveniently made.

The Serra da Estrêla is made up of a series of *mesas*, one set back above another, which have now mostly weathered into high rounded eminences with but few sharp crests. The bounding fault along the northwest is clear, and, although there is still discussion as to the geologic and tectonic history of the other border areas, it is commonly accepted that the southeastern boundary also may be delimited along a series of fault scarps. On the northeast the slopes grade into the plain of Transmontane Beira and on the southwest the granites of the Estrêla dip beneath the Triassic sandstones of Portuguese Estremadura.

THE COASTAL FRINGE (BEIRA LITTORAL PLUS ESTREMADURA)

Of all of the territory lying between the Douro and Tejo rivers only one important part can be said to be uniquely Portuguese and not a part of general Iberian landforms. This area lies to the west of a line drawn almost due north-south from Espinho through Coimbra to Tomar, and north of a line from Tomar to Lisbon. The area thus delimited includes virtually all of the modern provinces of Beira Littoral and Estremadura and has no companion-piece in Spain or north of the Douro in Portugal.

Its first and most obvious difference from the lands about which we have been speaking thus far is that of geologic age. It is a region in which the granites and schists, dominant in the north and in most of the center of Portugal, are totally lacking. Against these ancient rocks of the interior lies an almost continuous narrow band of Triassic sandstones reaching from Tomar, just north of the Tejo River to north of Coimbra and, discontinuously, as far north as the Vouga River. Westward and southwestward from these Triassic sandstones lies a broad band of limestones of Jurassic age, broken by considerable areas of Cretaceous sandstones and conglomerates. Still farther west, especially in the triangle bounded by a line drawn from Espinho to Coimbra and from there to Nazaré, are Tertiary layers, dipping on the seaward side under Quaternary deposits. Within these major, generalized rock areas are small enclaves of disparate character. For example, within the general zone

The Upper Alentejo: Plowmen with Quercus Ilex *in Background*

The Upper Alentejo: Olive Grove

of Jurassic and Cretaceous rocks are many areas of eruptives, the most important of which is that of basalts just to the west and northwest of Lisbon. Within the Tertiary zone are several minor areas where Mesozoic rocks are exposed. The small Berlenga Islands, lying offshore to the west of Cape Carvoeiro, represent an isolated fragment of the ancient mass separated from the latter by the Mesozoic area.

The differences in resistance to weathering of the limestones, sandstones, and volcanic rocks has produced a region with great variety of form. Occasionally one sees sandy hills or hills of basalt, and calcareous eminences that do not reach more than 2,500 feet in elevation. These eminences are striking because of their abrupt, sometimes karstic, arid, desolate slopes. On the seaward border from the Douro River to the Mondego the coast is low and slopes gradually inland. Against the ocean is one of the greatest areas of dune sand of western Europe. Broken only by Cape Mondego (near Figueira da Foz), sands have been deposited as far south as Nazaré, stretching along for over a hundred miles and averaging two to five miles in width.

THE ALENTEJO

If one wanted to describe the Beiras in a single word he would use "variety," but for the neighboring region to the south only the word "monotony" would serve. There could hardly be greater contrast than that between the Beiras in general and the Alentejo, even though Lower Beira at the east makes an imperceptible transition into the Upper Alentejo. The two areas meet where ancient rocks have been modeled by erosion into rolling countryside, with an average elevation of seven hundred to sixteen hundred feet above sea level and sloping generally toward the west and the south. On the west, Lower Beira makes an abrupt transition into the lands to the south, along a series of faults presently reflected in the topography of the area. The adjacent southern area is the Ribatejo (a subdivision of Lower Alentejo), which is part of a great sedimentary basin making up the lower section of both the Tejo and Sado river

The Upper Alentejo from Estremoz

The Caldeirão

Monchique: Schist Crests below Terraces on the Syenite

drainages, from which the sea withdrew in mid-Tertiary times. The Tertiary lands extend to the northwest of the river from ten to fifteen miles on the average, but to a far greater extent southward. There, its complex succession of continental sands, clays, and limestones are transgressive over the ancient rock as far as seventy-five miles south of the river, where the Tertiary materials meet the Carboniferous, sedimentary schists of the Lower Alentejo proper without a break in relief. The great level or gently undulating plain of the Lower Alentejo, largely under seven hundred feet in elevation, is a classic peneplain, with but a few widely separated crests of modest height breaking the monotony.

THE SOUTHERN RANGES OF PORTUGAL

Toward its southern limit, the great plain of the Lower Alentejo slopes upward to form mountain ranges, the Caldeirão Mountains on the east and the schist matrix of the Monchique Mountains on the west. The upfold of the schists resulted in faults normal to the fold, that is, somewhat parallel to the south coast of Portugal. The southern slopes of the mountains are rugged areas of the unconformable meeting of schists with the Mesozoic strata of the Algarve. The highest peak of the Caldeirão (Mú) is only 1,893 feet above sea level, but Monchique is a unique phenomenon, for there a laccolith of syenite has been exposed by erosion of the schists that formerly covered it. Being more resistant to erosion than its matrix, the syenite now towers nearly thirteen hundred feet above the highest crests of the schist (syenite Foia, 2,959 feet) around it.

These southern Portuguese mountains represent a purely Portuguese phenomenon, as they have no counterpart beyond the Portuguese boundary. Separating the two mountain areas is the Depression of S. Marcos, which represents a southern extension of the plain of Lower Alentejo. To the west of the Depression is a northwest-southeast trending fault, marking the eastern edge of the Monchique Mass. From the eastern side of the Depression the rise is gradual to the crests of the Caldeirão.

Another extension of the Alentejo surface is that to the west of the mountains of Monchique, where the plain surface, veneered by sands, can be identified along the Atlantic coast almost to the southern extremity of Portugal. A third extension lies to the east of the Caldeirão, where the Guadiana River has carved its course through a southern projection of the plain which reaches virtually to the southern sea coast.

THE ALGARVE

The most southern political province of Portugal is named the Algarve. It includes the mountains of Caldeirão and Monchique, but this is a political device and not the expression of either the people inhabiting the mountains nor those of the lowlands beyond. A mountain man speaks of the Algarve, meaning the limestone and littoral area of the extreme south, and the Algarvian proper speaks of the mountaineers who inhabit the schist uplands.

Several faults mark the approximate line of division between the schists of the mountains and the Mesozoic measures of the Algarve proper. Some of these faults have a northwest-southeast direction and some run almost due west-east. Along the edge of the schists, almost all of the way across the country, is seen an exposure of a steeply dipping deposit of red continental sandstones, conglomerates, and marls of the Triassic. To the south of the Triassic band are thick, hard beds of Dolomite and compact limestones of the Lower Jurassic, forming high crests separated by lowlands scoured out of softer marls. Southward are successively younger and generally softer beds, where the relief becomes one of crests (generally in east-west direction) diminishing in height, and rough slopes separated by increasingly broad valleys, excavated by streams where the limestones are softer. South of the Mesozoic area is the littoral of Late Tertiary deposits, including marine limestones of the Miocene, and sands, gravels, and clays of Pliocene to recent time. The littoral slopes from the sea edge to elevations of as much as four hundred feet.

It is easily apparent that Portugal, small though it is, is a place of physical diversity. Only the Beira provinces of the center show a considerable number of common characteristics. This has long been recognized by their being grouped together as "the Beiras." No one knowing the Minho, Trás-os-Montes, the Alentejo, and the Algarve, however, could think of them except as places with distinct physical character, each unlike the others.

CHAPTER 2

The Climate of Western Iberia

THE CONTRAST BETWEEN OCEANIC AND INTERIOR IBERIA

LANDFORMS of the northwest of Iberia are important geographical phenomena in themselves, but more important than slope and elevation per se is the relation of these to the Atlantic Ocean and to the climatic regions that result from it. These mountains are a barrier to the storms from the northwest and west, and oceanic influence strongly felt on the seaward slopes is absent in the interior of the peninsula (Fig. 2). There is a great contrast between the aspect of the north and west slopes and that of the *meseta* lying in the rain-shadow of the crests. In describing the transition from the *meseta* to the northern highlands and shores one Spanish geographer said, "In crossing the mountains of León, the beech and chestnut forests, the galleries of trees along the rivers, the meadows, the arborescent ferns announce one's departure from yellow, dusty Spain of the Castilian steppe and the entry into northern, rainy, green Spain." [1]

---

[1] L. Solé Sabarís and Llopis Lladó, *España, Geografía física*, p. 270.

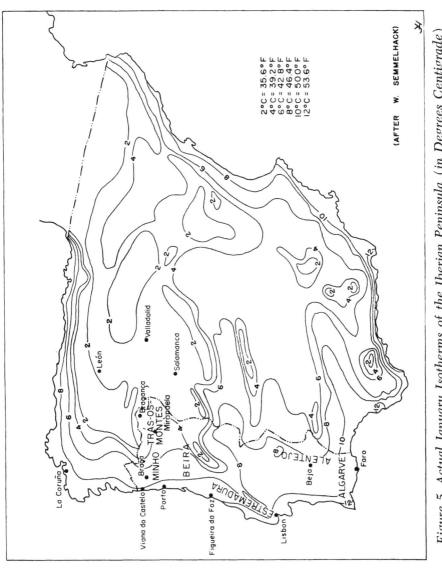

Figure 5. *Actual January Isotherms of the Iberian Peninsula (in Degrees Centigrade)*

The Meseta

The phrase "yellow, dusty Spain" recalls the scorching sun of summer as well as the aridity which is equally characteristic of the area. The *meseta*, denied the lenitive effects of the sea by the barrier of mountains, is continental in its climate. That is to say, there is a high annual temperature range between the means of its hottest and coldest months (an average of 33°F for stations of the north *meseta*) and, more than this, the diurnal range is also great. The temperature may drop to nearly zero during some winter nights—the mean of the minima for the coldest month of the northern *meseta* is 12°F—but the days are mostly bright even in winter, for cloudiness is slight and days with precipitation are few, averaging only eighty-five. Even though snow is not uncommon, falling on an average of fifteen days per year, it does not lie on the ground long, nor does much fall. The total precipitation for the months of December, January, and February is less than 4 inches (of water), on the average, at the typical stations of Valladolid and Salamanca.

In summer, the sun blazes down with hardly a cloud to obstruct its heating of the land. Days may be over 100°F (the mean of the maxima for the hottest month is 99°F), but nights cool rapidly. The persistently clear skies, allowing both heat in the daytime and counter-radiation at night, are not rain-producers. During July and August, the two hottest months of the year, precipitation, on the average, is one inch at both Valladolid and Salamanca. Nor is precipitation high during any month of the year. As the Gonzalez Quijano map shows, the greater part of the northern *meseta* receives less than 20 inches in an average year. There is reason for this area to be called "yellow, dusty Spain."

Oceanic Iberia

In strong contrast to the *meseta* is the area of the mountain rim and the seaward slopes on the north and the northwest. There the effect of the ocean reduces the extremes and eliminates drought, so that the two identifying characteristics of the *meseta* are entirely lacking. The temperature range between the mean of the coldest and the warmest months is moderate (under 22°F on the average), but as the diurnal range is also low, the absolute maximum and absolute minimum temperatures fall within relatively narrow limits. The searing heat of the interior is virtually unknown, as is the bitter cold of winter. Snow is hardly ever seen except on the high mountains. Of course, such boons carry their own deficiencies. The brilliant skies of the *meseta* are infrequent. The greenness and mildness of the Atlantic fringe is due to a high percentage of cloudiness through most of the year. The air is moist in all months (the yearly mean relative humidity of the city of Braga in the verdant Minho Province of Portugal—78 per cent—is higher than that of the month when the relative humidity of León is highest—77 per cent). Precipitation is persistent and copious. Everywhere, for example, in Northwest Portugal the yearly total is over 40 inches and a large part of the Portuguese Minho receives between 40 and 80 inches. (Compare Braga's 73 inches with less than 20 inches received at Valladolid, about 200 miles away, on approximately the same parallel of latitude.) The mountain slopes record totals up to one hundred and some crests over 120 inches.[2]

SEASONAL DROUGHT

On the north coast and the northernmost part of the west coast, where the winds are onshore throughout the year, rainfall is considerable during all months, but south of Cape Finisterre a summer drought is recorded during the period of the most northerly extension of the Azorean high. On the coast of southern Galicia the period of relative drought is almost two months long and this increases as one goes southward into Portugal. Actually the dry summer months of North Portugal

[2] Orlando Ribeiro, *Portugal*, p. 47. Rainfall increases upward on all windward slopes—presumably to the crests. None of these slopes is high enough to show diminution upward.

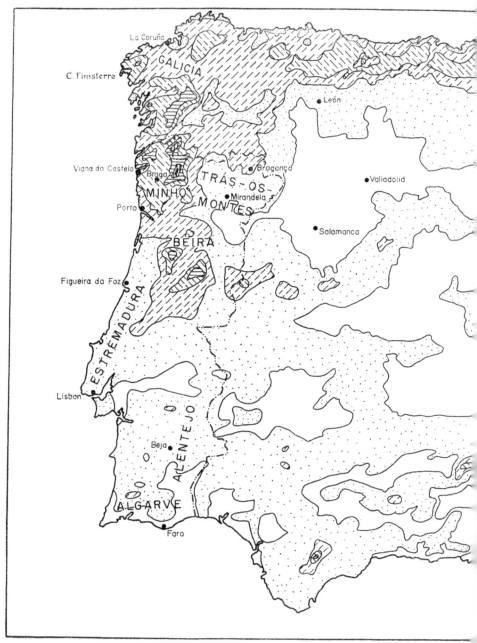

Figure 6. Yearly Precipitation

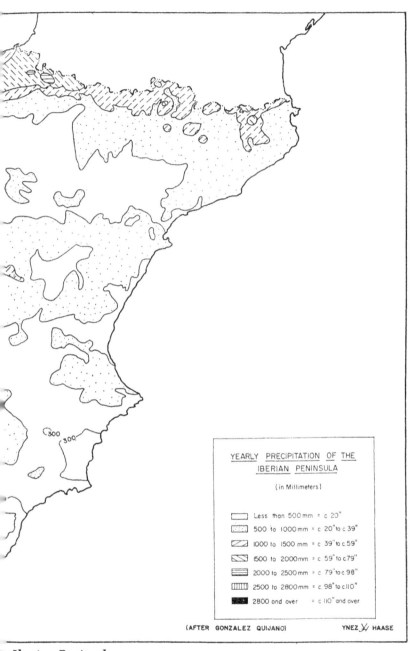

YEARLY PRECIPITATION OF THE
IBERIAN PENINSULA

(in Millimeters)

Less than 500 mm	= c 20"
500 to 1000 mm	= c 20" to c 39"
1000 to 1500 mm	= c 39" to c 59"
1500 to 2000 mm	= c 59" to c 79"
2000 to 2500 mm	= c 79" to c 98"
2500 to 2800 mm	= c 98" to c 110"
2800 and over	= c 110" and over

(AFTER GONZALEZ QUIJANO) YNEZ ⅄ HAASE

Iberian Peninsula

and Galicia would not seem dry to an inhabitant of the interior of the peninsula. For example, at Braga during July and August there are, on the average, 1 4/10 inches and 1 inch respectively of rainfall. Compare these figures with those for the wettest months of Valladolid which record, on the average, 1 8/10 inches each. In other words, the two dry months of Braga receive nearly 2 1/2 inches of rain, whereas the two wettest months of Valladolid show slightly more than 3 1/2 inches. There is reason for Portuguese to refer fondly to the "green Minho."

The "Mediterranean" South of Portugal

Within Portugal itself there is another important contrast in climate, that between the rainy, green north and the "Mediterranean" south.[3] Whereas in the Minho the summer drought represents a brief respite in a rainy year, for the extreme south the rainy period represents an interlude in a relatively dry year. The winter rainy season of the Algarve is scarcely longer than the Minho dry season of summer. However, the transition between heavy rainfall and relative drought is not made as abruptly from north to south as it is from west to east. The transition from oceanic climate in the Portuguese Minho to meseta-type climate of Trás-os-Montes occurs in a short distance due to the mountains that separate the two provinces. The transition from oceanic, "Atlantic" climate on the north, where the storm tracks dominate through most of the year, to "Mediterranean" climate of the south, where there is a dominance through several months of the Azorean high-pressure area with subsident, calm, stable, dry air and clear skies, however, is a matter of latitude and takes place over a longer distance.

[3] This contrast is expressed in the title and the text of the charming and perceptive book by Orlando Ribeiro, Portugal, o mediterráneo e o atlántico.

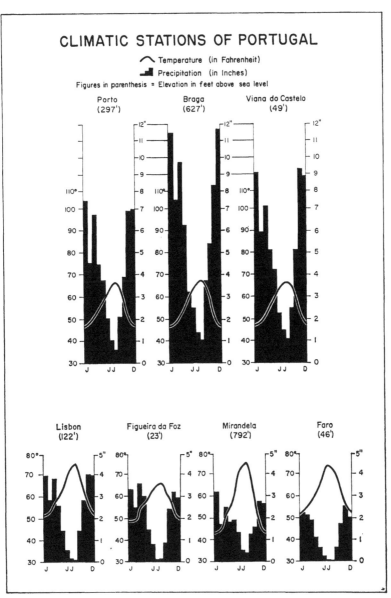

Figure 7. Climatic Stations of Portugal

CLIMATIC TRANSITION FROM NORTH TO SOUTH

The climatic transition from north to south in Portugal is clearly shown by the statistical records of representative stations along the coast. Viana do Castelo, in the Minho, receives 61 inches of rainfall in a year and records two months with less than 1 6/10 inches (40 millimeters). Porto, near the mouth of the Douro River, receives 50 inches of rainfall and shows less than three months with rainfall under 1 6/10 inches. From Porto southward to Figueira da Foz there is a notable change. Figueira receives only 24 inches of rainfall and has five months with less than 1 6/10 inches each. Still farther to the south, at Lisbon, the figures are approximately the same as those for Figueira da Foz. At the extreme south, the Algarve is distinct from the rest of Mediterranean Portugal, as mountains shelter it on the north. It faces out over the sea toward Africa and its climate is actually more like that of North Africa than it is, for example, like that of Lisbon. Faro, the capital of the Algarve, receives less than 16 inches of rainfall in a normal year and records six months with less than 1 6/10 inches rainfall. On the average, Algarvian stations receive less rainfall than the average received by *meseta* stations of Spain.

MECHANISM OF WEATHER OVER THE PENINSULA

Through the year, the Iberian peninsula comes under the influence of three meteorologic action centers: the Azorean high, the North Atlantic low, and the action center within the peninsula. The interior, the *meseta*, acts as a small continent to produce seasonal effects peculiar to itself.

SUMMER CONDITIONS

During the summer, the Azorean high of the South Atlantic extends to the north, covering the latitudes of most of the peninsula—at times even to the Bay of Biscay. At this season, Mediterranean summer, with stable air and clear, warm, dry days, blankets the south and west littorals up to southern

Galicia. The interior of the peninsula, isolated from the sea by mountains, is greatly heated, and becomes a low-pressure area in the midst of the great area of high pressures around it. Winds blow in toward the center of the low from all sides, but when the low is particularly pronounced in the midsummer months—especially July and August—little rain falls on the *meseta.* The winds from the south and southeast have their origin in dry Africa and absorb but little moisture in their traverse of the Mediterranean. Winds from the southwest and west, blowing in over relatively low and warm surfaces, are increasingly heated as they penetrate into the peninsula, and their moisture capacity is correspondingly increased. More significant than this, however, is the fact that the summer thermal low is relatively shallow. Above 10,000 feet the high of upper latitudes extends southward over it and establishes a condition of stability. During the rare periods when the Iberian depression spreads and joins that of Morocco, there are searing winds out of the east quarter, with temperatures well over 100°F and with a relative humidity as low as 10 per cent.[4] Only at the north and the extreme northwest do the inblowing winds yield summer rainfalls as they rise steeply over the mountains seeking the Iberian low; but rainfall occurs only on the windward side as the humid, oceanic air rises, cools, and condenses moisture. Within the mountain barrier, the *meseta* continues to be dry (Fig. 2), for the descending air masses show decreasing relative humidity.

WINTER CONDITIONS

In the winter, the Azorean high is reduced, and is replaced in the latitudes of the peninsula by the track of North Atlantic cyclones, which finally affect all of the peninsular peripheries and bring the influence of the ocean in over the land. Since from the end of November the temperatures of sea water are at their maximum in comparison with those of the air above them, conditions favor condensation. The humid masses of air

[4] Orlando Ribeiro, *Portugal,* p. 44.

are carried landward by a series of cyclones, sometimes in a chain that will last for days or even weeks without perceptible break. Such warm-front rains come in the form of drizzles that may be persistent for days, through the passage of the several consecutive lows. Occasionally, there may be a fall in temperature, accompanied by quick showers, and then the dissipation of the clouds marking the passage of a cold front. Such are brief interludes. To this frontal precipitation is added, on the westward slopes, orographic rainfall—produced when the humid masses are forced up the mountain slopes—and snowfall on the higher crests.

Again, as during the summer period, the *meseta* is anomalous, for it is then linked with the great high-pressure area of Asia and Central Europe. While the littorals of both Mediterranean and Atlantic Iberia (and also the Pyrenean slopes) are rainy, the interior is dry, clear, and cold. In fact, the high pressure of the interior increases the precipitation on the peripheries, for it often blocks the entry of cyclones. At times these stagnate at the edges, bringing large amounts of rainfall to the coasts and snow on the mountains.[5]

EQUINOCTIAL CONDITIONS

The rainfall of the interior differs seasonally from that of the border regions. It is dominantly that of spring and fall, taking place in the intermediate periods of change from one pronounced anomalous pressure condition to its opposite anomaly. These equinoctial seasons are times of unstable conditions and capricious weather, when one should be prepared for a beautiful, warm day with temperatures in the eighties to be followed by a freeze. With the onset of spring, cyclonic disturbances do not have the frequency, regularity, or duration of those of

---

[5] This is particularly notable in the Bay of Biscay. See Eduardo Hessinger, "La Distribución estacional de las precipitaciones en la península Ibérica y sus causas" (trans. from German by Valentín Masachs Alavedra), *Estudios Geográficos*, X, No. 34 (Feb., 1949), 124.

winter, and they are interspersed with periods of fine and increasingly warm weather. They may be, however, periods of hazard for the farmer, because of unpredictability. Due to increasing heating of the land in March, the high of the interior is being dissipated and the low of the Mediterranean broadens, increasing the flow of air into the *meseta*. Rainfall increases there until May, when, with the greatly increased warmth of the surface, frequent thundershowers make this the month of maximum rainfall. By July, the Azorean high has spread over the west coast, bringing stable air and replacing the track of the North Atlantic cyclones. Autumn conditions are roughly comparable, in reverse, to those of spring. It is a season of unstable air, of unpredictability, and a secondary maximum of rainfall is recorded then for the *meseta*.

SEASONAL TEMPERATURES

Throughout the year, temperatures are closely relative to oceanic exposure. Summer isotherms are roughly parallel to the ocean and closely spaced. Temperatures rise sharply inward to a maximum near the center of the *meseta*. The reverse is essentially true in winter, but not with the same degree of nicety; temperatures reach their minimum near the center of the peninsula. The west coast, with summer temperatures roughly homogeneous from the southern Alentejo[6] to the Minho, is somewhat differentiated in winter by the slightly lower temperatures of the Minho as compared with those of the south (Fig. 5).

The contrasts described in this chapter, first, between the

[6] The Algarve, isolated by the mountains of Monchique and Caldeirão, is distinct. It is largely untouched by even such cold as may affect the Alentejo in winter. However, an occasional outbreak of cold air may take place when a deep high spreads westward from the interior. This occurred in the winter of 1953–1954, and again in 1955–1956, bringing snow to most of the littoral of Portugal and freezing weather even to the Algarve. Such cold causes great distress, as it happens rarely and there is no preparation for it.

rainy northwest periphery and the *meseta*, that is, between Atlantic and continental climates, and second, between the Atlantic northwest and Mediterranean South Portugal, will be made even more obvious in the chapter on vegetation.[7]

[7] The following, in addition to the works cited above, have been most useful in the study of climate: Pedro M. González Quijano, *Mapa Pluviométrico de España*, text and map of nine sheets; Hessinger, *op. cit.*, 59–128; Wilhelm Semmelhack, "Beiträge zur Klimatographie von Nordspanien und Portugal," "Die Niederschlagsverhältnisse," *Archiv der Deutschen Seewarte*, XXXIII, No. 2 (Hamburg, 1910), pp. 1–90; "Niederschlagskarte der Iberischen Halbinsel," *Annalen der Hydrographie*, LX (1932), 28–32, and map; "Temperaturkarten der Iberischen Halbinsel," *ibid.*, pp. 327–333, with tables and maps; *O Clima de Portugal* especially Pts. I–V (1942–1946); H. Amorim Ferreira, *Distribuição da chuva no território do continente Português*, text of 14 pp. and map; E. Alt, *Klimakunde von Mittel-und-Südeuropa*, Vol. III, Pt. M, *Handbuch der Klimatologie*, ed. Köppen and R. Geiger.

CHAPTER 3

The Soils of Northern
and Western Iberia

N 1927 a General Map of the Soils of Europe was
published, giving the results of investigations made
under the auspices of the International Society of Soil
Science.[1] It is particularly useful for this study as its
soils regions are effectively simplified and allow a quick com-
prehension of the relations between regions of soils, climate,
and vegetation in northwestern Europe (See Fig. 8 and compare with Figs. 2, 6, 7, and 9).

CONTRASTS IN SOILS BETWEEN THE OCEANIC BORDER
AND THE *Meseta*

One is struck by the great stretch of "moderately podsolised
forest soils"[2] running from interior Asia, south of 60° latitude,

[1] *General Map of the Soils of Europe,* 1927, by the Sub-Commission
for the European Soil Map of the Fifth Commission of the International
Society of Soil Science, Chairman, H. Stremme, Danzig. German text
published in Danzig, 1927. Translation by Dr. W. G. Ogg, 1929.

[2] A podsol is a soil developed in cool, moist climates under forest
vegetation, commonly coniferous. It is leached in its upper layers and is

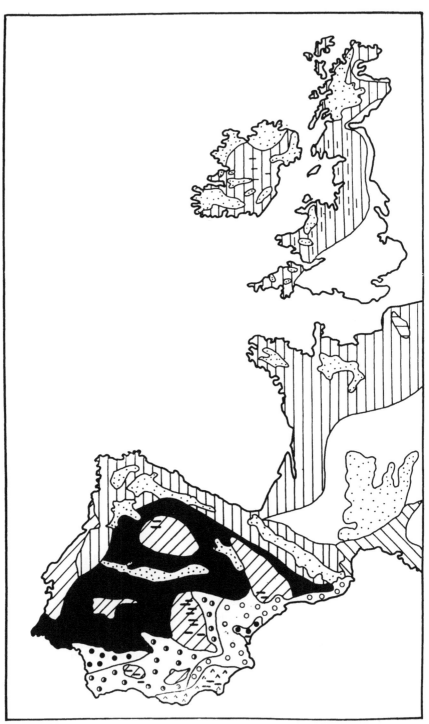

Figure 8. Soil Regions of Western Europe (Legend on Opposite Page)

SOIL REGIONS OF WESTERN EUROPE

⌈^^^⌉ GRAY AND BROWN DESERT STEPPE SOIL

☐ "BROWN" FOREST SOILS, SLIGHTLY PODSOLIZED

⊞ PODSOLIZED FOREST SOILS (MODERATE)

⌈ I I I⌉ RAW HUMUS IN THE REGION OF THE FOREST SOILS

⌈‾–‾⌉ MOORS MORE THAN 40% OF THE AREA IN THE REGION OF THE
FOREST SOILS

▨ LIGHT CHESTNUT-COLORED DRY FOREST SOILS

◩ RED EARTH

▤ RENDZINA, DEGRADED RENDZINA AND PODSOLIZED FOREST SOILS

⌈‾–‾⌉ SALINE SOILS

SKELETON SOILS AND SOILS RICH IN SKELETAL MATERIAL:

⌈:·:·:⌉ WITH PODSOLIZED SOILS IN HIGH MOUNTAINS, INCL. ICE

⌈o o o⌉ WITH RED EARTH AND LIGHT CHESTNUT-COLORED SOILS

⌈o o o⌉ WITH BROWN FOREST SOILS AND RED EARTH

■ BROWN FOREST SOIL, LIGHT CHESTNUT-COLORED DRY FOREST SOIL,
RICH IN SKELETAL MATERIAL

⌈• • •⌉ MEADOW SOIL AND SOIL OF RIVER MARSHES

(AFTER INTERNATIONAL SOCIETY OF SOIL SCIENCE)

along the coasts of the Baltic and North seas (not including the peninsula of Jutland), through northern and western France, the Pyrenees, the Cantabrians, Galicia, and the Minho Province of northwest Portugal. Only the western portion of this area is shown in Figure 8. To the south of the Minho Province a

usually strongly acid. Highly siliceous materials are most susceptible to podsolization. The soil has a characteristic grayish-white color. *Soils and Men, Yearbook of the United States Department of Agriculture,* 1938, pp. 972, 1020.

wide band of these soils extends along the humid interior upland of Portugal, reaching approximately to the Tejo River, but along the Atlantic Coast the Douro River marks its southern limit. This soils area can be equated with the area of oceanic influence, abundant rainfall, relatively mild temperatures, and mixed-forest vegetation.

In sharp contrast are the soils of the *meseta*, lying to the lee of the northern and northwestern mountains of Iberia, where wide areas are covered with brown forest soils or bright chestnut-colored dry forest soils, bespeaking the drought of the interior.

CLASSIFICATION BY DEL VILLAR

One of the contributors to the map of 1927 was Emilio H. del Villar, who presumably was responsible for the Iberian area. After that publication, however, he continued his work and in 1937 published a volume wholly devoted to the soils of the Iberian Peninsula.[3] In this text and its accompanying map he makes far more detailed specifications for the soils regions. In fact, the amount of detail makes this map less useful than the earlier, more generalized map of 1927. The text, however, is helpful, even though at first glance it seems to contradict his findings as published in the report of 1927. For example, the great area, mentioned above, of "moderately podsolized forest soils" is broken up into subareas, in terms of parent materials. The assumption is that here the parent materials were more important in the ultimate nature of the soils than was climate.[4] Those developed from granites are different from those derived from Silurian schists. Both of these are in separate categories from the soils derived from the calcareous Mesozoic materials.

[3] Emilio H. del Villar, *Los Suelos de la Península Luso-Ibérica.*
[4] *Ibid.*, p. 67.

OCEANIC AREA

From the Pyrenees to S. Vicente, thirty miles beyond Santander, is an almost solid zone of the "general occurrence of
humid siallitic soils." From S. Vicente to Oviedo is an area
where most of the soils are derived from calcareous materials.
To the south of this zone, and intermingling with it, are "humid
siallitic soils." To the west of Oviedo is a great zone of "the
general occurrence of the acid-humic type soils," which extends
through Galicia, North Portugal and along the humid highland
interior of the Beiras to the Tejo River. In spite of Del Villar's
differentiation according to parent materials, the great soil
areas indicate their intimate association with climate. Even the
area of soils derived from calcareous rocks is now broadly
similar to its neighboring areas, for under the climatic conditions of the rainy lowland the soils have been largely decalcified.[5] In general, all of these soils can be associated with
Marbut's pedalfers.[6] They are acid in reaction, but not to the
degree that would inhibit a healthy forest growth.[7]

THE INTERIOR

Within the angle of the northern and western mountains
appears a zone of "intermediate siallitic soils." Farther inland
begins the great zone of "xero-siallitic soils," which broadens
southward. In the interior areas the pedalfers become less and

[5] *Ibid.*, p. 199.

[6] *Ibid.*, p. 32. Marbut, former chief of the United States Soil Survey,
distinguished between two great soil groups in terms of the accumulation
of carbonate of calcium or the lack of such accumulation. The first he
named "pedocals," using the Greek *pedo* (ground) plus Latin *calcis* or
calx (lime). They are associated with dry or relatively dry areas. For the
other great group he coined the name "pedalfer," using the same Greek
prefix but adding the first two letters from *alumen* and *ferrum*, the Latin
words for aluminum and iron, respectively. The pedalfers usually show
not only the lack of a zone of lime accumulation but the positive accumulation of iron and aluminum compounds. They are to be associated with
humid areas. See *Soils and Men, Yearbook of Agriculture*, USDA, 1938,
p. 982.

[7] H. Gaussen, "Le Milieu physique et la forêt au Portugal," *Revue
Géographique des Pyrénées et du Sud-Ouest*, XI, Nos. 3–4 (1940), 240.

less acid as the elevations decrease and the land is drier, toward the Iberian interior. At Zamora on the west, and to the north of Burgos, begin the areas of pedocals that cover most of eastern Spain and most of the area to the south of the Sierra Morena.

"Agropedic" Soils

A large proportion of the acid-humic soils of the northwest occur at present in what Del Villar calls the "agropedic phase." The differences between them depend upon cultivation, improvement, and manuring. The Portuguese say that these soils are man-made. This situation seems to be a feature of areas where farming practices inherited from northern and Central Europe have been common since remote ages. Del Villar says:

> . . . the acid-humic soils are commonly considered poor; but it is necessary to qualify and adjust this judgment. . . . within this acid-humic region there are areas of agricultural production generally more intensive than that of the dry lands of the peninsula . . . soils of the same type dominate the greater part of the British Isles, Holland, North Germany, and Denmark, countries which show the most intensive agricultural production in Europe.[8]

The intensity of cultivation, especially in North Portugal, must come as a surprise to anyone seeing it for the first time. It certainly was surprising for one American who previously knew the somewhat comparable climatic environment of western British Columbia, where population is indeed sparse. To see the Minho Province of northwest Portugal, with a density of rural population as great as virtually any in Europe, is a revelation as to the capacity of a determined and ancient farming society. However, determination and skill cannot compensate completely for untoward natural conditions. That excessive rainfall and leaching are detrimental to the soils may be indicated by the use of the adjective *galega*, (referring to Galician areas where rainfall figures are especially high) in the common

[8] Del Villar, *Suelos de la Península*, p. 66.

SOILS

language of the Portuguese peasant. A soil thus described is light and infertile.[9]

SOILS OF TRÁS-OS-MONTES

The province of Trás-os-Montes lies east of the mountain barrier that limits the Minho Province. It is politically Portuguese because of its geologic and tectonic history, which has partially isolated it from Spain and has allowed more convenient communications with the west. In other ways it is more Spanish than Portuguese. Its soils have more the quality of those of León than those of the Minho. In the north of Trás-os-Montes and through much of the Spanish province of León are found "intermediate siallitic soils" (according to the Del Villar terminology),[10] and in this relatively dry area, parent-material differences are strongly reflected in the soils. The hard mica schists do not break down readily, and because of this fact there are large areas of shallow and essentially rocky soils[11] that support only a meagre heath. Other schists, somewhat more friable, break down more readily, the reflection of which can be seen in the easily established forest growth.[12] Southern Trás-os-Montes is characterized by the "general occurrence of xero-siallitic soils," that is, soils with neutral reaction and low organic content, which develop under conditions of relative dryness and from siliceous parent materials. They cover not only southern Trás-os-Montes but also an enormous area of the

[9] J. Leite de Vasconcellos, *Origem histórica e formação do povo Português*, p. 15.
[10] Del Villar, *Suelos de la Península*, III. He says that these are approximately the *braunerde* of Ramann, and Robinson calls them brown forest soils. According to the classification in the United States they would be listed as the most acid of the "non-calcareous pedocals" or "non-calcic brown soils." This is according to the information supplied by Raymond E. Storie, Department of Soils, University of California, Berkeley, California. Mr. Storie has recently spent several months in areas of the western Mediterranean studying soils and their distribution.
[11] Del Villar calls them "oropedic," so-named because they appear most frequently in mountains. In such soils the A horizon lies directly upon the C horizon, or parent material. Del Villar, *Suelos de la Península*, p. 33.
[12] Gaussen, *loc. cit.*

THE INDIVIDUALITY OF PORTUGAL

interior of Spain (the provinces of Salamanca, Cáceres, and most of New Castile, east to Ciudad Real), as well as most of the Alentejo in Portugal.

Terra Rossa SOILS AND DUNES

There are two other relatively dry areas of Portugal where soils reflect the parent material. These appear distinct on the Del Villar map by reason of their calcareous rock. This is a situation very different from that of the calcareous area of the humid north, to the east of Oviedo, where the lime is effectively leached. The larger of the two areas is clearly delimited on the east by the Lisbon-Tomar-Coimbra-Espinho line. Dominant within the region are *terra rossa* soils. This term is commonly used by European pedologists to describe a calcareous soil stained red by iron oxides, which is favored in development by the Mediterranean climate with its pronounced wet and dry seasons. The second area of *terra rossa* soils is that lying to the north of the Algarvian littoral. Under Algarvian rainfall conditions the limestone is not decalcified, and in many places the parent material is exposed at the surface, loose material on top being carried away as fast as it appears. Limestone rock and *terra rossa* soils reach to the sea in the western half of the southern coast.

Against the northern region of limestone lies the great quadrilateral area of dunes, and the eastern half of the Algarvian coast is likewise a distinct area of sand deposit. Such areas are shown on the Del Villar map as being of "sandy-skeletal coastal soils."

ESSENTIAL SIMILARITY BETWEEN STREMME AND DEL VILLAR CLASSIFICATIONS

In spite of the differences between subareas indicated by Del Villar, the fact remains that from the French border at the western end of the Pyrenees to central Portugal there is a great, unbroken stretch of either "humid siallitic" soils or of those pertaining to the series next to it in order of acidity, the "acid-humic" soils. According to the United States' classification, all would fall into the category of moderately podsolized soils, which brings us back, essentially, to the classification of Stremme.[13] Whichever classification or map is used, the general fact emerges that the great soils areas are in accord with the regions of climate of northern and western Iberia. The humid peripheries are clearly set apart, in soil types, from the dry interior and the south of the peninsula.

[13] For Portugal only, a useful map of soils has been elaborated and published under the direction of Luis Bramão, "Carta dos Solos de Portugal," Estação Agronómica Nacional, Direcção Geral dos Serviços Agrícolas. It is not serviceable for this chapter, as it does not show extensions of the soils regions beyond the political limits of Portugal.

CHAPTER 4

Vegetation Regions of Northern and Western Iberia

REGIONS OF WESTERN EUROPE

A GREAT VEGETATION zone, essentially homogeneous in character, stretches from Central Europe to Portugal (Fig. 9). Troll calls this the Holly Region. Nearest the ocean, it is the first of his three divisions of the forests of Western Europe.[1] The second is the Beech Region, some of whose species are found mixed with those of the Holly Region in Iberia; the third, and farthest from the ocean, is the Oak Region, with which we shall not be concerned, as it does not extend into the peninsula.

The Holly Region, an area of mild winters and summers and with rainfall in all seasons of the year, includes northwestern Iberia on the west, and northern and central Germany on the east. Besides the eponymous holly (*Ilex aquifolium*) it is characterized by common gorse (*Ulex europaeus*), several of the heathers (especially *Erica tetralix* and *E. cinerea*), and the primrose (*Primula acaulis*). Troll's Beech Region lies to the

[1] Karl Troll, "Ozeanische Züge im Pflanzenkleid Mitteleuropas," *Freie Wege Vergleichender Erdkunde*, pp. 307–325.

east and south of the Holly Region, but a large number of its species occur also in the latter and accompany it westward into humid Iberia. Some of these are: English oak (*Quercus robur*, which replaces beech in Galicia and Portugal), elm, ash, poplar, black alder, plane, birch (only in the extreme north of Portugal in the mountains), yew, sweet-gale (*Myrica gale*), foxgloves, the common fern, brambles, broom (*Sarothamnus scoparius*), wild plum (*Prunus spinosa*), hawthorne, ivy, and wild pear (*Pyrus communis*).

VEGETATION CONTRASTS BETWEEN HUMID IBERIA
AND THE *Meseta* [2]

The striking difference in floristic composition and physiognomy of the vegetation between the humid Iberian border and the *meseta*, in the lee of the mountains in interior Iberia, is immediately apparent. None of the plants given above as typical of the Holly Region can tolerate the climatic conditions of the *meseta*. The same is true of other plants of Central and Western Europe such as the heather (*Calluna vulgaris*) and the brake (*Pteris aquilina*). The maritime pine (*Pinus maritima*) and the edible European chestnut (*Castanea sativa*) of the northwest periphery of Iberia cannot tolerate the *meseta*

[2] With regard to the vegetation of Portugal I am chiefly indebted to J. Daveau, "Géographie botanique du Portugal." 1. "La Flore littorale du Portugal," *Boletim Sociedade Broteriana*, XIV (1897), 3–54. 2. "La Flore des plaines et collines voisines du littoral," *ibid.*, XIX (1902), 3–140. 3. "Les Stations de la zone des plaines et collines," *ibid.*, XXI (1904–1905), 16–85.

Also helpful has been H. Gaussen, "Le Milieu physique et la forêt au Portugal," *Revue Géographique des Pyrénées et du Sud-Ouest*, XI, Nos. 3–4 (1940), 219–267, and M. Willkomm, "As Regiões botánicas de Portugal," trans. from *Grundzüge der Pflanzenverbreitung auf der Iberischen Halbinsel* (*Die Vegetation der Erde*, Vol. I) in *Boletim da Sociedade Broteriana*, XVII (Coimbra, 1900), 89–154; and in this chapter, as in so many others, Hermann Lautensach, especially in his 1932 work on Portugal, "Das Land als Ganzes," *Petermann's Mitteilungen*, No. 213 (Gotha, 1932), as well as his "A Individualidade geográfica de Portugal no conjunto da Península Ibérica," *Boletim da sociedade de geografia de Lisboa*, XLIX (1931), 362–409.

THE INDIVIDUALITY OF PORTUGAL

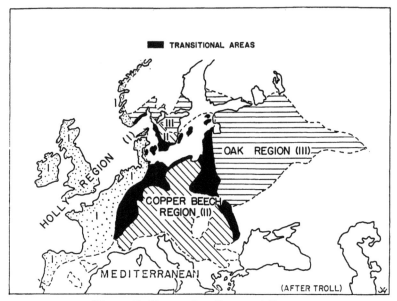

Figure 9. Vegetation Zones of Europe

because of its drought. The cultivated olive, almond, and fig, Mediterranean plants that are grown in North Portugal, are excluded by winter cold. Although it is true that many of the species of the Beech Region are found not only in the Holly Region, but also on the *meseta*, in the latter area they form a negligible part of the plant community, whereas in the former the individuals are more numerous, show exceptional growth and there reach their southwestern distributional extreme in Europe. On the contrary, some species find suitable conditions for existence on the *meseta* but cannot tolerate the dampness of the extreme north and northwest. Perhaps the most common example is that of the holm oak (*Q. ilex*).

Subdivisions of Humid Iberia

The humid outer edges of Iberia can be subdivided into a northern zone and a western zone. The first includes all of Galicia except for a narrow area of the west coast below the latitude of Santiago de Compostela. The second is essentially North Portugal but with an extension along the coast that includes the *rias* of Vigo, Pontevedra, and Arosa of Galicia. The western zone is distinct from the northern zone for two obvious reasons. In the first place, beech is not found in the western zone nor is birch (*Betula sp.*), except in remote, high mountains. Secondly, many of the Mediterranean species follow the west coast up into southern Galicia, but most of them are not to be found in the northern zone. Willkomm recognized the western zone as being one of special character because of the surprising combination of plants from diverse regions which thrive there. To quote him:

. . . this mixture of cultivated plants of south and central Europe is mostly in the north of Portugal and west Galicia, which gives to the picturesque valleys of this mountainous region an enchanting aspect, for there one sees trees of both pip and stone fruits, walnuts and chestnuts at the side of and mixed with figs, almonds, olives, oranges, vines, and maize fields next to fields of rye and meadows of trefoil. . . . one finds araucarias, eucalyptus . . . willows, poplars, elms, ashes, lindens . . . associated with ornamental trees of North America, Cape of Good Hope, Japan and China . . . [3]

It is to be noted that the division of Willkomm sets off political Portugal from Galicia to the north, with the exception of the narrow coastal strip, including the *rias* above-mentioned.

The change between the two vegetational areas results especially from the difference in rainfall, in total amount as well as seasonal distribution. The extreme northwest of Galicia is a region of rainfall in all months of the year and its total is the highest of any Iberian littoral, whereas the North Portuguese area, plus the extension into southwest Galicia, has less rainfall in total and a summer drought period (Fig. 7). The northern limit of intensive olive, grape, and citrus cultivation occurs at approximately this division line, the line of Santiago-Orense.

The North Portuguese area, i.e. Willkomm's Western Zone of Humid Iberia, in its floristic composition and appearance, is

[3] Willkomm, "As Regiões botánicas . . . ," p. 130.

similar to northwest Europe. The maritime pine, the principal species on the predominantly siliceous soils, is found on the western slopes of the mountains to an elevation of forty-six hundred feet. Along the open river valleys (i.e. especially the Mondego and Tejo valleys) it reaches into the interior. Even as far south as the valley of the Tejo it is the dominant tree. Associated with it, but more restricted in range—extending less far into the western littoral and not reaching to the same elevations on the mountain sides—is the oak common to northwestern Europe, *Quercus robur*, which is largely replaced above thirteen hundred feet elevation by the Pyrenees oak (*Q. toza*). Both oaks are almost entirely strange to the region south of the Tejo. This is also true of gorse (*Ulex europaeus*), *Armeria maritima*, *A. elongata* and *Rhododendron baeticum*, which are important members of the community. Endemics are few.

TRANSITION AREA OF MIDDLE PORTUGAL

Within Portugal itself, other vegetational subdivisions can be recognized. The area north of the Mondego River differs greatly from that south of the Tejo River. Between the two rivers is an area of transition, particularly marked on the coastal fringe. The sharp differences in floristic composition between the areas are due fundamentally to climate. It is in these latitudes that there are considerable contrasts in rainfall and in the length of the summer drought. From north to south there is a diminution in total rainfall and an increase in the period of drought, the combination of which reaches a critical point at approximately the mouth of the Mondego River. The yearly total of rainfall at this point is only half of that at the mouth of the Douro River (approximately 24 inches compared to 50 inches). The summer drought period lasts almost five months at the mouth of the Mondego River as compared to less than three months at the mouth of the Douro River.[4] It may be added that drought conditions are accentuated toward the south by an increasing rate of evaporation.

[4] *O Clima de Portugal*, Pts. V, VI.

This area is strongly affected by the seasonal alternation between the periods of dominance of North Atlantic cyclones, with rainfall, and of South Atlantic high pressures, with subsident, stable air and drought. Thus while one might expect a transition in vegetational complex from that of the north, an edaphic factor, actually, is responsible for the abruptness of the change. The Mondego River marks the meeting of the siliceous rocks of the north with the calcareous materials on the seaward fringe of Portuguese Estremadura, lying between the Mondego and Tejo rivers. A great number of the northwest European plants of northern Portugal are siliceous and cannot tolerate, or tolerate poorly, the limy soils of western Estremadura. Most of the species limited to North Portugal have their southern coastal limit to the north of the Mondego.

In this area there is nearly a balance, in terms of numbers, between the species of northwestern Europe and those of the Mediterranean region. Thirty-eight per cent of the species are those of northwestern Europe (compared to 58 per cent in the area north of the Mondego River), and 42 per cent belong to the Mediterranean. In contrast to the north, in this middle area Iberian species have importance, and there is a greater degree of endemism. African (Mauritanian) species are almost four times as numerous (85 to 22). Maritime pine is far less important, due both to lower rainfall and to the calcareous soils. The English oak (*Q. robur*), its northern companion, is found in the transition area also, but both are largely restricted to the wetter slopes and siliceous soils, whereas the Portuguese oak (*Q. lusitanica*), a pronounced calciphyte, grows vigorously. This tree belongs quite properly in a transition area, for it is intermediate in appearance and morphology as compared to the other Portuguese oaks, deciduous, but with a tendency toward permanence of its leaves. Both the wild and the cultivated olive grow in the transition area, although on the calcareous soils they appear more as spiny bushes than as trees. Among the bushy plants, *Quercus coccifera* and *Q. humilis* are common, although somewhat exclusive of each other. *Quercus humilis* requires siliceous soils, whereas *Q. coccifera*, although preferring siliceous, can tolerate calcareous soils. The genus *Cistus* is far more important here than in the area of the north (thirty species compared to nine) and *Genista* even more so (fifty species as compared to ten). The same relation exists with regard to certain members of the mint family (*Labiatae*). The genera *Phlomis* and *Sideritis*, common in the transition area, do not appear at all north of the Mondego. Of thirteen species of *Teucrium* in Portugal, only one appears in the north, and of twenty species of *Thymus* only two are found there.

SOUTHERN PORTUGAL

Portugal south of the Tejo River is quite a different floristic area. The species common to northwest Europe amount to less than one-third of the total, whereas Mediterranean species are the most numerous of all. While a few Iberian species are common and there is a liberal admixture of Algerian and Moroccan species, there is also an abundance of endemics. Maritime pine extends southward only to the Setúbal Peninsula, as it cannot tolerate the high summer temperatures and relatively low rainfall of the Alentejo. It is replaced, in the western Alentejo, by the Italian stone pine (*Pinus pinea*), which grows well on the quartzite sands of the region. However, the Alentejo in general is not a pine region. The dominant trees of the large eastern section are the cork and holm oaks (*Quercus suber* and *Q. ilex* respectively). Olives grow well, both the cultivated and, on the calcareous "islands," the wild olive. In large areas bushes are dominant, often to the complete exclusion of trees. Especially common is the gum cistus (*Cistus ladaniferus*), *Genista spp.*, and *Stauracanthus sp.* Important also are Kermes oak (*Quercus coccifera*), *Q. humilis, Halimium sp.*, various *Ulexes* and *Pterospartum sp.* The dwarf Mediterranean palm (*Chamaerops humilis*) and carob (*Ceratonia siliqua*), with their Portuguese center in the Algarve, reach their northern limit just to the south of the Tejo River in the Setúbal Peninsula.

The Effect of Man upon Vegetation

It is difficult, at best, to establish vegetation areas where complex mixing of species occurs. This is made more difficult through alteration by man. For at least three thousand years the nature and the extent of forests has been under attack. The results of this pressure are difficult to determine, but there can be no doubt that extensive changes have taken place. For example, in the western Minho the forest ordinarily reaches to no more than about eighteen hundred feet elevation. There is no evident pedologic or climatic reason why the forests do not extend to the summits of the mountains. As can be readily seen from present practices, the need for fuels, fertilizers (especially for the species of the nitrogen-fixing *Ulex*), and pastures has led to the destruction of trees and their consequent replacement by shrubby vegetation and weeds. It has also added to the erosion of the upper mountain slopes. Nevertheless, whatever changes have been made by man, it may be safely assumed that the broad vegetational distinctions between the humid northwest and the interior, and those between the area with the Central European complex and the region with the Mediterranean complex, exist in response to environmental conditions.

Perhaps no reader will be surprised at the close coincidence between the areas of landforms, climate, soils, and vegetation that has been indicated in this and in previous chapters, but it will do no harm to emphasize the fact again, as it has decisive bearing upon the differences between culture regions in this part of the peninsula, the subject now to be considered.

CHAPTER 5

Prehistoric Immigrants into Iberia

PALEOLITHIC HUNTERS OF THE NORTH

HOMO SAPIENS appeared in Iberia in that part of the Old Stone Age known as the Upper Paleolithic. He was a hunter, and in Spain as well as in southern France left evidence of his genius as an artist. Such men came to Iberia from Southern France prior to 10,000 B.C.,[1] entering through the low passageway between the shore and the west end of the Pyrenees. Following the slopes of the Cantabrian Mountains, they went westward at least as far as Asturias. For this there is direct supporting evidence. It can hardly be doubted that they knew also the country beyond. They may, indeed, have entered and hunted along the Mediterranean shores of Spain as well, for the wall paintings of the eastern provinces from Lérida to Almería have been attributed to them.

However, this credit now seems undeserved, in the light of the paucity of apparel shown in the pictures and also by the appearance of the dog, apparently as a companion to the men.[2]

[1] Luis Pericot García, *La España primitiva*, p. 111.
[2] Júlio Caro Baroja, *Los Pueblos del Norte de la Península Ibérica*, p. 28.

The hunters of the Paleolithic lived in the late Glacial Period, whereas the semi-nudity of the figures depicted in the paintings of northeastern Spain does not suggest such a climate but rather that of a subsequent, warmer period of time. The appearance of the dog is also disconcerting to the enthusiasts for the Paleolithic identification of these people. It is generally agreed that the dog's domestication took place in the Epipaleolithic Period, that is, in the epilogue to the Paleolithic, when the climate was warmer due to the recession of the ice sheets and when a new type of culture had succeeded that of the brilliant hunters. Nevertheless, it cannot be doubted that the Upper Paleolithic hunters-and-artists ranged broadly across the peninsula at times, for their paintings (clearly of the same type as those of the great Cantabrian center of their art) are found in the center of the peninsula, as well as in the province of Málaga in the south. The evidence, however, suggests that their numbers were small beyond Cantabria.

CAPSIAN CULTURE OF THE SOUTH AND *Meseta* CULTURE

While the hunters-and-artists of the Upper Paleolithic Period were living in the north, Capsian culture,[3] of a distinctly different basis and coming from Africa, spread into Mediterranean Spain. Between the two culture regions there was a "cultural abyss," according to Mendes Corrêa.[4] His expression is a good one if one keeps in mind that it indicates the existence of an intervening culture of a lower type, but it does not mean that the territory was uninhabited. People were living on the *meseta* (witness the traces of Magdalenian cave art in the provinces of Madrid and Guadalajara)[5] even though population was sparse. There is indisputable evidence that the *meseta* has been but thinly settled from as long ago as the middle of the second

---

[3] Pedro Bosch Gimpera, "Los Iberos," *Cuadernos de Historia de España*, IX, 7.
[4] A. A. Mendes Corrêa, "A Lusitânia pré-romana," *História de Portugal*, I, 105.
[5] Pericot García, *La España primitiva*, p. 68.

millenium B.C. to the present,[6] and there is no reason to believe that earlier inhabitants either were more numerous or were lacking. It is reasonable to assume that the ancient ways of the Lower Paleolithic Period were continued by a thinly spread population, except where thrusts were made into the interior by the peoples of more advanced cultures from the northern and the Mediterranean fringes. This was the case in the west of the peninsula, where even such thrusts as those of the hunters may have been lacking. This land-end area was largely unaffected by changes taking place elsewhere in the peninsula. The record of the Upper Paleolithic is scanty; in Portugal there is very little to be so identified. Techniques of the Lower Paleolithic continued there, while migrants from northern and Central Europe and from Africa were bringing Upper Paleolithic techniques into the northeast and the southeast of present Spain.[7]

POST-PALEOLITHIC CULTURES

It was toward the end of the Paleolithic Period that the west was drawn into a larger Iberian culture area by an intrusive ethnic wave of southern origin.

MUGE

The evidence for this change is found at Muge, a site on the Tejo River about thirty miles northeast of Lisbon, where large shell mounds of the transition stage between the Old and the New Stone ages have been excavated and studied. The skeletons revealed are those of men of short stature and long heads, very similar to those of the Natufians of Mount Carmel and also closely similar to those of the Carthaginians, Libyans, and

[6] Juan Maluquer de Motes, "Los Pueblos de la España céltica," *Historia de España,* Tomo I, Vol. III, Pt. 1, 10.

[7] Mendes Corrêa, "A Lusitânia pré-romana," *História de Portugal,* I, 104.

Phoenicians.[8] This offshoot of a culture area stretching from western Asia across north Africa came into Iberia at the end of the Glacial Period, when modern climatic conditions were being established. Magdalenian hunters were either withdrawing northward or were being eliminated, due to the lack of the game upon which they had fed.[9] At Muge, Epipaleolithic people lived within reach of the tide, where their food was to be had,[10] making their characteristic small geometric flints, until they were overwhelmed by subsequent migrants. There is no satisfactory agreement as to how this elimination took place. Guiart[11] believes that the Muge people were pushed to the north, to become part of the stock of the present province of Beira. Mendes Corrêa believes that it was a north European stock that eliminated or absorbed them.[12]

ASTURIAN

In northern Iberia at approximately the time of the prosperity at Muge another Epipaleolithic group, the Asturian, dominated a narrow coastal band fronting on the Atlantic from Bayonne, in southwest France, to the area at the mouth of the

[8] Jules Guiart, "Anthropologie des populations dolichocéphales de l'Europe Méridionale et de l'Afrique Septentrionale," *Congresso do Mundo Português*, XVII, 374.

[9] Mendes Corrêa, "A Lusitânia pré-romana," *História de Portugal*, I, 109.

[10] The *Lutraria compresa* upon which they subsisted is not found beyond tidal range. As the tide now does not reach within twenty miles of this area, it is obvious that there has been a change. Perhaps the land has risen in the ten thousand years since the culture flourished. *Ibid.*, p. 107. Júlio Martínez Santa-Olalla (*Esquema paletnológico de la Península Hispánica*, p. 48) would shorten the time span to from six thousand to eight thousand years. Or perhaps sedimentation has altered the area in such fashion that the water is now fresh. See J. Carríngton da Costa, "Evolução do meio geográfico na Pré-história de Portugal," *Congresso do Mundo Português*, I, 50.

[11] Guiart, "Anthropologie des populations dolichocéphales," *Congresso do Mundo Português*, XVII, 384.

[12] Mendes Corrêa, "A Lusitânia pré-romana," *História de Portugal*, I, 139.

Douro River in Portugal.[13] These Asturians found their living along the sea-edge by prying shellfish from the rocks with hand-axes, made by chipping the ends of water-worn cobbles. That they were not the same people as those of Muge is evident from the fact that at Muge the hand-axes of the Asturians were lacking. Nor were they Magdalenians, at least not those of the great hunting and painting stage. They may have represented a pauperized remnant of Magdalenians, or they may have represented a continuing remnant of a substratum of Lower Paleolithic stock which had been overlaid by Magdalenian culture.[14] Or they may have represented a transition culture between the Paleolithic and the Neolithic,[15] perhaps a transition between the cultures of the north and the south.

NEOLITHIC CULTURE

During the period of time in which the Asturian culture flourished in the north, peoples of the Neolithic entered and developed their culture along the Mediterranean coast of Iberia.[16] In its early years this culture clearly showed influences of the makers of the small geometric flints, but pottery makers and agriculturists were at work, and other Neolithic influences from the eastern Mediterranean were increasingly evident, coming both by land through North Africa and by sea along the Mediterranean. This culture, having strong African traits, with a pastoral base but also with rudimentary farming, af-

[13] Probably slightly later than the period of settlement at Muge. See Martínez Santa-Olalla, *Esquema paletnológico*, p. 49; Caro, *Los Pueblos del Norte*, p. 40; Abel Viana, "Os Problemas do Asturiense Português," *Congresso do Mundo Português*, V, 170; Hermann Lautensach, "Die diluviale Umwelt des Menschen in Portugal," *Congresso do Mundo Português*, XVIII, 748–749.

[14] Pericot García, *Las Raíces de España*, p. 27.

[15] Mendes Corrêa, "A Lusitânia pré-romana," *História de Portugal*, I, 115.

[16] According to Pericot García (*La España primitiva*, p. 112) the Neolithic phenomena started about 5000 B.C. The full Neolithic in Spain may be dated from 3500 to 2000 B.C. Martínez Santa-Olalla, *Esquema paletnológico*, p. 53.

fected a large part, perhaps all, of the peninsula. It was, however, chiefly along the Mediterranean coasts that it was important.[17] Again Portugal remained largely to one side of the stream of events, showing nothing more than a slight infiltration of elements of the more advanced culture. Discoveries there of the early and even of the full Neolithic are few.[18]

ALMERÍA CULTURE

At the beginning of the third millennium B.C., the Metal Age came to Iberia through the migration of a Saharan group, which established itself in the area of present Almería. This culture complex included from the outset articles of copper, especially a large number of weapons.[19] Almería culture spread into Andalusia on the one side, and into the valley of the lower Ebro River on the other. It may have been the foundation of what later became known to the Greeks as Iberian culture. At least from that time onward, in this area there is no evidence of any ethnic change of importance until the time of the first historical record, when the Greeks encountered the Iberian Tartessians and other littoral peoples of the south of the peninsula.[20] Obviously this does not prove direct connection and lineal descent of the Iberians from the Almerians, but as Mendes Corrêa points out, the assumption is not unreasonable even though there is no direct evidence.[21]

[17] *Ibid.*, pp. 53–54.
[18] Mendes Corrêa, "A Lusitânia pré-romana," *História de Portugal*, I, 116.
[19] Alberto del Castillo, "El Neoeneolítico," *Historia de España*, Tomo I, Vol. I, Pt. 4, 523, 571.
[20] Bosch Gimpera, "Los Iberos," *Cuadernos de Historia de España*, IX, 6; Hugo Obermaier and António García y Bellido in *El Hombre prehistórico y los orígenes de la humanidad*, pp. 258–259; Juan Maluquer de Motes, "Pueblos Ibéricos," *Historia de España*, Tomo I, Vol. III, 306.
[21] Mendes Corrêa, "A Lusitânia pré-romana," *História de Portugal*, I, 155.

THE INDIVIDUALITY OF PORTUGAL

MEGALITHIC PHENOMENA

About a thousand years after the appearance of Almería people, came the dramatic appearance of great stone burial structures. Many authors refer to a Megalithic culture, but as Pericot has pointed out, in view of its distribution and of the diverse peoples and cultures involved—e.g., the herders of the Cantabrians and Pyrenees as well as the agriculturists of the Guadalquivir valley—it can hardly be called a culture. It is better to refer to the Megalithic phenomena.[22] This cult use of great monoliths with capstones for burials, called dolmens (from two Breton words meaning "stone" and "table"), involves thousands of such structures and brings western Iberia to the center of the stage for the first time. There are especially great numbers of them in northern Portugal where their construction probably spanned a period of time from the late Neolithic Age into the Bronze Age.[23] It is argued by many Spanish and Portuguese scholars that their point of origin is to be sought within the Iberian Peninsula.[24] If concentration of numbers is the basis of decision this argument is a strong one. However, it ignores the existence of far older Neolithic dolmens

[22] Pericot García, *La España primitiva*, p. 144.

[23] Mendes Corrêa, "A Lusitânia pré-romana," *História de Portugal*, I, 118.

[24] The phenomena were widespread. But from where did the idea come? One finds proponents for theories of origin for any of the countries from Portugal to those of the eastern Mediterranean. Mendes Corrêa ("A Lusitânia pré-romana," *História de Portugal*, I, 140) suggests that it might have been Portugal. Obermaier and García y Bellido (*El Hombre prehistórico*, p. 174) agree fundamentally with him. Martínez Santa-Olalla (*Esquema paletnológico*, p. 59) points to southeast Spain. Bosch Gimpera says ("Los Iberos," *Cuadernos de Historia de España*, IX, 14) that the Megalithic culture in Portugal owed its origins to an indigenous non-Capsian culture but with Capsian infiltrations from the south, Andalusia, and the *mesetas* of Spain, this mixture constituting the basis of the pre-Celtic indigenous population of Portugal which appeared later as the historical Lusitanians. Pericot suggests (*La España primitiva*, p. 146) that the idea of the Megalithic tomb was introduced into Iberia in simple form, perhaps in several places, and in these different places took its diverse forms. Carleton Coon expresses the idea (*The Races of Europe*, p. 490) that the phenomena were the result of the spread by maritime Mediterraneans.

of Palestine, apparently built in imitation of earlier habitations.[25] Whatever may have been the place of origin, certainly the development of the cult seems to have been of basic importance in Iberia, from where certain local features spread to northern Europe on the one side and along the Mediterranean on the other.[26]

Toward the end of the Bronze Age another feature, almost surely of Andalusian derivation, the campaniform vase, spread widely throughout Europe.[27] This source of contact, as well as those of the cult associated with the dolmens, created a bond and an interchange between the peoples of Iberia (including Portugal, which so frequently has stood out of touch with European developments) and wide areas of the rest of Europe, as well as with the eastern Mediterranean shores. Whether the dolmens originated in Portugal, Spain, or elsewhere, is less important here than the fact of the obviously important contact between western Iberia and the world of Europe and western Asia during the early Bronze Age.

In southern Portugal, as a variation upon the sepulchral structures of the other Portuguese Megalithic, there developed a special type of dolmen, named for the site of Alcalá and hence called Alcalar. Instead of monoliths supporting the great slab on top, pillars were made of small stones, either fitted or cemented together. The precise dating of these dolmens can not be given. They may have been coexistent with those of the middle and the north of Portugal, or they may have developed later, representing a continuation of the traits of the early Bronze Age into a period of time when much of the remainder

[25] W. F. Albright, *The Archaeology of Palestine*, Penguin Books, p. 64. Pericot (*La España primitiva*, p. 146) favors the idea of eastern origin.

[26] The simple architecture of present North Portugal is strongly reminiscent of that of the dolmenic period.

[27] For the European distribution, see Obermaier and García y Bellido, *El Hombre prehistórico*, p. 171. The campaniform vase, presumably of Andalusian derivation, has been found in many Portuguese sites, although, strangely, not in the Algarve, the adjacent Portuguese area usually thought to be culturally closest to Andalusia, and but few in the Alentejo. Mendes Corrêa, "A Lusitânia pré-romana," *História de Portugal*, I, 130.

of the peninsula was far more advanced in the use of metals and in agricultural techniques.

PROBLEMS OF CHRONOLOGY

Actually, it is not always possible to speak positively in the comparison of peninsular regions and the time of their development. Throughout Iberia the problems of chronology and sequence are great. At various periods of time there have been cultures of greatly differing stages existing near each other. For example, in the later Bronze Age of other Western European countries much of Portugal remained in the stage in which copper was dominant. It did not really take part in the full Bronze Age developments. In fact, in Portugal there is a notable hiatus in the record between early Bronze Age developments and those of the second Iron Age, the latter intrusive from Central Europe and taking root among early Bronze Age cultures. Such unconformity does not exist through most of the rest of Iberia.[28] For example, in Spain the period of dolmenic phenomena was also one of a flourishing agriculture, as well as one of an increasing use of metals.[29] Portugal, the site of great energy in the construction and elaboration of the structures themselves, did not keep pace in other respects with the neighboring parts of the peninsula. Portugal not only lagged in the use of metals, but probably in the advancement in agriculture. Barley at least was cultivated,[30] but there is no evidence to show that agricultural development in general was anything but meagre.

PORTUGAL'S OFFSIDE POSITION

Portugal lost subsequently even the energy of its period of dolmen construction and then drifted into what seems to have

[28] Mendes Corrêa, "A Lusitânia pré-romana," *História de Portugal*, I, 146–147.
[29] Martínez Santa-Olalla, *Esquema paletnológico*, pp. 59–60.
[30] Jorge Dias, *Os Arados Portugueses e as suas prováveis origens*, p. 92.

been a cultural backwater. It scarcely took part in the splendid, basically Mediterranean culture, the Argaric, which brilliantly developed techniques in the use of silver, copper, and bronze. This culture, named for the site of El Argar in southeast Spain, spread into southern and northeastern Spain and even into the Balearic Islands, but in Portugal only into the Algarve.[31] Although Portugal gained very little from these developments which took place elsewhere in the peninsula, she did contribute raw materials to them. Such middle and late Bronze Age finds as have been made in Portugal are all related to the distribution of metals. During the period of Argaric culture, the copper of South Portugal was exploited. In a later period of the Bronze Age the tin of North Portugal became important. The south, with most of the copper deposits of Portugal, and the north, with most of the tin, have yielded remains of Bronze Age axes, whereas the Center, lacking for the most part both of these metals, is almost entirely devoid of the ax remains. However, none of the finds later than those of the dolmenic period suggest local developments or inventions. All indicate that they were of foreign provenience and that they were intrusive into an otherwise little changed older culture.[32]

[31] It probably did not spread beyond the Algarve in Portugal, although there have been isolated finds in the Alentejo. Mendes Corrêa, "A Lusitânia pré-romana," História de Portugal, I, 148; Bosch Gimpera, "Los Iberos," Cuadernos de Historia de España, IX, 42, 44.

Bosch Gimpera, "Los Iberos," Cuadernos de Historia de España, IX, 43) dates it 1900–1200 B.C. Martínez Santa-Olalla, on the other hand, shortens the span (Esquema paletnológico, p. 61); his dates are 1500–1200 B.C.

[32] Mendes Corrêa, "A Lusitânia pré-romana," História de Portugal, I, 152.

CHAPTER 6

Early Central European Influences
in Iberia

Indo-European Migration into Iberia

NEAR THE END of the second millennium B.C. great cultural changes took place in Iberia, but how and by whom is still an open question. Traces of Central European bronze culture first appeared in the north, and presumably not long after that introduction the first Indo-Europeans arrived. The first Celts may have arrived by 900 B.C., bringing small groups of Germans with them. Such is the belief of Bosch Gimpera.[1] But his is not the only theory regarding the immigrants. Júlio Martínez Santa-Olalla thinks that the earliest Indo-Europeans were pre-Celtic Bronze Age people who arrived in Iberia about the year 1000 B.C. and were followed by other Bronze Age, pre-Celtic Indo-Europeans, the Urnfields people.[2] Almagro finds it difficult to distinguish be-

---

[1] Pedro Bosch Gimpera, "Two Celtic Waves in Spain" (Sir John Rhŷs Memorial Lecture of November 8, 1939), *Proceedings of the British Academy*, XXVI (1940), 29.

[2] Júlio Martínez Santa-Olalla, *Esquema paletnológico de la Península Hispánica* (2nd ed.), pp. 62–68, 78–79.

CENTRAL EUROPEAN INFLUENCES

tween Urnfields, Ligurian, Illyrian, and Celt, and suggests that after 800 B.C. the Indo-European peoples filtered into Iberia throughout a considerable period of time and that they were essentially of the same stock.[3] Pericot cautiously inclines to the belief that there were numerous peoples entering Iberia after 900 B.C., differing considerably from each other but ultimately dominated by Goidelic Celt culture.[4] Maluquer suggests greater complexity, the first Celts entering by the eighth century at the latest, but perhaps considerably before that date.[5]

The above data, seemingly contradictory, are not presented pointlessly. They indicate fairly well the present state of indecision—or at least lack of firm knowledge—concerning the migrations of the Indo-Europeans into western Europe. Furthermore, they are not completely at sixes-and-sevens. It is to be noted that all of the authors cited point to the movement of Central European peoples into Iberia during the late Bronze Age. Whether such migrants are to be identified as Celt or pre-Celt may be secondary to the fact of their place of origin. One other fact must be kept in mind, however; these earliest Indo-Europeans, Celt or not, were not acquainted with the use of iron. This metal was no doubt introduced into Iberia by Celts, but so far there is no reason to reject the traditional belief that its introduction is to be credited to the Goidelic Celts of the seventh century.[6] By the middle of that century iron was in common use in Catalonia,[7] but so far there have been no earlier data established for its use in Iberia.

THE SPREAD OF THE CELTS

But who were the Celts, what kind of culture did they have, and what were the areas of Iberia affected by them? These are

[3] Martín Almagro, "La Invasión Céltica en España," *Historia de España*, Tomo I, Vol. II, 262–272.

[4] Luis Pericot García, *Las Raices de España*, pp. 47, 50.

[5] Juan Maluquer de Motes, "Los Pueblos de la España céltica," *Historia de España*, Tomo I, Vol. III, Pt. 1, 135.

[6] Júlio Caro Baroja, *Los Pueblos de España*, p. 94.

[7] Martínez Santa-Olalla, *Esquema paletnológico*, p. 78.

questions of fundamental importance in the historical geography of Iberia, which are again, after a period of neglect, being investigated by Iberian scholars.[8] That early Celts entered the peninsula through the western passes of the Pyrenees and that they left a strong impress upon the north of Iberia is beyond doubt. However, there are gaps to be explained. For example, in the present Spanish provinces of Vizcaya, Guipúzcoa, and Navarra, there is no record of Celtic dominance. Yet Celts did find their way through this presently largely Basque area. It seems that the local population and culture were sufficiently strong to resist, and finally to absorb and transform them.[9] Farther to the west, however, there was a different situation. In many parts of Alava, Santander, León, and Asturias, Celts either displaced or dominated the older stocks of people.[10] Still farther west, especially in present northwest Portugal and Galicia, they settled in numbers among, and blended with, a firmly rooted farm population—one made up of earlier farmers from Central Europe (probably including some of Germanic stock) and primitive, metal-using farmers harking back in their ancestry to the Megalithic Period of the early Bronze Age.[11]

The extent of Celtic spread in Iberia is still argued, but as time and linguistic inquiry go on, much is being added to our

[8] The Celtic question in Iberia has had periods of both attention and neglect. Early culture historians focused great attention upon them, but following upon that period of interest there was a period of neglect, when enthusiasm for the culture of the Iberians of the Mediterranean coasts eclipsed everything else. Only in the last quarter century has there been a renewed interest and enthusiasm for Celtic culture and its effect upon the Iberian peninsula. Now, indeed, the problem is considered with an enthusiasm that goes to extremes which may counterbalance earlier neglect but which hardly conduces to balanced judgment. Fortunately the men most greatly concerned, realizing the danger of the situation, are tempering enthusiasm with moderation. See Pericot García, *Las Raices de España*, pp. 47–48.

[9] Bosch Gimpera, "Two Celtic Waves," p. 109.

[10] Júlio Caro Baroja, *Los Pueblos del Norte de la Península Ibérica*, p. 213. Many provinces of present Spain, such as Alava, Santander, and León, bear the name of the most important city of the region. In such cases, to avoid crowding on the place-name map, only the city is identified.

[11] Maluquer, "Los Pueblos de la España céltica," *Historia de España*, Tomo I, Vol. III, Pt. 1, 10, 12, 77–79, 179.

knowledge of the matter. Probably Celtic tongues spread from southern France throughout most of the north of Iberia and on the west extended southward to include the Lusitanians of central Portugal.[12] They probably predominated in the interior of the peninsula prior to the Roman advent.[13] In some areas they reached the Mediterranean coasts,[14] and long before the Roman entry—probably soon after the arrival of the first iron-using Celts—connections had been re-established between the peninsula, plus western France, and the British Isles.

ECONOMY OF THE CELTS—HERDING

The Celts came into Iberia with their families, flocks, and wagons—and it is not without interest that the type of Central European wagon that they introduced is still used in Galicia and Asturias.[15] In their economy they represented a continuation of the Bronze Age cultures of western Germany.[16] They were agriculturists certainly, but also pastoralists. It is difficult to determine which type of economy was dominant. Possibly stock-raising was more important than farming, as in the case

[12] Caro Baroja, *Pueblos del Norte*, pp. 82–84; Adolfo Schulten, *Historia de Numancia*, p. 21.

[13] Caro Baroja, *Pueblos del Norte*, pp. 82–85; Maluquer, "Los Pueblos de la España céltica," *Historia de España*, Tomo I, Vol. III, Pt. 1, 10.

[14] Maluquer, "Los Pueblos de la España céltica," *Historia de España*, Tomo I, Vol. III, Pt. 1, 9; António García y Bellido, *La Península Ibérica en los comienzos de su historia*, p. 58.

[15] Maluquer, "Los Pueblos de la España céltica," *Historia de España*, Tomo I, Vol. III, Pt. 1, 171.

The *carro chillon* (or *chirrión*), typically with the axle firmly attached to and turning with the wheels, is certainly not Roman. See Fritz Krüger, *El Léxico rural del noroeste Ibérico*, p. 47. Caro Baroja (*Pueblos del Norte*, pp. 144–149 and map) says that it is pre-Indo-European. Its historical distribution is that of the northern and western peripheries, the lands of pre-Celtic farmers and herders, with only limited extensions into the edges of the *meseta*. See Krüger, *El Léxico rural del noroeste Ibérico*, pp. 46–47. Also see Luis de Hoyos Sáinz and Nieves de Hoyos Sancho, *Manual de Folklore*, pp. 436–437.

[16] Jorge Dias, *Os Arados Portugueses e as suas prováveis origens*, p. 101; Maluquer, "Los Pueblos de la España céltica," *Historia de España*, Tomo I, Vol. III, Pt. 1, 11.

74

A Verraco in Ciudad Rodrigo

of the Neolithic communities of northern Europe.[17] In the northern forests of Iberia there was an abundance of everything necessary for their animals—beech mast and acorns for pigs, and food for horses, cattle, sheep, and goats.[18] Interesting evidence of the importance of herding in northwest Iberia is found in the large number of so-called *verracos*, testifying to the great importance ascribed to certain animals, especially pigs.[19] The region of these granite sculptures centers in the Spanish provinces of Avila, Salamanca, and Zamora. From there the sculptures—crude, if you will, but so then is modern abstract sculpture—spread into the adjacent areas of North Portugal and to some extent into Galicia. The earliest examples are probably to be credited to sixth-century Celts,[20] but the highest

[17] Grahame Clarke, "Farmers and Forests in Neolithic Europe," *Antiquity*, XIX, No. 74 (June, 1945), 67.

[18] *Ibid.*, p. 70.

[19] Jesus Taboada, "La Cultura de los verracos en el noroeste hispánico," *Cuadernos de Estudios Gallegos*, IV, No. 12 (1949), 15; Maluquer, "Los Pueblos de la España céltica," *Historia de España*, Tomo I, Vol. III, Pt. 1, 25.

[20] Taboada, "La Cultura de los verracos . . . ," *Cuadernos de Estudios Gallegos*, IV, No. 12 (1949), 17.

development of the work was accomplished by later Celts, probably between the fourth century B.C. and the first century A.D.[21]

The veneration of the animal did not preclude the enjoyment of its flesh. At about the beginning of the Christian era, Strabo spoke of Cantabria (mountainous northern Iberia) as being an area of fine hams,[22] and Varro said that "it was asserted that once when a pig had been killed in Lusitania (present Middle Portugal) there was sent as a present to a senator two ribs with meat attached which weighed twenty-three pounds, and that in the pig the depth of flesh from skin to bone was one and a quarter feet." [23] That the veneration of animals was not unique to Iberian environment is shown by the fact that Irish Celts kept sacred cattle, and "royal" oxen, swine and sheep.[24]

ECONOMY OF THE CELTS—AGRICULTURE

Northern and northwestern Iberia was wonderfully suited to the tastes of the Celts and to those of their herds of pigs, sheep, cattle,[25] and goats.[26] Men here could pursue the male tasks of herding, fighting, and hunting, and as these are rainy lands of mild weather, women could cultivate wheat for bread,[27] barley for beer,[28] and flax for textiles,[29] with the

[21] Maluquer, "Los Pueblos de la España céltica," *Historia de España,* Tomo I, Vol. III, Pt. 1, 120, 138.
[22] Caro Baroja, *Pueblos del Norte,* p. 26.
[23] *M. T. Varro on Farming,* trans. by Lloyd Storr-Best, p. 172.
[24] R. A. S. Macalister, *Tara, a Pagan Sanctuary of Ancient Ireland,* p. 124. See also Christopher and Jacquetta Hawks, *Prehistoric Britain,* Pelican Books, p. 135.
[25] Maluquer, "Los Pueblos de la España céltica," *Historia de España,* Tomo I, Vol. III, Pt. 1, 176, 183.
[26] Strabo reported that in this area goat's meat was eaten by preference. Caro Baroja, *Pueblos del Norte,* p. 46.
[27] Maluquer, "Los Pueblos de la España céltica," *Historia de España,* Tomo I, Vol. III, Pt. 1, 99, 172.
[28] Barley and beer were old in the region at the time of Strabo. See Caro Baroja, *Pueblos del Norte,* p. 44.
[29] Maluquer, "Los Pueblos de la España céltica," *Historia de España,* Tomo I, Vol. III, Pt. 1, 172, 176. In Europe specialized hunting (highly disciplined and in large bands) had passed out of existence prior to the

gathering of nuts and fruits as a supplementary means of providing food. Actually, farming may well have been more important than it would seem from the records. It is possible that the simple activities, especially of women, in this patriarchal society may have received less notice than they deserved. It is of interest to observe that the Irish branch of these peoples convened their assemblies to coincide with the critical days in the agricultural year.[30] Or, indeed, it may be possible that the men were more involved than the record shows. When the Celts came into Iberia they brought with them their plow, although it was not everywhere used.[31] There can be little doubt, in view of the universal association of plows and males, that men were to some degree involved in planting, but the distribution of the use of the plow indicates that the association of males with agriculture was either casual or that they were easily dissuaded from it. For example, there was probably no plow used in North Portugal prior to the advent of the Romans.[32] This situation can probably be explained by the fact that this northwest area preserved strong matrilineal remnants.[33] Here, men considered farming unmanly and woman's work.[34] Nor is this difficult to understand (given their back-

period about which we are writing. However, hunting by individuals and sometimes by small groups was common. In no sense was it the fundamental basis of life but always a supplement to the dietary.

Something the same can be said of gathering. None of the Europeans of that time were fully dependent upon gathering in the sense in which some of our primitive contemporaries depend. However, there is no doubt that the women gathered nuts, fruits, greens, and perhaps many other foods as a standard part of their domestic occupation.

[30] Macalister, *Tara*, p. 155.

[31] Caro Baroja, *Pueblos del Norte*, p. 211. See also Júlio Caro Baroja, "Los Arados españoles, sus tipos y repartición," *Revista de Dialectología y Tradiciones populares*, V, No. 1 (1949), 93, 94, and Figures 15 and 17; Júlio Caro Baroja, "La Vida agraria tradicional reflejada en el arte Español," *Estudios de Historia Social de España*, I (1949), 92–94; and Maluquer, "Los Pueblos de la España céltica," *Historia de España*, Tomo I, Vol. III, Pt. 1, 171.

[32] Dias, *Arados*, pp. 103, 107.

[33] Caro Baroja, *Pueblos del Norte*, p. 205.

[34] Maluquer, "Los Pueblos de la España céltica," *Historia de España*, Tomo I, Vol. III, Pt. 1, 72.

ground), for it should not be overlooked that in the hilly northwest, where people lived on the uplands, the plow was of little
use. Until the Romans put men to work on the valley lands
where plows were serviceable, the area, reasonably enough,
remained an area of hoe farming.[35]

Nevertheless, parts of Iberia were exploited by men with
plows. The Vacceos, living along the middle course of the
Duero River and also occupying the area to the north around
the present cities of Zamora, Valladolid, and Palencia, were
skilled grain farmers using plows.[36] Large quantities of wheat
were harvested, especially around Palencia, at the time of the
Celtiberian war.[37] It is true, however, that the Vacceos were
Celtiberians of late entry into the peninsula. They came especially late into the west, where they were in the act of appro-
priating lands from earlier Celtic settlers at the time of the
Roman conquest.[38] It happens that this area can be equated
with the zone of "dry and intermediate calcareous soils" shown
on the map of Del Villar.[39] They are approximately *rendzinas*
and are now considered to be one of the really excellent soils
for cereals.[40] So the question might well be raised as to whether
the Vacceos, admittedly plow-and-grain farmers, would have
taken precisely this area, so fitting to their desires, if it had not
been previously demonstrated to be desirable for use with their
tools.

The Vacceos were an interesting people from another point of
view. They were organized into a firmly controlled collectivist
society. At the time of the grain harvest, division was made
officially—and equally—and the death penalty was exacted for
holding out any of the grain from the collective pool.[41] It seems
that neither the Romans, nor their successors in authority
over this part of Iberia, destroyed the traditions of community

[35] *Ibid.*, p. 170.   [36] Jorge Dias, *Rio de Onor*, p. 60.
[37] Caro Baroja, *Pueblos del Norte*, p. 215.
[38] Maluquer, "Los Pueblos de la España céltica," *Historia de España,*
Tomo I, Vol. III, Pt. 1, 24.
[39] Emilio H. del Villar, *Los Suelos de la Península Luso-Ibérica* (map).
[40] Raymond E. Storie, personal statement.
[41] Caro Baroja, *Pueblos del Norte*, p. 45.

78

effort (and perhaps the Germanic Swabians strengthened them again), for there are many parts of remote, mountainous Portugal and northwestern Spain where such practices are continued today—attenuated, but still fundamental to the economy.[42]

In the northern mountains, there may have been a primitive combination of herding, farming, hunting, and gathering, without particular accent upon one or the other. Strabo, a Mediterranean, was struck by the fact that these people lacked olive oil and in place of it used butter—or at least he is translated to have said this. However, it seems possible that it was not butter, for there is no positive evidence of milch cows in the area, and the grease used may have been that of the pig.[43] In either case there was a dependence upon animal fat.

Gathering seems to have had considerable importance.[44] Strabo reported that the northern people depended upon acorns for their food during three quarters of the year; but probably he exaggerated the importance of the acorn and neglected that of chestnuts, for the great forests of edible chestnuts in this area have been eliminated only during the last few generations. In the nineteenth century they still flourished and were an important source of food.[45]

[42] Dias, *Rio de Onor*, pp. 20, 28, 63. I have oversimplified the problem in my statement. There are various and greatly differing opinions as to the origins of collectivism in Iberia. Maluquer ("Los Pueblos de la España céltica . . . ," pp. 94, 170) states his belief that such collective economy may be a typical expression of the organization of a migrating group. This contention is hard to accept in view of the persistence of collective practices among the anciently rooted people in the present northwest of Spain and North Portugal. Mendes Corrêa (*Raízes de Portugal*, pp. 73–74) has called attention to the strong collective organization of the Megalithic culture groups. A further view is that of some Spanish medievalists, who now think that such organization is likely to be of medieval provenience. Orlando Ribeiro in "Villages et communautés rurales au Portugal," *Biblos*, XVI (1940), Tomo II, 420–421, shows how collective systems in Trás-os-Montes hark back to pre-Roman times and attributes them to necessary arrangements in a grain-pasturage-fallow rotation.

[43] Caro Baroja, *Pueblos del Norte*, p. 46.

[44] *Loc. cit.*

[45] Alberto Sampaio, "As Vilas do Norte de Portugal," *Estudos históricos e económicos*, I, Pt. 1, 28.

First Contacts between Celts and Earlier Inhabitants of Iberia

The difference between Celtic culture, as commonly considered, and that of the earlier settlers is partly of degree and partly of kind. The Celts had a background of culture not dissimilar to that of some of the inhabitants encountered upon their entry into that peninsula.[46] Similar background and tastes may have allowed them to settle among the indigenous groups in amity and cooperation, but we do not know this as a fact. They may have pushed in by force, but in view of the disparity between Celtic tribes it is probable that the situation varied according to time, place, and tribe. The Celts of the seventh century B.C. knew iron and were fighters. Their possession of superior weapons and their propensity for battle may have resulted in the forcible eviction of earlier peoples from parts of Iberia. Some authors maintain that the sword should be considered the badge of these Celts, that aggression was their preference, and that the large number of fortified settlements used by them in strategic locations supports this thesis.[47] Such authors are apt to credit to the Celts, both in origin as well as in later development, the predominantly Portuguese hilltop fort settlements known as *castros* and *citânias*.[48] There can be no doubt at all that *castros* were greatly elaborated by the Celts in the centuries just before the birth of Christ and that some of them during that time were converted into real fortified cities.[49]

[46] Maluquer, "Los Pueblos de la España céltica," *Historia de España*, Tomo I, Vol. III, Pt. 1, 11.

[47] Martínez Santa-Olalla, *Esquema paletnológico*, p. 79; Dias, *Arados*, p. 99.

[48] Some authors distinguish between a *castro* and a *citânia*, saying that the former was merely a fort and the latter both a fort and a place of settlement. This distinction, according to an eminent authority on the matter, has no value, since there is increasing evidence that all such structures were used as settlements. See Mário Cardozo, *Citânia e Sabroso*, pp. 9–10.

[49] Martínez Santa-Olalla, *Esquema paletnológico*, p. 103; Taboada, "La Cultura de los verracos en el noroeste hispánico," *Cuadernos de*

THE INDIVIDUALITY OF PORTUGAL

The Problem of the Castro and Its Origin

However, there is strong evidence adduced to support the belief that the *castros* were pre-Celtic, for the quality and style of the *castro* seems to indicate an origin out of the remote past of Portugal itself. In all periods they were rude and showed a continuation of archaic forms. The pottery associated with them was often virtually the same as that of the earliest period of the Bronze Age.[50] It may be of importance to observe that the *castro* area of concentration in Iberia is approximately that of the earlier area of dolmens in the peninsula,[51] that is, an area with a strong Megalithic tradition, where the knowledge of stone working is age-old,[52] and where the curved structure is of ancient tradition.[53] Although *castros* were of a variety of

Estudios Gallegos, IV, No. 12 (1949), 26; Maluquer, "Los Pueblos de la España céltica," *Historia de España,* Tomo I, Vol. III, Pt. 1, 15.

The development of large fortified cities here, however, did not involve cultural improvements in other respects. The area is known to anthropologists as one in which there was a continuance of early ways, in which there was a prolongation of Hallstatt type culture generally, and in which La Tène items were rare, as the connections with south and east Iberia remained tenuous until the time of the Roman conquest. See A. A. Mendes Corrêa, "A Lusitânia pré-romana," *História de Portugal,* I, 174, 181.

[50] Mendes Corrêa, "A Lusitânia pré-romana . . . ," pp. 181–182.

[51] A. de Amorim Girão, *Geografia de Portugal,* maps, pp. 214–216.

[52] It is far from lost. In the Minho today props for grape trellises are hewn from granite—an unlikely material for such a purpose.

[53] Maluquer, "Los Pueblos de la España céltica," *Historia de España,* Tomo I, Vol. III, Pt. 1, 50. This is in keeping with the thought of Richthofen that circular structures were pre-Celtic and non-Indo-European (António Jorge Dias, "Las Construcciones circulares del Noroeste de la Península Ibérica y las citânias," *Cuadernos de Estudios Gallegos,* VI (1946), p. 176, and with Dr. Edwin Loeb, who argues that circular structures probably originated with Hamitic peoples (personal statement).

Another point of view is that of Florentino López Cuevillas and Joaquín Lorenzo Fernández ("Las Habitaciones de los Castros," *Cuadernos de Estudios Gallegos,* II, Nos. 5–7 [1946–1947], 7–74. See particularly pp. 10, 30, and 62–63), who argue that stone houses in northwest Iberia were late and took their form from an earlier native round house, built by interlacing branches for the walls and by roofing the structure with straw. They point out that, although round houses were known in Gaul, they were so different in other respects that they cannot be compared with the structures of northwestern Iberia. Their argument in support of the belief in the "petrifaction" of the round *cabaña* of branches is seduc-

shapes—round, elliptical, and some of no simple form but with broken lines—sharp angles were few and the curve predominated.

In another argument against the Celtic origin of the *castro*, Maluquer points out that the earliest Celtic houses in Iberia were not circular, but quadrangular,[54] and Bosch has shown that Celtic structures south of the Mondego River were quadrangular.[55] However, it would seem again (as in the case of relating one type of economy to a Celtic group and assuming that this was the only type of economy to be found among Celts in Iberia) that it may be a bootless procedure to try to relate one type of house to all Celts. Obviously they used structures of a variety of shapes in the northwest of Iberia. This may indicate, indeed, what has been suggested above, that the Celts, especially the early Celts, were adjustable when they entered Iberia not only in the choice of a means of livelihood, pastoralism or agriculture, but also in the acceptance of the building practices of the local area. The northern Portuguese structures may probably be associated in the origin of their type with the ancient dolmen area, whereas the rectangular structures south of the Mondego River can, perhaps, be associated with a distinct culture area with connections eastward into the interior of the peninsula.[56]

---

tive, but it does not dispose of the authors cited above nor of the ancient tradition of masonry in the area.

[54] Maluquer, "Los Pueblos de la España céltica," *Historia de España*, Tomo I, Vol. III, Pt. 1, 181. If one wanted to confuse the issue even further he might cite Maluquer again (*ibid.*, p. 97), where he states his belief that the *castros*, at least of the *verraco* area, go back to the early Bronze Age and that they were later inhabited by Indo-Europeans. It should be noted that these *castros* of the *verraco* area—at least those that have been excavated—have rectangular structures quite different in general character from the edifices of the North Portuguese-Galician *castro* area (*ibid.*, p. 100).

[55] Bosch Gimpera, "Two Celtic Waves," p. 80.

[56] *Ibid.*, p. 83.

THE INDIVIDUALITY OF PORTUGAL

ROMAN IDENTIFICATION OF CELTS IN IBERIA

The problem of the extent of the spread of Celtic cultures might be largely solved if we could be sure as to which of the tribes of the peninsula first encountered by Greeks and Romans were Celtic, but this is no easy task. It is a matter of confusion and disagreement among scholars, all of whom can quote classical authors to their own satisfaction. For example, one of our best sources of information for early Greek contacts is the *Ora Maritima*, the work of a geographer of the first century B.C., which was based upon the geography of Eforos, a work composed in the fourth century B.C. Eforos, in turn, had incorporated into his manuscript material from a Massaliote narrative of the sixth century B.C., adding data from the period subsequent to the time at which the Greek author from Massalia had written the document. The origin of the information can be established, however, as being even earlier than the sixth century, for the Greek of Massalia almost surely used information from Punic sources antedating his time. In any event, the early material is not entirely lost by passing through so many hands.[57] In this document it is not clear that the tribes of central Portugal and Spain, the Cempses and Sefes, were Celts;[58] yet Herodotus said that the Celts lived next to the Cinesios (usually called Cynetes or Cónios) of the Algarve of present South Portugal. Aristotle, on the other hand, said that they were "above Iberia in a very cold region" (which does not suggest Portugal), immediately to the north of the Cinesios. Rather, it suggests the interior of Old Castile. Polybius, Strabo, and Pliny, as well as many other Romans, said that the Celts lived between the Tejo and Guadiana rivers,[59] which would bring them more or less in accord with Herodotus.

[57] Casimiro Torres, "Las Kassitérides," *Cuadernos de Estudios Gallegos,* IV (1945), 623. Francisco José Velozo (*Oestrymnis*, pp. 39–40) expounds the view, and supports it with considerable evidence, that the *Ora Maritima* was based ultimately upon Punic sources.

[58] Almagro, "La Invasión Céltica en España," *Historia de España,* Tomo I, Vol. II, 245.

[59] Mendes Corrêa, "A Lusitânia pré-romana," *História de Portugal,* pp. 164–165.

DISPARITY OF MODERN OPINIONS REGARDING
CELTIC IDENTIFICATION

Modern authorities on the Iberian Peninsula have a tendency to expand Celtic culture beyond the limits acceptable a generation ago. Bosch Gimpera, Schulten, and Dixon defend the idea that the Cempses and Sefes were Celts.[60] Maluquer goes even further, stating that not only these peoples, but the Cinesios as well,[61] were Celts. Dixon would not quibble with the first part of this view, but he believes that the Cynetes (Cinesios) were Ligurians.

If the authorities cannot agree, it may be asked how one can use the material in making judgments as to historical geography of the area involved. There must be some attempt at clarification, but if one thinks of Celts as being all essentially the same and responding to differing environmental conditions always in like manner, confusion is hard to dissipate. Understanding may be had, however, with the realization that "Celtic" may mean a variety of things in terms of economics and social structure. It seems probable that classical authorities may have judged native tribes and their ethnic associations in terms of language and economic practices.

Among the several groups of Celts, at least three fundamental subdivisions should be made on the basis of language. The Goidelic Celts, with Hallstatt techniques, must be kept distinct from the Brythonic Celts with their elements of eastern grassland culture and the strong admixture of Mediterranean traits that came to be associated with Celtic La Tène culture.[62] A third group, the Belgas, who may be roughly equated with

[60] Almagro, "La Invasión Céltica en España," *Historia de España*, Tomo I, Vol. II, 245; Pierson Dixon, *The Iberians of Spain and Their Relations with the Aegean World*, end map.
[61] Maluquer, "Los Pueblos de la España céltica," *Historia de España*, Tomo I, Vol. III, Pt. 1, 9.
[62] Carleton S. Coon, *The Races of Europe*, pp. 186–187; Hugo Obermaier and António García y Bellido, *El Hombre prehistórico y los orígenes de la humanidad* (2nd ed.), p. 306.
The Iron Age came tardily into Central Europe from the Mediterranean. However, it was taking clear form in the early part of the first millennium B.C. The earliest period is termed "Hallstatt" after the type

84

the Celtiberians, must be recognized as distinct from the other two.[63] The Belgas were the last of the major groups of Celts to find their way into Iberia. For recognition of the special qualities of these peoples we are indebted to the work of Maluquer, whose evidence as to their individuality is far more convincing than the thesis of Schulten that makes the Celtiberians merely a mixture of an early Celtic group with Iberians.[64]

VARIATIONS AMONG THE CELTS

All of the above facts make it obvious that there were many differences among the Celts.[65] They were a mixed group racially, although dominantly Nordic, and they were mixed culturally as well.[66] They were both agricultural and pastoral, but the emphasis may have been quite different among the various groups, for when they entered the Iberian peninsula they were still in the formative stage of their culture. Any one of several cultural trends might have been chosen. Some were strongly influenced by native groups that had been firmly rooted in their own areas and had developed well-integrated cultures.[67] Obviously, it is equally possible, and perhaps more probable, that migrants who were both agricultural and pastoral would have made their choice in terms of the place in which they elected to settle or which was available to them for settlement. Where farming proved to be more profitable, they would concentrate

site in eastern Austria. Its duration was roughly from 800 to 400 B.C.

"La Tène," following the name of a type site in western Switzerland, is the name associated with the later Iron Age in Central Europe, which developed under frequent and intimate contacts with the Greek world, especially through Greek Massalia (Marseilles). It was carried largely by Celts and is usually dated as being from 400 B.C. to about the time of the birth of Christ. It was a far more sophisticated culture than that of Hallstatt.

[63] Maluquer, "Los Pueblos de la España céltica," *Historia de España*, Tomo I, Vol. III, Pt. 1, 12.

[64] Schulten, *Historia de Numancia*, p. 27.

[65] Maluquer, "Los Pueblos de la España céltica," *Historia de España*, Tomo I, Vol. III, Pt. 1, 13–15.

[66] *Ibid.*, pp. 8, 10.

[67] Pericot García, *Las Raices de España*, p. 51.

upon it; and where pastoralism was advantageous, this would be their emphasis. The Celts that went to the Mediterranean region came under Phoenician, Iberian, Greek, and Etruscan influences.[68] Those that went to the area of the rainy, green, northwestern edge of Iberia, where there were agricultural populations in some cases harking back to the Bronze Age, settled themselves on the land, raising grains, flax, and animals. The *meseta*, on the other hand, in most parts offered a more promising opportunity for herding, and this occupation was the choice of most Celts who settled there.[69]

In the third century B.C., the northern mountains of Spain were dominantly agricultural and matrilineal (which was pre-Indo-Germanic), whereas the *meseta* was predominantly pastoral[70] and, typical of Celts, dominantly patrilineal. It seems that the numerically greatly superior peoples of the northern mountains maintained their fundamental way of life in spite of the Celts who settled among them and asserted control over them. The Celts fitted into the culture pattern of these earlier inhabitants—one that had had connections with the immemorially old culture area of Central Europe. The peoples of the sparsely settled *meseta* apparently were more largely changed by Celtic customs.[71] With their pastoral-agricultural background, adjustment to either one or the other type of economy presented no serious problems to the Celts.[72]

[68] There are other possible ones. See "Le Mobilier Funéraire de la Tombe de Vix," *La Revue des Arts*, No. 4 (1953), 202; Raymond Bloch and René Joffroy, "L'Alphabet du Cratère de Vix," *Revue de Philologie*, XXVII, No. 11 (1953), 175–191; "Le Grand Cratère de Vix: produit de l'Italie meridionale ou 'vase etrusque'? Quelques théories à ne pas prendre 'à la lettre,'" *Revue Archéologique*, Ser. 6, XLIII (Jan.–March, 1954), 71–79.

[69] Maluquer, "Los Pueblos de la España céltica," *Historia de España*, Tomo I, Vol. III, Pt. 1, 184.

[70] Caro Baroja, *Pueblos del Norte*, pp. 29, 205, 226.

[71] Bosch Gimpera, "Two Celtic Waves," p. 113.

[72] There is another factor also, that of the non-Celtic Central Europeans who accompanied the Celtic invasions. In some cases it may have been these peoples who established the economic pattern. Many small Germanic groups are perhaps involved in the Celtic invasions. See note 1 above, and Maluquer, p. 10.

CHAPTER 7

Contacts between the Ancient Civilizations of the Eastern Mediterranean and Iberia

First Direct Contacts

ONE FREQUENTLY meets claims that there was contact between the far western coasts of present Spain and Portugal and Crete of Minoan times. It is not only a seductive idea but it makes a reasonable hypothesis, for the Minoans were good navigators, traders, and seekers of metals. Had they known anything of the Iberian Peninsula they might well have been attracted; however, while it is quite possible that the Mediterranean island route to the west was used by them,[1] as yet there is no convincing evidence that it was. The excavations of Almería culture at Los Millares, which may be dated as of 2000–1800 B.C., presented certain items reminiscent of Aegean cultures, but there is no evidence that would clearly demonstrate connection. Such items may represent nothing more than casual parallelism. Other finds of a somewhat later period in Spain make better evidence of con-

[1] Rhys Carpenter, *The Greeks in Spain*, p. 17.

tact with the eastern Mediterranean lands, for they can be neatly equated with materials of Egyptian Tell-el-Amarna of 1400–1200 B.C. The Egyptian trade items of this period of time are well known to Spanish archaeology and almost surely may be associated with Phoenician intermediaries. As of the present date, such items may be taken as the earliest evidence of direct contact between Iberia and the eastern Mediterranean navigators.[2]

A WESTWARD MOVEMENT

It could not have been long after this time that easterners gained a greatly increased knowledge of Iberia and interest in it. In a sense, there was a westward movement that was the southern counterpart of a similar movement in the north. The chronology of contacts between the eastern Mediterraneans and Iberia is roughly comparable to that of the Central European contacts with north and northwest Iberia. The earliest passage of Phoenician ships through the straits of Gibraltar was probably made during the general period of time when the Central European farmers and pastoralists were first entering the Cantabrian region. These events preceded the first millennium B.C.

Later, Greek exploration and trade grew, following the example given by neighboring Phoenicia, perhaps as early as the ninth century and certainly by the end of the seventh century B.C. Such contacts can be equated in time with the acceleration of the east-west movement of peoples and cultures which took place in the north with the advent of the Celts, who may have appeared in Iberia as early as 900 B.C., and the main force of which was felt by the sixth century. Between the sixth and the third centuries B.C., while the lands of the western Mediterranean were developing under the influence of active and aggressive Greeks and Carthaginians, northern Iberia was changing under the influence of Celts of later arrival from beyond the Pyrenees.

[2] António García y Bellido, *Hispania Graeca*, I, 5–7.

Salt-evaporating Basins in the Algarve (Probably Operating in the Same Way and at the Same Place as in Phoenician Times)

There was a difference, however, between the early contacts along the Mediterranean coasts and those of the Central Europeans with northern Iberia. It was not opportunity for settlement that drew men along the southern coasts, but trade and quite probably fishing, and perhaps evaporation of sea water for salt. Sidon, the mother of many other Phoenician settlements at home and abroad, bore a name meaning fishers' town, and the Phoenician settlement, in approximately the present location of Málaga, bore the name Malach, which means salting place.[3] It was the attraction of metals that drew the early Greeks beyond the straits of Gibraltar and along the western coasts of Spain.

CONTACTS WITH THE WEST COAST OF IBERIA

It is possible that the early merchant wayfarers sailed up the west coast to trade directly with Galicia. But if they did, the coast of present Portugal represented a gap in their interest, for there is almost no record of them there.[4] It would seem that Portugal was then, as through so many periods of time before and after, apart from the main stream of events. It possessed no great source of silver such as the mines of Andalusia, nor of copper or tin (with slight exceptions in both cases). With her metals, Spain was a magnet for the early traders, whereas Portugal attracted casual traders at most. A few Punic settlements in the south were devoted to fishing, salt-making, and perhaps some farming, but none of these has left a record of importance. There is sufficient knowledge of such settlements, however, to assure us that Portugal was not entirely unknown or untouched by developments, even though it was offside. In part, it was affected directly, but the more important results were indirect.

The history of the revolutionary events involved in the con-

[3] Charles L. Cutting, *Fish Saving*, pp. 18, 21.
[4] There are slight exceptions; for example, there is the Egyptian scarab of the seventh century B.C. that was found in a pre-Celtic level at Alcácer do Sal. See Pedro Bosch Gimpera, "Two Celtic Waves in Spain," *Proceedings of the British Academy*, XXVI (1940), 79.

tacts between Phoenicians, Greeks, and Carthaginians in their commerce with Iberia is the basis for the understanding of the ultimate domination of the whole peninsula by Mediterraneans from Rome. In order to understand the effect upon Portugal we must use, for the most part, evidence dealing with Spain; indirect as it is, it has important bearing upon the development of the Portuguese character and nation.

HOMOGENEITY OF THE IBERIAN MEDITERRANEAN REGION

At the time of their first contacts with the west, the earliest Phoenicians and Greeks encountered a culture area with fundamentally similar characteristics throughout. It extended along the Mediterranean coasts, slopes, and adjacent interior valleys, from the Pyrenees to the Guadiana River.[5] The population had been long rooted in the area, probably as far back as the Neolithic period or even earlier.[6] With their usual perspicacity, the Greeks recognized this area as being essentially homogeneous and sharply different in culture from the Celtic territories of the interior and of the north and west peripheries.[7]

EARLY POLITICAL GROUPS AND CONFUSION OF NAMES

This cultural homogeneity was not reflected, however, in political unity, which has led to confusion in interpreting the early accounts of peoples. Many politically disparate peoples were essentially of the same culture, and the application in many cases of several different names to the same group has not increased understanding.

For example, frequently met are the names Ligurian and

[5] And perhaps even to the Rhone. See Juan Maluquer de Motes, "Pueblos Ibéricos," *Historia de España,* Tomo I, Vol. III, Pt. 2, Chap. 1, 309.

[6] *Ibid.,* p. 306; António García y Bellido, *La Península Ibérica en los comienzos de su historia,* pp. 51–52; Luis Pericot García, *Las Raíces de España,* p. 55.

[7] Maluquer de Motes, "Pueblos Ibéricos," *Historia de España,* Tomo I, Vol. III, 306, 309.

Turditanian, but the precise identification of these peoples is almost impossible to make. The first, according to Hesiod, were the oldest inhabitants of the Iberian peninsula.[8] Eratosthenes and Strabo mention them as being at the extreme west of the peninsula, including, it would seem, Andalusia and the Algarve of Portugal. Many writers believe them to have been the ur-stock of the peninsula, dislodged from the south (except for the Algarve) by the Iberians, and from the north by the Celts (except for the Basques, whom Schulten believes to be a remnant of the Ligurians). However, the evidence is more contradictory than enlightening, and the question remains vexed.[9]

The derivation and distribution of the Turditanians is also far from clear. Probably they may be equated with the Tartessians of the middle and lower Guadalquivir valley and perhaps the term should include the people of the area of Huelva and beyond to the present Portuguese border.[10] Merchants and miners from this general area may have found their way into Portugal and established colonies at the time in which Argaric culture was flourishing in Spain. The *Ora Maritima* indicates that some of them may have been as far north as the location of present Alcácer do Sal of the western Alentejo. Ptolemy mentioned them as being in the areas of present Moura and Beja of the eastern Alentejo[11] and their influence may have spread as far north as the Mondego River in Middle Portugal; but for none of this do we have firm and conclusive evidence.

In the earliest Greek texts the term "Iberian" is found, referring to peoples at the extreme southwest of present Spain, the region of Huelva.[12] Yet in later texts of the Greeks the term is applied to all peoples of the Mediterranean area of present

---

[8] Pierson Dixon, *The Iberians of Spain and Their Relations with the Aegean World*, p. 2.

[9] Pedro Bosch Gimpera, *Etnología de la Península Ibérica*, pp. 631–634.

[10] Maluquer de Motes, "Pueblos Ibéricos," *Historia de España*, Tomo I, Vol. III, 310–311.

[11] See Pedro Bosch Gimpera, "Los Iberos," *Cuadernos de Historia de España*, IX (Buenos Aires, 1948), 71.

[12] García y Bellido, *La Península Ibérica*, pp. 45–47.

92

Spain.[13] Still later all non-Celtic peoples of the interior and north were called Iberians, and ultimately the name became generalized for the peninsula.[14] Originally the term had cultural and perhaps ethnic meaning, but this was lost in its later use.

Indisputably, one of the important Iberian groups was that of the Tartessians, wealthy farmers and traders in metals.[15] It was their knowledge of the sources of metals that first brought them in touch with the Phoenicians and Greeks. They knew the coasts to the west and northwest of their home, for the tin and gold that they traded came from Galicia.[16] They were also able to furnish silver, copper, and lead, which came to them from the Guadalquivir River basin.[17] It appears that tin was the product of greatest importance at the time. The early centuries of the pre-Christian millennium were times of great opulence along the coast of Galicia. That this wealth was due to tin may be inferred from the fact that the Greeks used the term *Cassiterides* to identify the area. However, the question as to the ultimate source of tin is moot. In spite of the lack of archaeological evidence it seems likely that, in the earliest years of trading, it came from alluvial deposits along the river banks of Galicia. There is a possibility, however, that Bronze Age connections with French Brittany and with the British Isles had

---

[13] *Ibid.*, p. 51. Martínez Santa-Olalla and Almagro have been inclined to deny the existence of an ethnically distinct group to be called Iberians (Pericot, *Las Raices de España*, p. 54), but as time goes on this anti-Iberian position is becoming more and more difficult to maintain. Almagro himself in his later publications has altered his earlier view (*Ibid.*, p. 56).

[14] Bosch Gimpera, "Los Iberos," *Cuadernos de Historia de España*, IX, 6.

[15] Pericot García, *Las Raices de España*, p. 56; Dixon, *The Iberians of Spain*, p. 9; Maluquer de Motes, "Pueblos Ibéricos," *Historia de España*, Tomo I, Vol. III, 309; Bosch Gimpera, "Los Iberos," *Cuadernos de Historia de España*, IX, 5.

[16] C. Torres Rodríguez, "La Venida de los Griegos a Galicia," *Cuadernos de Estudios Gallegos*, VI (1946), 211, 218; Casimiro Torres, "Las Kassitérides," *Cuadernos de Estudios Gallegos*, IV (1945), 624; Maluquer de Motes, "Pueblos de la España céltica," *Historia de España*, Tomo I, Vol. III, Pt. 1, 78.

[17] Maluquer de Motes, "Pueblos Ibéricos," *Historia de España*, Tomo I, Vol. III, 339.

continued and that the Galicians were merely purveyors of tin from those places.[18] This basic necessity of bronze-users was scarce in the other parts of the Phoenician and Greek world. There was no tin in all of North Africa, Asia Minor, Caucasia, Cyprus, mainland Greece, and the Greek islands. The mines of Tuscany were small.[19] It is no wonder that both Galicia and the Tartessians were prosperous and that the Phoenicians and Greeks were attracted to the area.

The Tartessians were named after the region in which they lived, Tartessós, probably the Biblical Tarshish with which Hiram of Tyre traded for metals in the tenth century B.C.[20] It is likely that the name at first had no geographical significance, merely meaning, to the Phoenicians, the market place for metals.[21] Later, with the overriding importance of the lower Guadalquivir Valley in such traffic, the name was pre-empted for it, especially after the foundation of Gadir (Cádiz) by the Phoenicians.

PHOENICIAN SETTLEMENT OF GADIR AND CARTHAGE

The ancient Tyrian settlement, Gadir, may be dated from 1000 B.C. There are numerous and convincing arguments supporting such a date,[22] even though archaeology does not as yet bear it out, and some pre-historians deny it vigorously. Dixon would bring the date down to the eighth or seventh century B.C,[23] but not all of his arguments are convincing. He claims

[18] Torres, "Las Kassitérides," *Cuadernos de Estudios Gallegos,* IV (1945), 624–632.

[19] Torres Rodríguez, "La Venida de los Griegos a Galicia," *Cuadernos de Estudios Gallegos,* VI (November 6, 1946), 218, quoting Quiring.

[20] António García y Bellido, *La Península Ibérica en los comienzos de su historia,* pp. 170–171.

[21] Bosch Gimpera, "Los Iberos," *Cuadernos de Historia de España,* IX, 51.

[22] António García y Bellido, *Hispania Graeca,* I, 32–37. Phoenician ivories from Carmona, east of Seville in the Guadalquivir Valley, can probably be dated as of the tenth century B.C. See W. F. Albright, *The Archaeology of Palestine,* Pelican Books, p. 123.

[23] Dixon, *The Iberians of Spain,* p. 23.

that Gadir, being farther from the mother city, could not have been founded before Carthage, in spite of the fact that history is replete with examples demonstrating that the maxim, "the nearer, the sooner," is not valid in the matter of colonization.[24] It seems obvious that its foundation was due to its position facing the metal market of Tartessós. Also, it was an excellent place for the settlement of traders who, in the tradition of the eastern Mediterranean, were probably pirates as well, and if not, were certainly conscious of the threat of piracy. The site, at that time, was not connected with the mainland but separated from it by a deep channel, sufficiently wide to serve for defense. With its numerous wells of potable water and fine pasture for cattle, it was a stronghold of obvious attractions. In fact, the name Gadir, or Agadir, probably signified fortress or castle.[25] Its location is much like the sites of early Tyre, Sidon, and other cities of Phoenicia.

Some time after the settlement of Gadir, the Phoenicians founded the city that was to become the most famous of their colonies; Carthage was founded in 814 B.C.[26] In the same general period of time, numerous little fishing and salting settlements were founded along the coasts that stretched from Cape S. Vicente in the west through the south of Portugal and along the Mediterranean to Cape Gata of modern Spain.[27]

GREEK EXPLORATION AND SETTLEMENT

The earliest Greek ventures may perhaps be dated as of the ninth or the eighth century B.C. Possibly Rhodian and Chalcidian sailors were in the western Mediterranean at this time.[28]

[24] H. R. W. Smith, in his review of García y Bellido's *Hispania Graeca* in the *American Journal of Archaeology*, LVII, No. 1 (January, 1953), 31–36. The earliest Greek find in Spain is that of the Jerez helmet of the seventh century B.C. This also is the find farthest from Greece bar only one, the Huelva helmet.

[25] García y Bellido, *Hispania Graeca*, I, 34.

[26] *Ibid.*, p. 46.

[27] António García y Bellido, "Colonización Púnica," *Historia de España*, Tomo I, Vol. II, 331.

[28] García y Bellido, *Hispania Graeca*, I, 61, 77.

García believes that for the last half of the eighth century there is clear evidence of traffic with the islands and along the western coasts of the Mediterranean, picking up the metals for which the Phoenicians had long been trading. The line of Ionian names stretching along the islands and coasts of the western Mediterranean and to the Atlantic coast of Portugal— the names with the *oussa* termination—can probably be ascribed to this early period.[29] These names are interesting and important in dating the arrival of the Greeks in western waters.[30] They mark the island route of the early Greek navigators. Starting from Syrakoussai in eastern Sicily, they may be followed through Ichnoussa (Sardinia), Meloussa (Menorca), Romyoussa (Mallorca) and Pityoussa (Ibiza). The latter three, even now, are identified on maps as the Balearics or Pityusas (for example, in the Stieler Atlas). The *oussa* names extend westward to the straits of Gibraltar and up the Atlantic coast of Portugal to Ophioussa, in the region of Lisbon, and the general area of Portugal plus Galicia may have been vaguely termed Ophioussa.[31]

If one could merely say "Greek" and thus clear up the question of early contacts, the matter would be much simplified. However, various Greeks were involved, and as they were not all of the same viewpoint and intent, it is of some value to try to determine which groups were concerned in these earliest contacts.

THE PHOCAEAN GREEKS

Herodotus said that it was Greeks from the city of Phocaea in Asia Minor who were first to navigate in the western Mediterranean waters. It may seem temerous to question the facts of the father of history, but García does so convincingly. The Phocaeans, says he, arrived late upon the scene, profiting by

[29] *Ibid.*, p. 77.
[30] Carpenter, *The Greeks in Spain*, p. 33. Schulten first recognized them, and later the idea was more fully exploited by Carpenter.
[31] García y Bellido, *España en los comienzos de su historia*, map, p. 186.

earlier maritime contacts. Nor does he accept the statement that the interesting and important voyage of Kolaios, the Samian, was a voyage of discovery of Tartessós for the Greeks. This widely heralded seventh century journey was, to him, merely one—although perhaps the most profitable and spectacular up to that time—of many such voyages that had been made by Rhodians, Chalcidians, Samians, and others.[32]

Whatever the dating may be—and the archaeological inquiry has far to go—the Phocaeans certainly became the most active and effective Greeks in the area. Their colonization had energy and breadth and was the only one in the western Mediterranean with lasting results.[33] If one can believe that necessity is the mother of invention, or at least of effort, one can understand why relatively humble Phocaea achieved her success. Situated upon a good harbor near the mouth of the important Hermos (Gediz) River in Asia Minor, it was limited by the earlier activities and monopolies of more important neighbors, Miletus, Ephesus, and Samos, which had colonized vigorously around the eastern Mediterranean. Phocaea had to look farther afield for a sphere of profitable activity. There is no specific evidence that this activity was connected with the decay of Tyre, but there is such a coincidence in time. Tyrian decline had begun by the end of the eighth century B.C. and was notable during the following century. This was the time of the voyage of Kolaios the Samian (650 B.C.), the founding of the Phocaean colony of Massalia, present Marseille (600 B.C., or approximately then),[34] and the founding of Alalia in Corsica (640 B.C., or approximately forty years prior to Massalia).[35]

[32] García y Bellido, *Hispania Graeca*, I, 121, 124. Another point of view is expressed by H. R. W. Smith in his review of García y Bellido's *Hispania Graeca*, *American Journal of Archaeology*, LVII, No. 1 (January, 1953), 33. Smith does not deny the thesis of García but says that he can find no reason to believe that the Phocaeans reached Tartessós prior to the time of Arganthonios, the Tartessian king friendly to the Greeks, or before the voyage of Kolaios.

[33] García y Bellido, *Hispania Graeca*, I, 97.

[34] *Ibid.*, p. 115.

[35] *Ibid.*, p. 156.

Some time before the end of the century, Mainake, the most westerly of Phocaean colonies, was founded near Málaga.[36] This century was one of intimacy between Phocaeans and Tartessians. The reign of Arganthonios of Tartessós began in the seventh century B.C.[37] The ancient sources spoke of his eighty-year reign but probably, in typical Greek fashion, they dramatized a dynasty or a period by creating a mythical longevity for a single ruler. Whether this represented one ruler or several does not alter the fact that there was frequent and close contact between Tartessós of the period and Phocaea. This was the period of the Phocaean maritime dominance [38] and also the period of time during which the Tartessian king lent money to the Phocaeans to build their fortifications against the threat of the Persians.[39]

DIFFERENCES BETWEEN GREEKS AND PUNIC PEOPLES IN THEIR RELATIONS WITH IBERIA

The period of the decline of Tyre was not only important for the Ionian Greeks, but also for the Tyrian colony of Carthage. During the time of Phocaean colonization, Carthage too was expanding. As early as 653 B.C. it had established the colony on Ibiza of the Balearics, which lay athwart the Greek island route to the west.[40] After 573 B.C., when Tyre fell to the Babylonians, Carthage showed increasing independence. Competition for western metals was growing between the two great rivals, Carthage and Greece. It is reasonable to assume that the friendship of Arganthonios (or that of his dynasty), through

---

[36] Within twenty miles to the east, says García y Bellido (Hispania Graeca, I, 130–131). Smith suggests (in a review of Hispania Graeca, op. cit., p. 34) that it might even be at approximately the outskirts of present Málaga.

[37] 630–550 B.C., according to García y Bellido, Hispania Graeca, I, 129; or 620–540 B.C., according to Dixon, The Iberians of Spain, Appendix.

[38] 584–540 B.C., according to García y Bellido, Hispania Graeca, I, 144; or 577–533 B.C., according to Dixon, The Iberians of Spain, Appendix.

[39] Dixon, The Iberians of Spain, p. 48.

[40] García y Bellido, Hispania Graeca, I, 103.

almost a century of time, was more than mere affection and amiability. It probably represented a form of alliance in which the Tartessians aided the Phocaeans in their struggle against the threat to their mother city. In return, Greeks supported the westerners against the growing aggressiveness of Carthage and the Punic colony of Gadir, which threatened the area of Tartessós.

Almost from the time of their founding of Gadir the Phoenicians showed their expansionist tendencies. It was not long before they were using the island as a base of attack against the mainland and the Tartessians.[41]

The Greeks were usually neither pacific nor friendly neighbors when the prospect of gain was apparent. In this they differed little from the Phoenicians. However, in their relations with the Tartessians they had no desire, it would seem, for control of land or people, but merely wanted to trade their products, especially olive oil and wine, for Tartessian metals.[42] In fact, the history of Greek contacts with Iberians is one of amity, and the hospitality of the Iberians toward Greeks was proverbial.[43] The purposes of both peoples were served by friendly intercourse and mutual support against the common enemy, especially after the increased importance and the expanded ambition of Carthage. A major clash and a final deci-

[41] García y Bellido, "Colonización Púnica," *Historia de España,* Tomo I, Vol. II, Pt. 3, 331–332.

[42] Dixon, *The Iberians of Spain,* p. 15, and Carpenter, *The Greeks in Spain,* p. 96, state that the olive and the vine were introduced into Spain by the Greeks. Olive oil was exported from Greek Akragas to Carthage in the first half of the first millennium B.C. See T. J. Dunbabin, *The Western Greeks,* p. 221. There is no reason to suppose that it was not also sent to Iberia, even though J. G. D. Clark in *Prehistoric Europe, the Economic Basis,* p. 116, doubts such an early introduction into the west. Wine made from grapes is very old in the countries of the eastern Mediterranean, and the Phoenicians were famous merchants of wine. No doubt the Greeks traded in wine with Iberia, but it may have been Phoenicians who introduced it there. See H. F. Lutz, *Viticulture and Brewing in the Ancient Orient,* p. 31.

[43] Maluquer, "Pueblos Ibéricos," *Historia de España,* Tomo I, Vol. III, 307.

sion as to complete dominance of the area was inevitable. This was speeded by events in the eastern Mediterranean area.

THE ALALIA COLONY AND ITS EFFECTS

In the middle of the sixth century B.C., events took their course in a rapidly changing scene. In 546 B.C., Cyrus, the Mede, captured Sardis and the Lydian monarch, Croesus. The fright that this occasioned among Ionians nearby caused a mass migration of perhaps half of the population of Phocaea from Asia Minor to their Corsican colony of Alalia.[44] When the generals of Cyrus took Phocaea, all the men in this city of probably five to seven thousand people had gone.[45] This population figure suggests the large number of available vessels, and points to the commercial importance of the city at that time.

The Alalia settlement proved to be of short duration, for its position on the Tyrrhenian Sea, through which so much traffic moved between Carthage and Etruria, made it a threat to this major route of commerce. It must be remembered that in those days along the Mediterranean only small distinction existed between trade, fishing, and piracy. The Greeks were as cold-blooded and grim a group of predators as could be found. All ships were prepared to exploit any possible opportunity of gain. Not only was the trade route threatened, but so also were Punic interests in Sardinia. Obviously, neither the Carthaginians nor the Etruscans could tolerate such a situation. They united their forces, each furnishing sixty vessels to a battle fleet. This fleet was opposed by sixty Phocaean vessels which, although trimmer and more effective, were decisively defeated, sometime between 540 and 535 B.C.[46] Carthage may then have sealed the straits of Gibraltar, as Carpenter suggests.[47] More likely, the

[44] García y Bellido, *Hispania Graeca*, I, 177, 181.
[45] *Ibid.*, p. 183.
[46] *Ibid.*, pp. 185–186. Carpenter dates it as 535 (*The Greeks in Spain*, p. 18). Herodotus speaks of the Phocaean victory. If they did achieve a victory, it was Pyrrhic, for the result was disastrous.
[47] Carpenter, *The Greeks in Spain*, p. 34.

Alvôr, Where People Have Fished since Phoenician Times

straits had been largely sealed for a long time, but after the battle the land route between Mainake and Tartessós was also blocked. Mainake itself was destroyed by the Carthaginians toward the end of the century,[48] to end its traffic and its competition with the Carthaginian settlement in the location of present Málaga.[49]

This period of Carthaginian supremacy may have given rise to the legends of sea monsters and other dangers of the Atlantic. Pindar, in the middle of the fifth century, spoke of the dangers beyond the Gates of Hercules. The Greek capacity for mythologizing real events may have given birth to the superstitious fears which plagued at least some mariners down to the time of the Age of Discoveries. There were sea monsters certainly, after Carthaginian dominance of the western Mediterranean, but they were under the command of Carthaginians.

ECONOMIC CHANGES IN THE WEST

As Carthage had inherited the western empire of Tyre, so did Massalia fall heir to that of her mother city, Phocaea. Greek trade became centered here, with the end of Phocaean maritime enterprise in the west of the Mediterranean. Trade through France to Brittany and beyond had been undoubtedly important to the Massaliotes previous to this time, but the record had been obscured by the greater drama of the struggle on the Mediterranean.

During the last half of the sixth century B.C., during which time Carthaginians grasped complete power in the west, the prosperity of Galicia—presumably based upon tin—declined.[50] This decline may have been due simply to the change from the sea route, by way of the straits, to that from Massalia, via the

[48] García y Bellido, *Hispania Graeca*, I, 149.
[49] Founded probably in the eighth century B.C. Dixon, *The Iberians of Spain*, p. 24.
[50] Torres, "Las Kassitérides," *Cuadernos de Estudios Gallegos*, IV (1945), 627.

French rivers, to the northwest and ultimately to Britain. But the question must be raised as to why Carthaginian control would have reduced the importance of the Galician area if it had been a primary producer of tin. The Carthaginians were aggressive traders and presumably would not have appropriated a productive area from the Greeks just to watch it languish.

There are several possible explanations. (1) It may have been simply a matter of the playing out of the placer tin in the Galician area. (2) More likely, the Galicians had for some time been not producers, but purveyors, of tin from French Armorica or the British Isles. If this were true, the direct land route from Massalia would have skirted the Carthaginian barrier and eliminated Galician middlemen. (3) It is possible that interest in tin diminished because of the increasing use of iron. (4) The Carthaginians had little coinage until the fourth century B.C., and that for payment of mercenaries. The great demand for bronze by Greeks was for armor and sculpture. As Carthaginian archaeology indicates little interest in either, tin may have had little importance to them.[51] Moreover, at approximately the same period of time there was an increased interest in silver. The Phoenicians had early been interested in silver,[52] and during the centuries of the rise of Greek trade the demand was increased by the avidity with which the Greeks of Asia Minor sought it for coinage.[53] Metal from the rich mines in the area of the headwaters of the Guadalquivir River[54] was brought downstream to Tartessós. Perhaps the richest of ancient silver mines was that of Mastia (or Massia), a region second only to Tartessós in commercial importance. The ancient prosperity of the region and of its most important city, also named Mastia (or Massia), the later Cartago Nova, and probably the site of the present Cartagena, was based upon silver mining[55]

[51] H. R. W. Smith (personally transmitted note).
[52] García y Bellido, Hispania Graeca, I, 30–31.
[53] Dixon, The Iberians of Spain, p. 33.
[54] Mines near present Linares. Carpenter, The Greeks in Spain, p. 37.
[55] Ibid., pp. 28–29. Cartago Nova, present Cartagena, was founded by the Carthaginians in 221 B.C. Ibid., p. 91.

through several centuries. Great amounts were mined under the direction of Hannibal in the third century B.C., and it was still a large operation at the time of Polybius in the succeeding century.[56]

CARTHAGINIAN DOMINATION OF THE WESTERN MEDITERRANEAN

Prior to the battle of Alalia the Carthaginians had conquered Sardinia[57] (one of the *oussa* links in Greek traffic), partly by the use of mercenaries recruited from their seventh-century colony of Ibiza (another *oussa* link). Beyond the straits of Gibraltar the early Punic settlement of Gadir gave them strategic control of that region. Besides these important strongholds, there were others, of lesser importance but adding to total Carthaginian strength. Greek commercial activity in Iberia was ended and Carthage was less inhibited in the spread of its control. Tartessós, which had feared the Carthaginians and had allied itself with the Greeks, was left without support and was destroyed.[58] In the following century, probably twenty thousand Iberian mercenaries were fighting in Sicily for the Carthaginians.[59] Fourth-century evidence indicates that some Celts were also serving as mercenaries in the Carthaginian forces.[60]

There was an increasing reliance upon mercenaries from the peninsula, not only from the fringes but from deep within the interior as well. In the late third century B.C., Hannibal's army included Celtiberians from the northern interior, Galicians from the extreme northwest, Lusitanians from Middle Portugal,

[56] Dixon, *The Iberians of Spain*, p. 34.
[57] García y Bellido, *Hispania Graeca*, I, 147.
[58] If there was no one city of that name, it is not important to the larger fact that the area as a whole was put under the control of the Carthaginians of Gadir. Carpenter, *The Greeks in Spain*, pp. 34–35.
[59] The Carthaginians made a bargain to save themselves before Syracuse, leaving their allies and mercenaries behind. The Iberians were then enlisted as a unit into Syracusan forces. Later, some of them served in Greece.
[60] García y Bellido, *Hispania Graeca*, I, 23–24.

Vetones from the middle Tajo drainage—and these do not complete the list.[61] Such troops, however, were something other than pure mercenaries; many had been forcibly impressed into service. In spite of Hannibal's amazing campaigns in Italy, it may be wondered if they might not have been even more spectacular had there been no bitter opposition in Iberia to his forcible draft of troops. During earlier centuries no general antagonism in Iberia seems to have been engendered by the Carthaginians. Locally there may have been antagonism, such as probably existed between the Carthaginians and the Tartessians, but for the tribes of the interior the Carthaginians may have had a friendly appeal. They offered an opportunity to fight with pay. It was later, when the Carthaginians had expanded their power and increased their need for troops, that their tactics changed with regard to these tribes of the interior, which had long served as a source of manpower. When Hannibal, in desperate need for troops and under economic pressure, forcibly impressed some of them into his armies, the others reacted in bitter opposition. The tribes of the interior were a bellicose lot. An opportunity to fight for pay was not distasteful to them but a demand that they submit to enslavement was another matter. According to Strabo they resisted Hannibal as they later did the Romans for somewhat the same reasons.[62]

Nevertheless, tens of thousands of mercenaries were introduced to new lands and cultures of the middle and eastern Mediterranean. Since this process had been going on from as early as the sixth century B.C. and many men had returned to the peninsula, the effect upon attitudes of the peoples of the *meseta* and even some of the remote western coasts may have been considerable.

In the area of present Portugal, Carthage recruited a few

[61] A. A. Mendes Corrêa, "A Lusitânia pré-romana," *História de Portugal,* I, 175.

[62] J. García Mercadal (trans. and ed.), *Viajes de extranjeros por España y Portugal,* p. 115.

Figs in the Algarve

mercenaries, but aside from this it apparently had interest only in coastal stations. For example, there is no record of Carthaginian exploitation of the copper of the Alentejo, which Romans later mined at Aljustrel.[63] As all of southern Portugal is poor in tin, silver, and gold, there was little there to distract them from their preoccupation with such places as Andalusia and Murcia, except for the profitable fishing for tuna, mackerel, and other less important species, and the evaporation of salt for the preparation of fish for export. This was the basis of several Carthaginian settlements along the Algarvian coast and even up the west coast to the mouth of the Sado River.[64] One wonders also if they may not have been interested in certain aspects of farming on the Algarvian littoral. Carthaginians were good farmers, and although their expeditions were concerned with commerce primarily, and not with settlement for its own sake, dried figs had long been an item of their commerce out of Ibiza.[65] As figs thrive now in the Algarve and have been important in its economy through all time for which we have information, one wonders if the Carthaginians had not added this item to their list of commercial products by introducing the tree to southern Portugal.

The events related in this chapter are concerned with the Mediterranean shores of present Spain, and only slightly with those of Portugal. During the centuries which have been considered, commerce and communications were bringing the southern shores of Iberia in contact with the affairs of the East, whereas the western coasts of Iberia, the Portuguese coasts, remained isolated and out of touch with the more advanced civilizations of the eastern Mediterranean. It is part of a per-

[63] Manuel Torres, "La Península hispánica, província romana, 218 a. de J. C.–409 de J. C.," *Historia de España*, II, 333. This may also be due to Carthaginian lack of interest in bronze.

[64] García y Bellido, "Colonización Púnica," *Historia de España*, Tomo I, Vol. II, 385.

[65] *Ibid.*, p. 379. However, whatever was the Carthaginian contact with southern Portugal, it was not sufficient to alter, materially, the indigenous stratum. A. A. Mendes Corrêa, *Raízes de Portugal* (2nd ed.), p. 83.

sistent pattern of history in Iberia. The character of Spain was shaped, in part, by the contact with the eastern Mediterranean lands during the millennium prior to the birth of Christ. Such contact had little effect upon Portugal.

CHAPTER 8

The Period of Roman Conquest and Control

CULTURAL UNITY OF THE HUMID FRINGE

WHEN ROME conquered the Iberian peninsula there was a kinship and a cultural similarity between the peoples of Aquitaine (present southwest France) and Cantabria. This was made clear by Caesar and others.[1] From the Pyrenees to Galicia there were peoples similar to each other in their ways of life. Strabo said (and others bear him out) that all of the people of this northern, mountainous strip of Iberia lived essentially the same sort of life and had customs that were virtually identical (Fig. 10).[2] It was a matriarchal, agro-pastoral civilization, the vestiges of which are still to be found in parts of the region.[3] Farming-and-herding peoples of this oceanic fringe had been settled in the area since before the beginning of the first millennium B.C. In spite of subsequent changes, brought about by incursions of new peoples (most of whom had somewhat the same Central European background as that of the earlier arrivals), they had main-

---

[1] Júlio Caro Baroja, *Los Pueblos del Norte de la Península Ibérica*, p. 82.
[2] *Ibid.*, p. 38.　　　　[3] *Ibid.*, p. 205.

Figure 10. Iberian Culture Areas as Delimited by Strabo

tained an affinity for each other and considerable differences from the societies of patriarchal herders who occupied most of the *meseta*.[4] There is abundant evidence that to the south of present Galicia, in what is now North Portugal, there was an extension of many of the same culture attitudes. The intimate, friendly association of the peoples of the area of present Galicia and those of the area of the present Minho Province of North Portugal cannot be doubted, for it was difficult to make a clear dis-

[4] *Ibid.*, p. 227. See also Chapter 6 on Celtic immigration. It was true not only when the Romans first knew the territory but also as late as the twentieth century, according to Abelardo Merino ("El Regionalismo peninsular y la geografía histórica," *Boletín de la Real Sociedad Geográfica*, LVIII (1916), 293–294): "To all of the zone of Cantabria and Atlantic to Porto can be applied Murgia's dictum (except for the maritime villas of Santander): a life more internal than external with no effect on the balance of the peninsula . . . through all of its historical experiences it continues to be 'fishing and agricultural,' in a word 'primitive.'

"In vain did foreigners with their pilgrimages try to make Santiago a cosmopolitan urb. . . . One can not exaggerate Vascocantabrismos, Asturianismos or Gallegismos."

Figure 11a. Area of Primitive Granaries

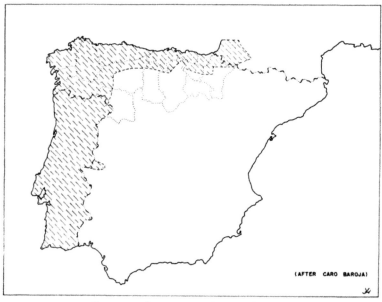

Figure 11b. Area of the Chillon Cart

tinction between them at that time. Callaeci north of the Minho River were not of precisely the same tribe as the Callaeci to the south of the stream, but the two were sufficiently alike in their ways to be conveniently grouped together for administrative purposes. Caro Baroja has shown by his maps, two of which are reproduced in Figure 11,[5] that several fundamental culture items were common to all of the north and northwest fringe of Iberia, down at least to the Douro River. These maps not only show similarities among the peoples along the humid fringe but emphasize the differences between the periphery and the dry *meseta* in the interior.

Furthermore, there seems to have been a fundamental similarity between the peoples of the area of present North Portugal (between the Minho and Douro rivers) and the Lusitanians in present central Portugal. These Lusitanians probably harked back to a pre-Celtic period of time in Portugal. They were not descended from Central European peoples of the same stock as were the agriculturists and pastoralists of the north. Nor, on the other hand, were they originally Iberians (in the strict sense), although they may represent an Iberian sub-group that later, but prior to our first record of them, had become Celticized, culturally and perhaps even physically.[6] They were a distinct sub-group that lived between the Tejo and Douro rivers, but had been acculturated and mixed with peoples to the north of the Douro to such an extent that it was sometimes difficult to make a neat separation. This was notably so in comparison with the Callaeci. Silius Italicus distinguished the difference, but texts and archaeology show them to be difficult to separate culturally or ethnically.[7]

There was, then, a basic cultural similarity among peoples, extending from present France through northern Spain and down into Portugal to the Tejo River. This is not to say, how-

[5] Caro, *Pueblos del Norte*, maps 6 and 7, pp. 208 and 210 respectively.

[6] A. A. Mendes Corrêa, "Celtas na Beira," *Boletim da Casa das Beiras*, X (1943), No. 6, 5–11, and "A Lusitânia pré-romana," *História de Portugal*, I, 182.

[7] Mendes Corrêa, "A Lusitânia pré-romana," *História de Portugal*, I, 183.

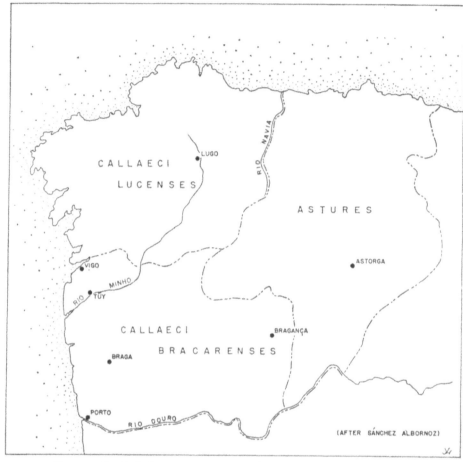

Figure 12. Tribal Divisions in Northwestern Iberia during the Roman Period

ever, that there were not differences among them, clearly recognized and strongly felt by the tribes themselves. They were in a sense cousins, rather than brothers. The Lusitanians were distinct from the Callaeci Bracarenses to the north of the Douro River (Fig. 12). These latter were divided from the Callaeci Lucenses to the north of the Minho River, and history and philology agree that the boundary between the Callaeci and the Astures lay along the Navia River, not far to the east of the present boundary separating Galicia from Asturias.[8] With this diversity amid unity it is not surprising that confusion came about in the record of the various writers of the time. It seems that this was even furthered by the peoples involved. For example, prior to the campaign of Decimus Junius Brutus along the west of the peninsula (137 B.C.) the word "Callaecia" merely referred to a tribal territory, but we have Strabo's word for the fact that after that time the land farther south might be suggested by the term as some of the Lusitanians, impressed with the fame of the Callaeci, took to using their name.[9] The Lusitanians under their own name gained fame somewhat later. Either because of this change in names by local groups or because of the blending of the various culturally akin peoples, and also undoubtedly due to confusion or carelessness on the part of Roman writers, the name Lusitania at times was used for all of the peninsula.

ROMAN ENTRY INTO THE PENINSULA

The Roman advance along the western Mediterranean, like that of the Greeks, was made, not by plan or with a predetermined goal, but by steps taken one at a time as the opportunity or necessity occurred. In Iberia many steps were forced upon the Romans. Carthage was a growing rival and was expanding eastward along the Mediterranean. In Iberia when this advance reached into the northeast, as far as present Catalonia, the maneuver was obviously threatening to Rome. The peninsula was a base of supplies, both material and human, for the Carthaginian armies, and Roman action was mandatory.

The history of contacts between peoples in the peninsula and Mediterraneans farther to the east contributed to the ease of Roman entry along the Mediterranean coasts. In the first place

[8] Claudio Sánchez Albornoz y Menduiña, "Divisiones tribales y administrativas del solar del reino de Asturias en la época romana," *Boletín de la Real Academia de la Historia*, XCV, No. 1 (July–Sept., 1929), 317.

[9] J. Leite de Vasconcellos, *Religiões da Lusitânia*, I, xxii.

Carthage had become increasingly severe in her demands—especially for levies of troops—and Carthaginian popularity had not been increased by it. On the other hand the peoples of the urbanized Mediterranean coasts of Spain were thoroughly acquainted with European Mediterraneans to the east of them. The Greeks had long been friendly traders and the people of the Phocaean colony of Massalia had continued to maintain contact even after the battle of Alalia and the Carthaginian dominance of Mediterranean waters of Iberia. The Massaliotes and the Romans recognized a common enemy in Carthage and struck an alliance as early as 348 B.C.[10] By reason of all of these conditions the way was opened for the Romans, and they advanced without difficulty along the littoral in the third century B.C.

RESISTANCE TO ROMAN CONQUEST

It was with the Celts and the Celticized groups of the interior and west that Rome faced her greatest difficulties. Here, too, it was more a matter of one step demanding another, than desire to possess either of these areas, that drove Rome to further conquest.[11] There is little reason to suppose that either the bleak *meseta* or most of the remote west had any attraction for the Romans. The sanguinary battles with the Celtiberians on the one hand and the Lusitanians on the other were not worth the cost in terms of the territory involved. The fact was that these dissident peoples were a threat to Roman control of the Mediterranean regions and they had to be subdued.

In the non-Mediterranean areas the Romans were not dealing with essentially peaceful, urbanized folk of the kind that were known along the Mediterranean shores. Both the Celts of the interior and, especially, the Celticized hill folk of the west were of a different stamp. They were anything but complacent with

---

[10] António García y Bellido, *Hispania Graeca*, I, 238.

[11] Except for gold in the northwest. Juan Maluquer de Motes, "Los Pueblos de la España céltica," *Historia de España*, Tomo I, Vol. III, Pt. 1, 79.

regard to Roman assumption of authority over them. They were a bellicose lot, famous for their interest in physical exploits, and were reputed to like fighting their neighbors better than cultivation of the soil.[12] That they felt themselves to be different from the city people of the Mediterranean slope is made manifest by their resistance to the Romans. Viriathus was the most flamboyant among them and had a quality of leadership fitting to his opportunities. But the spectacular sweep of Lusitanian armies under his command across the width of Iberia, decimating Roman legions on their way, was not inspired by their leader; it was not forced upon his people; nor was it the achievement of mercenaries. Rather it represented the upsurge of an independent group of strong character that had found an effective leader. This dire threat to Roman control of the peninsula was averted by hiring the assassination of Viriathus. Whatever one may feel about the judgment and the deed, he must recognize that it was effective of the end it sought. There was no comparable leader among the Lusitanians, and opposition, although continued, was dogged rather than aggressive. The remnants of the Lusitanian forces withdrew in separate, small groups to the *castros* of the rural northwest and maintained resistance for several generations.[13]

It was this sort of danger that forced the Romans to continue their conquest to the last remote outposts. The quality of the land, except for the lower Tejo valley and parts of the littoral, was of small attraction to them. In the rural northwest there were gold sands, but little else to catch their interest. Yet it was obvious that rebellious remnants, with a history of truculence and raiding of settled places, could not be tolerated by imperial Rome. However, the reduction of the territory was far more difficult than Rome could have suspected at first. It took more than a century and a half, compared with seven years for the conquest of all of Gaul.[14]

[12] A. A. Mendes Corrêa, "A Lusitânia pré-romana," *História de Portugal*, I, 191–192.
[13] Vergílio Correia, "O Domínio Romana," *História de Portugal*, I, 218.
[14] *Ibid.*, p. 217.

THE INDIVIDUALITY OF PORTUGAL

CONQUEST AND SETTLEMENT OF THE WEST

The Consul Decimus Junius Brutus, after fortifying Lisbon, advanced to the north, destroying settlements as he went. He established a fortified position at Viseu, crossed the Douro River, and reached the Lima River by 137 B.C.[15] Ultimately, according to Strabo, he conquered to the Minho River.[16] At the end of his campaigns, Rome controlled the territory between the Douro and Minho rivers plus probable extensions along the coast and in the interior.[17] It was only under Augustus, however, at the last of the first century B.C. that present North Portugal and Galicia were fully pacified and put under Roman control. The cities of Asturica Augusta (Astorga) and Bracara Augusta (Braga) were then founded. To the south, Emerita Augusta (Mérida) was settled in 25 B.C. with the *emeriti* of the fifth and tenth legions. It became the capital of Roman Lusitania, that is, the territory lying between the Tejo and Douro rivers and extending eastward to present Talavera de la Reina.

Roads were built to connect these and other settlements, in order to maintain firm control of this long-resistant area.[18] Villas were established. These large estates, rather like plantations in the New World of a later time, had the necessary structures and retainers grouped around the manor house.[19] Many of the names of these Roman villas have persisted until now as names of parishes or small towns. The *quintas*, the large and middle-sized properties of present northwest Portugal, perhaps represent subdivisions of the villa.[20] The total number of Romans

[15] *Ibid.*, p. 218.

[16] Francisco José Velozo, "A Lusitânia Suevico-Bizantina," *Bracara Augusta*, II, No. 2 (July, 1950), 118; No. 3 (Oct., 1950), 221–256; No. 4 (Feb., 1951), 389–402; IV, Nos. 1–3 (Dec., 1952), 46–69.

[17] Casimiro Torres, "Límites geográficos de Galicia en los siglos IV y V," *Cuadernos de Estudios Gallegos*, IV, No. 14 (1949), 367–368.

[18] See A. de Amorim Girão, *Geografia de Portugal*, map facing p. 366, for Roman roads.

[19] Velozo, "A Lusitânia Suevico-Bizantina," *Bracara Augusta*, II, No. 2 (July, 1950), 151.

[20] António Jorge Dias, *Os Arados Portugueses e as suas prováveis origens*, p. 117.

settled in the north was comparatively small, for this rainy, forested country was not to their taste. Compared to the rest of Iberia, it was Romanized late and poorly.[21] The south of Portugal, Mediterranean Portugal, was somewhat more to their liking.[22] This was sunny country, wheat country, good for olives and grapes. Evora, of the Alentejo, became known to them as Cerealis, a place of obvious attraction to the wheat-eating Romans.

ADMINISTRATIVE DIVISIONS

In the control of the west, Rome did not set up divisions contrary to previous tribal and cultural arrangement, except for reasons of military strategy or police requirements.[23] The administrative organization of Roman Lusitania was ethnically reasonable if not perfect. It grouped together people with fundamentally similar attitudes and values.[24] The province of Tarraconensis, extending in a broad band across all of the north and including most of the east of the peninsula, was an exception to this policy. It included greatly disparate culture groups. The Romans realized the awkwardness of the arrangement and tried on several occasions to remedy the matter by establishing borders more in keeping with ethnic distribution. But they faced a twofold problem. Administration boundaries suitable to tribal (that is, cultural) boundaries conduced to smooth operation of control, and wherever possible the Romans followed this precept.[25] However, in dealing with belligerent subjugated peoples, the matter of military strategy took primacy over all other considerations. This fundamental conflict be-

[21] Claudio Sánchez Albornoz y Menduiña, *Ruina y extinción del municipio romano en España e instituciones que le reemplazan*, p. 118.

[22] Dias, *Arados*, p. 103.

[23] António Jorge Dias, *Rio de Onor*, p. 56.

[24] Exception here could clearly be taken to the inclusion of the Cónios of the Algarve. However, they were a small group, inhabiting a small territory. Obviously Rome could not establish administrative subdivisions for each minor group.

[25] Velozo, "A Lusitânia Suevico-Bizantina," *Bracara Augusta*, II, No. 2 (July, 1950), 126.

118

tween civil and military control was nowhere more evident than in the northwest of Iberia.

The first division of the country under Augustus put all of northwest Iberia into the province of Lusitania.[26] Later, probably between the years 15 and 1 B.C., the area down to the Douro, that is, inclusive of present North Portugal, was put under the control of Citerior Spain, which later became the Tarraconensis Province. This military device was made necessary by the administrative insecurity of the remote, intransigent, newly conquered province.[27] It obviously was not satisfactory, and Tiberius made a separate unit of approximately the territory of present Galicia and Asturias.[28] Later Caracalla set up other boundaries for a short-lived northwestern province under the governor, Cerealis.[29]

It seemed impossible to arrange the exterior boundaries of the province satisfactorily for both the people of the area and for the Roman government. In setting the boundaries of the subdivisions within the province, difficulty was mostly avoided by equating such limits with the culture groups affected. The territory of the Callaeci Lucenses (Fig. 12) became, with but slight difference, the Roman judicial district (Conventus Iuridicus) centered upon Lucus Augusti (Lugo) which included approximately the present territory of the Spanish province of Galicia. The territory of the Callaeci Bracarenses fitted well to the judicial district centered upon Bracara Augusta (Braga).[30] It foreshadowed the modern North Portugal.

[26] C. Torres, "Límites geográficos . . . ," *Cuadernos de Estudios Gallegos*, IV, No. 14 (1949), 371.

[27] *Ibid.*, p. 372; Claudio Sánchez Albornoz y Menduiña, "Divisiones tribales y administrativas del solar del reino de Asturias en la época romana," *Boletín de la Real Academia de la Historia*, XCV, No. 1 (July–Sept., 1929), 377.

[28] C. Torres, "Límites geográficos . . . ," *Cuadernos de Estudios Gallegos*, IV, No. 14 (1949), 372.

[29] Sánchez Albornoz, "Divisiones tribales . . . ," *Boletín de la Real Academia de la Historia*, XCV, No. 1 (July–Sept., 1929), 384.

[30] In fact, the boundaries of the Roman judicial districts fit nicely with the present national boundaries of Portugal. Velozo, "A Lusitânia Suevico-Bizantina," *Bracara Augusta*, II, No. 2 (July, 1950), 126; António García y Bellido, *La Península Ibérica en los comienzos de su historia*, p. 393.

EFFECT UPON SOCIAL AND ECONOMIC LIFE

The Romans had certain fixations with regard to organization and ways of life. They effectively imposed their language upon the peninsula. Their code of law was applied. Changes were made in ways of living where it seemed necessary to administration. The hilltop dwellers of the northwest were largely transferred to the bottom lands. This was presumably done to eliminate raiding. By this action, however, an even more fundamental change was made in society. Present information indicates that men had taken, at best, a casual interest in agriculture. That had been woman's work, to be done with the hoe. In the bottom lands the problem was completely different, for not only was plow agriculture possible but it was obviously a superior mode of operation. Furthermore, the heavier sods of the bottom lands are harder to cut than those of the hill lands and probably offered a real obstacle to the hoe. Perhaps of greater importance was the invariable association of men with the care and use of animals. With the introduction of the draft animal into agriculture men were immediately involved. Being involved, however, does not necessarily mean that they took to it whole-heartedly.

Even today the transfer of responsibility seems not to have been complete. This is shown by the fact that in Galicia and in the Minho of Portugal there is little distinction between the duties of men and women in the fields. In Galicia, women may perform any of the tasks (although rarely plowing). In the Minho, one is told that the heavier tasks go to the men, but this usually means merely that the job involving the use of an animal is a male responsibility, whereas other tasks, seemingly as heavy, are accomplished by women. In the bottom lands, where agriculture with plowmen became fundamental, raiding was eliminated, and the importance of herding was reduced.

All of this altered the social structure in the area. Formerly it had been based fundamentally on extended family units. Each *castro* had been an individual autarchy, with collective

120

occupancy of the land. This was changed with the Roman introduction of individual ownership of the land.[31]

The changes in Iberia effected by the Romans were not only great but also lasting. This resulted partly from the fact that the Romans were dealing, in many areas, with peoples who had "Mediterranean" ways not too different from those of the Romans themselves. Rome's troubles in the conquest and pacification of the interior and remote exterior areas of Iberia came from the bellicose Celtic or Celticized peoples, who were not "Mediterranean" in their points of view. Ultimately, however, Rome brought all of the dissidents to heel, and, through social and economic organization, as well as consideration for cultural differences where they did not interfere with administration, made the peninsula an effective unit in the empire.

[31] Dias, *Arados*, p. 103. It eliminated much of the primitive collectivism, but not all. Traces are still to be found in northwest Spain and in northern Portugal. See Caro, *Pueblos del Norte*, p. 45, and Dias *Rio de Onor*, especially Chapters V and VI, and *Vilarinho da Furna*, especially Chapters IV and VI.

Even with Roman efficiency the *castro* was not entirely eliminated as a fort and place of resistance, for in 430 A.D. when the Swabians "desolated" the interior of Galicia the local inhabitants defended themselves in strong *castel-forts*. Manuel Torres ["Las Invasiones y los Reinos Germánicos de España (Años 409–711),"] *Historia de España*, III, 27; Velozo, "A Lusitânia Suevico-Bizantina," *Bracara Augusta*, II, No. 3 (Oct., 1950), 249.

CHAPTER 9

The Germanic Conquest

I N THE EARLY fifth century the weakening Roman Empire relinquished power in Iberia to the migrating Germanic peoples who entered the peninsula, not with the intent of replacing Roman power, but in a search for lands upon which to settle.[1] Nevertheless, absolute power was ultimately theirs. Partly it fell into their laps from the debile hands of the Romans; partly, it came as a result of their changed attitude after Roman weakness became obvious. Ultimately the assumption of complete authority was a clearly indicated, easy step for them to take.

DIFFERENCES AMONG GERMAN TRIBES

To say that the Germans[2] took power should not imply that the exercise of it was everywhere the same, for these migrants

[1] F. Newton de Macedo, "O Domínio Germânico," *História de Portugal,* I, 313.

[2] The word "Germans" will be used instead of "German peoples" to avoid the awkwardness of the latter phrase, even though the usage may not be precisely accurate. It makes no major distortion of fact.

from Central Europe were not homogeneous in culture. One must be wary of the term "German" in such a context, for the Germans, in fact, differed greatly among themselves. It is helpful in understanding the most fundamental of the differences to distinguish between eastern and western Germans. The Visigoths and Vandals were eastern Germans, whereas the Swabians came from the west. Another tribe, not German at all but ultimately derived from the region of the Caucasus, was that of the Alans,[3] who accompanied the Germans in their migration into Iberia. After battles in which they were decimated by Visigoths, their remnants finally merged with the Vandals and they left Iberia at the same time as the Vandals.

An important distinction is to be made between western and eastern Germans in terms of their attitudes toward the land. Although both were at once agriculturists and herders, the easterners were predominantly pastoralists,[4] whereas the westerners paid greater attention to farming. For example, the Visigoths were primarily dependent upon herding, although they were never ignorant of agriculture. This, presumably, was the result of their migration from northern Europe southeastward to the area near the Black Sea, several centuries before their move into Iberia. It was on the grazing lands near the Black Sea that they developed the complex of herding and agriculture which, blended with the attitudes and techniques that they had acquired through propinquity to the Roman Empire, gave them their character. At the time of their entry into the Iberian peninsula they were known to be the most Romanized of the barbarians. It was for this reason that the Romans selected them to protect Roman interests against the other Germans.

The Swabians were western Germans and very different in their attitudes from the eastern Visigoths. They had long occupied Saxony and Thuringia and had early gone south, where they had come in contact with the Helvetians (Celts) near the Main River. So in the centuries just prior to the Christian era,

[3] Joseph M. Piel, *Os Nomes germânicos na toponímia portuguesa*, p. 5.
[4] Ludwig Schmidt, "Teutonic Kingdoms in Gaul," *Cambridge Medieval History*, I, 287.

the ways of Germans and Celts were blended and the two groups shared a common culture.[5] Although Tacitus said that the Swabians thought it more honorable to fight than to harvest, and that they left the farm work to the women and the old men,[6] he is also our authority for the fact that they had a cult of "mother earth."[7] Reminiscent of the early Celts in Iberia, the Swabians were both farmers and fighters. There was a division of labor, so that women accomplished most of the farming, while the major attention of the men was focused upon care of the animals and fighting. Notwithstanding their taste for fighting and raiding, they were rooted in the soil. For Tacitus and others to call attention to Swabian truculence and taste for war is natural in a writer, but it distorts the facts, nevertheless. One must be wary of writers when they deal with simple peoples and humble pursuits. As long as the account of human activities has been written, the concern has been almost exclusively with dramatic events, while the undramatic but abiding bases of culture are apt to be overlooked. Warfare, weapons, and cities call attention to themselves, whereas peace, agriculture, and the simple ways of the countryside often escape notice. The great contribution that the Swabians made to Portugal was in the use of the land.

The effect of this has been durable. It was they who introduced the Central European quadrangular plow into northwest Iberia.[8] These Central Europeans had a preference for the north and northwest of Iberia with its mild summers and with rainfall throughout all or most of the year. The climate was suitable to their crops, as was the natural vegetation to their animals. They found here a more propitious type of the same kind of environment which they had known previously in Central Europe. They brought to the area techniques and attitudes similar to those of its previous exploiters and well suited to its

[5] Martin Bang, "Expansion of the Teutons (to A.D. 378)," *Cambridge Medieval History*, I, Chap. VII.

[6] Francisco José Velozo, "A Lusitânia Suevico-Bizantina," *Bracara Augusta*, II, No. 2 (July, 1950), 152.

[7] *Ibid.*, p. 137.

[8] Jorge Dias, *Os Arados Portugueses e as suas prováveis origens*, p. 129.

124

further development. Much of the basis of living in present Galicia and North Portugal is a direct inheritance from the Swabian period of dominance. It differed sharply from attitudes and customs dominant in the *meseta*,[9] and toponymy illustrates the contrast. As Castilian is rich in martial terms, Galician is rich in agricultural words and the number of local terms associated with agriculture is greater in Galicia than in any other part of Spain. The evidence for this has been collected only for Galicia, the northern part of the former Swabian kingdom, but one can reasonably infer that this judgment made by a Galician concerning Galicia can also be applied to the southern part of the kingdom, present North Portugal.[10]

THE SPREAD AND ASSUMPTION OF POWER BY THE GERMANS IN IBERIA

The Swabians, Vandals, and Alans crossed the Pyrenees in 408 or 409 A. D.[11] Within two years, parts of them had spread to the western edge of the peninsula and lands had been apportioned to each tribe. If difficulties were made either by the local inhabitants or by the local Roman administration, there is no record of it. In the statement of an early document, the areas originally apportioned to these tribes were assigned by lot.[12] This may have been the fact, and it may have been fortuitous circumstance that placed the Swabians, by 411 A. D., in lands that were eminently to their taste, but it seems a little hard to believe. It is more likely that the Swabians, who later clung to these lands with determination, chose them. In fact, there is

[9] Ramón Menéndez Pidal in *La España del Cid*, p. 56, says that Cantabria and Vasconia were always hostile to Visigothic Toledo.

[10] José Ramon and Fernández Oxea, "Toponímias agrícolas gallegas," *Cuadernos de Estudios Gallegos*, V, No. 16 (1950), 221–222. National barriers frequently impede scholars from encompassing all of a logical area of study.

[11] Manuel Torres, "Las Invasiones y los Reinos Germánicos de España (Años 409–711)," *Historia de España*, III, 21.

[12] Piel, *Nomes germânicos*, p. 5; Schmidt, "Teutonic Kingdoms in Gaul," *Cambridge Medieval History*, I, 304.

some reason to believe that they did so, and later, compelled by the more powerful Vandals, had to relinquish a portion of them.[13] The Alans, at that time the strongest of the tribes, took a large area in the center and south, approximately the area of Roman Lusitania. The Silingian Vandals settled to the southeast of the Alans, and the Asdingian Vandals were in interior Galicia next to the Swabians.[14]

In 415, when the Visigoths entered, at the behest of Rome,[15] the peninsula was at peace.[16] By this time the Swabians had been in the northwest for six years, as had been the Alans and Vandals in their allotted areas. They had settled among the local Luso-Romans, who may have welcomed them and who at least offered no effective opposition to their settlement. The Luso-Romans apparently preferred "barbarian" control to the onerous pecuniary demands of the central Roman government.[17] There was no major opposition to the Swabians until the advent of the Visigoths who, allied with Rome, entered the peninsula, supposedly to re-establish Roman authority.

The Visigoths met and decisively defeated an army of Alans and Silingian Vandals in 416. After that, neither of these tribes was to be reckoned with in peninsular affairs.[18] Their remnants were ultimately absorbed by the Asdingian Vandals who, like the Swabians, were settled in a remote corner of the peninsula. Presumably the fact of their geographical position saved these two tribes from the fate of their quondam companions, but it did not keep them at peace, for warfare broke out almost im-

[13] Velozo, "A Lusitânia Suevico-Bizantina," *Bracara Augusta,* II, No. 2 (July, 1950), 242.
[14] Torres, "Las Invasiones y los Reinos Germánicos de España," *Historia de España,* III, 22; Schmidt, "Teutonic Kingdoms in Gaul," *Cambridge Medieval History,* I, 304; Velozo, "A Lusitânia Suevico-Bizantina," *Bracara Augusta,* II, No. 2 (July, 1950), 144.
[15] Macedo, "O Domínio Germânico," *História de Portugal,* I, 309.
[16] Velozo, "A Lusitânia Suevico-Bizantina," *Bracara Augusta,* II, No. 2 (July, 1950), 144.
[17] *Ibid.,* p. 143.
[18] Torres, "Las Invasiones y los Reinos Germánicos de España," *Historia de España,* III, 22.

The Spanish Meseta between Valladolid and Salamanca. A Threshing Ground

mediately between them. In 419 the Swabians were driven into the northern mountains by the Vandals and only Roman intervention saved them from extermination.[19] It is apparent that Rome did not think of all German tribes as being of the same stamp.

Not long after this event, the Asdingian Vandals, presumably dissatisfied with their environment in the northwest and under pressure by Romans and Visigoths, moved southward to join the remnants of the Silingians and the Alans. From there they went to Africa. Whether they went there by their own inspiration, or by the invitation of the Roman governor, is a disputed question. Boniface, the governor, was in difficulties with Rome at the time and there is reason to believe that he may have induced these fighters to aid him by the promise of territory.[20] On the other hand, Africa was an area of famed productivity [21] and was country far more to the taste of the Vandals than the rainy northwest of Iberia. Nor was this the first time that east Germans had evinced an interest in Africa. When in Italy, the Goths had planned to go there; again later, when they reached Cádiz, they went so far as to build a fleet to transport themselves thither and were diverted only by the destruction of their ships in a storm.[22] With the departure of the Vandals and the remnants of the Alans for Africa in 429, the most important Germans left in Iberia were the Swabians and the Visigoths.[23]

VISIGOTHIC VERSUS SWABIAN SETTLEMENT IN IBERIA

The Visigoths showed their taste for grazing country and settled by choice in the *meseta*, allowing the formerly prosper-

[19] *Loc. cit.*; Schmidt, "Teutonic Kingdoms in Gaul," *Cambridge Medieval History*, I, 304.
[20] Macedo, "O Domínio Germânico," *História de Portugal*, I, 315.
[21] Torres, "Las Invasiones y los Reinos Germánicos de España," *Historia de España*, III, 22.
[22] Macedo, "O Domínio Germânico," *História de Portugal*, I, 312.
[23] *Ibid.*, p. 315.

A Farm in the Minho

ous peripheries to languish. Coastal cities declined in importance, while a few *meseta* cities grew. Cartago Nova was
relinquished as the capital in favor of Toledo. Cádiz faded
almost completely as Mediterranean commerce declined.[24] The
bleak central land, unattractive even to Romans, was good
pasture land and attractive to Visigoths. Even less than the
Mediterranean fringes did the humid lands under the grey skies
of North Portugal and Galicia appeal to them. Only a few
individual Visigoths ever stayed to settle there.[25]

How different were the attitudes of the Swabians. They
chose to settle in the rainy, green Minho of North Portugal and
in Galicia, and clung to it. They had come from an area in Germany very similar to it in climate, vegetation, and opportunities for farming and grazing. The Swabians had had contact
with Celts to their south in Central Europe and with the
Romans throughout centuries of time. Many Swabians had
served in Roman armies.[26] They had absorbed techniques and
ways of life from both peoples. It was this combined culture
that they brought with them into northwest Iberia. It fitted
neatly into the patterns of use and wont of the area, which had
been submitted earlier to both Celtic and Roman—and probably some German—influences. The effect of this is brought
out by the fact that in the sixth century, A. D., toward the end
of the period of the Swabian kingdom in the northwest, after
nearly two centuries of Swabian tenure, the Minho was the
best organized and developed of all of the parts of northwest
Iberia.[27]

Braga, situated in a fertile valley in the central Minho, had

[24] António Domínguez Ortiz, "La Población española a lo largo de
nuestra historia," *Boletín de la Real Sociedad Geográfica*, LXXXVI, Nos.
4–6 (April–June, 1950), 266.
[25] Velozo, "A Lusitânia Suevico-Bizantina," *Bracara Augusta*, II, No. 2
(July, 1950), 150.
[26] Torres, "Las Invasiones y los Reinos Germánicos de España," *Historia
de España*, III, 18–19.
[27] Pierre David, *Etudes historiques sur la Galice et le Portugal du VIe
au XIIIe siècle*, p. 118.

Mondego River Valley, East of Coimbra in Central Portugal

been the Roman provincial capital and the ecclesiastical metrop-
olis. Roads led into it from the south, north, and east. Its
tradition of authority, its communications and, above all, its
storehouse quality, recommended it to the Swabians, who made
it their capital at the outset. They never relinquished it as their
center, even at the time of their one great expansionist burst
which carried them across the width of the peninsula and into
southern France.[28] It not only had the virtues that had served
the Romans but for the Swabians it was central to the core of
their kingdom, which extended from the Bay of Biscay on the
north, to the Douro River on the south, and from the Atlantic
Ocean on the west to the Sierra de Rañadoiro, in present Asturias on the east, that is, approximately the present Portuguese
province of the Minho plus the present Spanish province of
Galicia. If the Swabians made thrusts farther east into Asturias
they did not remain to control it.[29]

TRANSITIONAL MIDDLE PORTUGAL

The area to the south of the Douro River is transitional
physically. Through most of recorded time this fact has been
reflected in the culture, for it has exhibited an intermingling of
northern and southern culture types. Perhaps the transitional
nature of the area is well indicated by the fact that the four
dioceses of Lamego, Coimbra, Viseu, and Idanha, during the
centuries of Germanic kingdoms in Iberia, did not clearly belong to either the north or the south. The fact that control
shifted back and forth between the Metropolitans of Mérida
and Braga points to the lack of clear orientation.[30] Swabian
control and influence came into the area, but not completely or
even dominantly. At times, their control speared through this

[28] Torres, "Las Invasiones y los Reinos Germánicos de España," Historia
de España, III, 31; Velozo, "A Lusitânia Suevico-Bizantina," Bracara
Augusta, II, No. 3 (Oct., 1950), 248–249.
[29] Júlio Caro Baroja, Los Pueblos del Norte de la Península Ibérica,
p. 109.
[30] Pierre David, Etudes historiques sur la Galice et le Portugal du VIe
au XIIIe siècle, pp. 19–20.

One of the Valleys of the Center of the Minho

central region to the Tejo River [31] and perhaps even beyond, but this was temporary and the effects were not lasting.

THE SWABIAN LAND SYSTEM

Where the Swabians were dominant, the record of their presence remains even today in the types of land holdings. Tacitus, speaking of German settlements, said that they were unlike the Roman, which had contiguous structures, whereas the Swabians built houses with an "empty space" about each one.[32] That is to say, the Swabians were accustomed to small holdings. The idea of dispersed, small, privately owned farms probably was their contribution to the northwest of Iberia, which had previously known the collectivism of the *castros* and the large, private estates of the Romans. Today the area of their early kingdom, the Minho of Portugal and Galicia of Spain, is a land of small proprietors, whereas the country south of the Douro, where their influence was attenuated, shows a reflection of this fact in present land holdings. The region south of the Tejo, where the Swabian influence was virtually absent, is the area of greatest concentration of large estates.

The Swabians, however, were not less than human. In the areas under their control, favored individuals took over Roman villas and even established new villas of their own. So there were large estates for a few individuals, even though the area, then as now, was predominantly that of small owners.

PERSISTENCE OF ROMAN INSTITUTIONS

During the period of Swabian dominance the Roman administrative structure was not eliminated, nor were other important institutions, such as the church. Even during the periods of

[31] Francisco José Velozo, "Contribüição Luso-Galaica para a reconquista," *Minia*, I, No. 2 (May, 1945), 103. See also Abelardo Merino, "El Regionalismo peninsular y la geografía histórica," *Boletín de la Real Sociedad Geográfica*, LVIII (1916), 291.

[32] Velozo, "A Lusitânia Suevico-Bizantina," *Bracara Augusta*, II, No. 2 (July, 1950), 151, 154.

The Lower Alentejo near Beja

their paganism or heretical inclinations, they showed consideration for the ecclesiastical authorities, allowing them to function
with freedom. For example, Idatius, the Bishop of Aquae Fla-
viae (Chaves) protested bitterly against what he thought to be
Swabian perfidy. He went to Gaul to complain about it, and
returned to this Swabian territory to protest loudly and bitterly
—all with impunity.[33] The conversion of the Swabian Rechi-
arius, subsequently king, to Catholicism (probably in 447
A. D.), over fifty years prior to that of Clovis, must also indicate
that there was great freedom of action for the church and
sympathetic support by the Swabian authorities.[34]

If the northwest was tolerant of orthodox Catholicism, it was
also willing to listen to other doctrines; it was a stronghold of
Manichaean heresy.[35] It was probably the birthplace of Priscillian, and certainly the great center of Priscillian heresy,
which actually was less heresy than merely asceticism. Whatever it was, the idea swept through the peninsula in the fourth
century. By the year 400, all of the Galician bishops except two
were Priscillianists and Braga was the headquarters of the dis-
sent, but by 563 it had virtually disappeared as a publicly held
creed, almost two centuries after Priscillian himself had been
burned alive at Trèves (in 385 or 386) for his heresy.[36]

Orthodox Catholicism became official under the rule of Rech-
iarius. Seventeen years later the superficiality of the conversion
was demonstrated by Swabian acceptance of the Arian creed
as part of an international marriage agreement arranged by
Theodoric, the Visigothic king, and Remismund, the king of
the Swabians.[37] Arianism, too, was dropped after the middle of
the century, when the orthodox belief was accepted again, this

[33] Ibid., No. 3 (Oct., 1950), 250–252; No. 4 (Feb., 1951), 398.
[34] Sergio Silva Pinto, "O Bispo de Braga, Balcónio e a primeira conversão dos Suevos," Braga, Boletim do Arquivo Municipal, I, No. 13
(Dec., 1949), 407–416; also Velozo, "A Lusitânia Suevico-Bizantina,"
Bracara Augusta, II, No. 2 (July, 1950), 250.
[35] Velozo, "A Lusitânia Suevico-Bizantina," Bracara Augusta, II, No. 4
(Feb., 1951), 397.
[36] H. V. Livermore, A History of Portugal, pp. 13–14.
[37] Torres, "Las Invasiones y los Reinos Germánicos de España," Historia
de España, III, 37.

time permanently, about thirty years earlier than the decision of the Visigoths to accept Catholicism.[38]

The Minho Province of North Portugal appears immediately as distinct from all other provinces of Portugal. It resembles only one other part of the peninsula, Galicia, which, with the present Minho, formed the great bulk of the Swabian kingdom. Certainly the landscapes of the formerly Swabian lands have a personality immediately apparent. More than this, their personality is felt to be even more impressive when one lives in the area and observes the quality of life that in so many ways is to be credited to the Germanic folk.

[38] *Ibid.*, p. 39.

CHAPTER 10

Moslem Domination

Visigothic Decline

FOR ALMOST two centuries, until 585 A.D., the Swabians maintained their kingdom in the northwest, while the Visigoths controlled the remainder of the peninsula. The Swabian area was remote, obscure country, as it has been throughout virtually all of its history, and the Visigoths had little interest in it. This is perhaps fittingly expressed by the letter of Braulius of Saragossa to St. Fructuosus of Braga: "Do not think yourself worthy of scorn because you are relegated to the extremity of the west in an ignorant country, as you say, where naught is heard but the sound of tempests, . . ." [1] Near the end of the sixth century the Visigoths, hard-pressed by rebellious Swabians, removed that thorn in their sides by putting an end to Swabian independence. The little kingdom, which had occupied but a small part of the Iberian peninsula, was absorbed by the Visigothic state. Actually, the ways of life in the northwest were little altered by this fact except for whatever involvement it caused in the devious and violent politics of Toledo. For the most part, inso-

[1] H. V. Livermore, *A History of Portugal,* p. 25.

138

far as there is a record of the matter, the remote west was not greatly involved in the bloody, feudal struggle, always near the surface in Visigothic affairs.

By the year 711, the condition of affairs within the Iberian Peninsula was such that the success of almost any well-organized body of men bent upon conquest was a foregone conclusion. It should be a surprise to no one that it occurred, but perhaps one might wonder why it had not occurred some time earlier. The incredibly easy Moslem conquest of the whole peninsula, except for small areas in the northwest undesirable to Africans, can be explained only in part by their fervor and organization. The Visigothic kingdom had been dreadfully pauperized, materially and in spirit, by the continuous internal conflict between king and nobles or between Catholicism, Arianism, and the Jews.[2] Added to this confusion was a general restiveness, due to the gradual disappearance of small properties. Such change and its accompanying economic maladjustment had been brought about by the necessary grouping around feudal strongholds in times of persistent warfare.[3]

The immediate cause of Moslem entry into Iberia and its original success was due to the bitterness engendered when the Visigothic nobles rejected the claims of the family of King Vitiza to hereditary rights. Rebelling against the decision of the nobles, the Vitiza party—probably by the intervention of Archbishop Oppa, brother of Vitiza—invited Tarik, the leader of the Moslem forces, to land on the Iberian shore to fight in their cause. Rodrigo, the Visigothic king, not realizing the facts of the situation, entrusted two wings of his army to Oppa and to Oppa's brother, Sisbert. Sanguine because of the numerical superiority of his forces, Rodrigo confidently entered the battle, only to be betrayed by Oppa and Sisbert.[4]

[2] The Byzantine conquest of the south may have been possible because of this.

[3] F. Newton de Macedo, "O Domínio Germânico," História de Portugal, I, 340, 342.

[4] Manuel Torres, "Las Invasiones y los Reinos Germánicos de España (Años 409–711)," Historia de España, III, 138.

MOSLEM CONQUEST

Tarik, with his relatively small army made up of Berbers, swept through the country virtually without opposition, reaching probably as far as southern Asturias, from where he withdrew to the south to meet Muça, the governor of Africa. Muça came with an army made up mostly of Arabs.[5] Neither he nor the Arabs in Africa wanted to miss the opportunities beckoning to them in Iberia. Tarik and Muça made a second sweep through the interior of the peninsula, reaching Astorga where Tarik turned back, while Muça continued on to Lugo in present Galicia.[6]

The Moslems were amazed by the ease with which they were able to sweep through the peninsula in the first years of their conquest. However, after the first shock was over Christian groups in various parts of the peninsula planned and attempted revolts, especially in the west. In 713 a rebellion in Seville was aided by the people of Beja, who had received fugitives from the first conquest of Seville.[7] The revolt was quickly quelled and the Moslems extended their victorious advance through the Alentejo of present southern Portugal. By 715, another Moslem commander, Abde Alazis, had conquered Evora, Salacia, (Alcácer do Sal), and Egitania (Idanha a Velha). Lisbon had acceded apparently without a struggle. (Many times in its history Lisbon has decided that discretion was the better part of valor.) In 716 Abde Alazis pressed into central Portugal, where he took Coimbra. Continuing farther to the north he entered the present Minho Province. It was here, at the Douro River, that he met the first of a series of intransigent cities. Portucale (Porto) and then Braga, Túy, Orense, and Lugo tried to oppose him. Their attempts were penalized by the destruction of the settlements.[8]

[5] David Lopes, "O Domínio Arabe," *História de Portugal*, I, 393.

[6] Claudio Sánchez Albornoz y Menduiña, *La España Musulmana*, I, map facing p. 42. Also his "Itinerário de la conquista por los musulmanes," *Cuadernos de Historia de España*, X, 39, 43–45, 51–55, 57, 64, 69.

[7] Francisco José Velozo, "Contribüição Luso-Galaica para a reconquista," *Minia*, I, No. 2 (May, 1945), 108.

[8] Francisco José Velozo, "Ainda a contribüição Luso-Galaica para a

The rebellious cities represented a spirit, rather than preparation. Certainly their resistance gave little pause to the sweep of conquest, but it was a harbinger of things to come. The northwest was not only psychologically constituted to resist the African invaders but—and this was of much greater importance —it was geographically distant from the center of Moslem strength.

LANDS UNWANTED BY MOSLEMS

Furthermore—and also of fundamental importance—it is not the kind of country and climate to attract either Arabs or Berbers. Of all the regions of Iberia this probably would be the least attractive to them. It is the rainiest lowland area of the peninsula (Fig. 6). That they had little or no interest in it is indicated by a diploma of Ordoño II, of the 29th of January, 915 A. D., which states that the territory of the diocese of Iria— that is, all or most of the present province of La Coruña, plus a contiguous band of Pontevedra—was never occupied by Moslems, although there had been some thrusts into it. The same fact is borne out by the Chronicle of Alfonso III, which excludes Iria Flavia in the enumeration of the cities taken from the Moslems by Alfonso I. As an additional proof, when the bishops of Lamego and Túy fled from their homes to escape the Moslem invasion, they came as refugees to the diocese of Iria and were there given sufficient lands for their support.[9] In all ways it was better situated for revolt than most of the rest of the peninsula; this is demonstrated by the fact that the Moslems held no territory beyond the Douro River after the first two generations following the conquest. None of the forays that they made into the territory had lasting results.[10] Changes that were brought about in North Portugal by the Moslems were

reconquista. A primeira invasão de Entre-Douro-e-Minho pelos Arabes," *Braga, Boletim do Arquivo Municipal*, I, No. 12 (Aug., 1949), 318.

[9] Velozo, "Contribüição Luso-Galaico para a reconquista," *Minia*, I, No. 3 (Dec., 1946), 235.

[10] Particularly notable were those of al-Mansur (Abu Amir Mafamede) in the last quarter of the tenth century.

mostly indirect. The threat of possible attack effected a transformation of the Christian lands into siege areas which altered political and social conditions, especially in the urban centers. The countryside was less affected, indeed, in many places hardly at all.

LANDS PREFERRED BY MOSLEMS

The area of present Portugal pre-eminently to the taste of the Moslems was the dry south, below the Tejo River, the present Portuguese provinces of the Alentejo and, especially, the Algarve,[11] with its climate more African than European and with fine opportunities for irrigation. The Romans had also preferred this Mediterranean area, although they had shown no marked interest in most of Portugal. The Arabs had more than casual interest. Although they did not introduce irrigation, they elaborated it greatly.[12] Moslems from Egypt were settled near Faro (on the south coast) and in Beja (of the Alentejo),[13] and Yemenite Arabs built the lovely city of Silves amidst gardens and orchards in the Algarve.[14] Here, particularly, is the Moslem stamp strong upon the country today.

Middle Portugal, the country between the Douro and the Tejo, fulfilled its long-time function as a transition area during the Moslem period also. It was a battleground throughout the centuries. Wherever the armies marched there was desolation. Fortunately, due to its broken terrain, armies were limited to specific routes and ordinarily did not deviate greatly from them. Roadway areas and cities were damaged, but it is improbable that the independent, small farms of the hills were reduced in productivity, although their owners, at times, may have been oppressed by levies. Certain areas had an especial appeal for the Arabs, notably the lower valley of the Mondego River, near

[11] Al-Gharb—the west—that is, the westernmost part of Moslem dominions in Europe.
[12] António Jorge Dias, *Aparelhos de elevar a Agua de Rega*, pp. 180 *et seq.*
[13] Lopes, "O Domínio Arabe," *História de Portugal*, I, 407.
[14] Abu-Abd-Alla-Mohamed-al-Edrisi, *Descripción de España*, pp. 16–17.

the city of Coimbra,[15] an area where the great "Persian" water wheels are still in use. Another area of attraction for them was the Tejo Valley between Lisbon and Santarém. Edrisi speaks of the prodigious harvests of grain there.[16]

Near the Guadiana River, just beyond the present Portuguese border, is Mérida, the Roman provincial capital which was maintained by the Visigoths. The Arabs were awed by its splendor when they first saw it; [17] yet ultimately it did not meet their requirements. They preferred a small settlement on the broad flood plain of the Guadiana, which offered a greater opportunity for the expansion of irrigation. Here an upstart out of the northwest, Ibn Jalaqui (which means son of Galicia), established an independent kingdom, with its capital in the newly selected site of present Badajoz. He not only established a new kingdom, but a dynasty that lasted from 875 to 930. He founded a new religion (a combination of Islam and Christianity) and made friends of the Christian princes, especially of Alfonso III (the Great), king of León.[18] This development marked the decline of Mérida,[19] which reached its nadir prior to the time of Edrisi, who referred to its interesting "vestiges."[20] It remained obscure until comparatively modern times.

Lisbon is mentioned but briefly in the Moslem records of the time.[21] That it was a city of importance is not to be doubted. Edrisi reported it as being a charming place, protected by a castle and surrounded by walls,[22] large portions of which remain today, as does much of the castle. But it did not have the supremacy among Portuguese cities that it enjoys now. Alcácer do Sal, less than fifty miles to the southeast, is now a pleasant

[15] *Ibid.*, p. 20.

[16] *Ibid.*, p. 22–23.

[17] Louis Bertrand, *The History of Spain*, p. 4.

[18] Francisco José Velozo, "As Origens Nacionais de Portugal e de Espanha e o domínio Islâmico na península," Reprint from the journal *Gil Vicente*, p. 9.

[19] Evariste Lévi-Provençal, *Histoire de l'Espagne musulmane*, III, 350–351.

[20] Edrisi, *Descripción de España*, p. 19.

[21] Lévi-Provençal, *Histoire de l'Espagne musulmane*, III, 342.

[22] Edrisi, *Descripción de España*, p. 20.

little city of four thousand inhabitants. Under the Moslems it may have been a rival of Lisbon, for it was the port from which the vessels of Al-Mansur sailed and about which Edrisi speaks fondly, particularly noting its commerce and shipbuilding.[23] For an essentially nonmaritime people, Alcácer do Sal may have served in many ways better than Lisbon. The Sado Valley presents an open route across the Alentejo, whereas the Tejo River is a barrier between Lisbon and the southeast.

On the whole, as one regards the Moslem history of Portugal, he is struck with the relative disinterest in the area when compared with the concentration upon such areas as the valley of the Guadalquivir and the Mediterranean coasts of present Spain. The Algarve must have been a delightful place then, as it is now, a place of modest endowments made charming by the application of skills in the use of the land. There were no great areas for tremendous wealth, although, no doubt, there were prosperous Moslems living in the cities and towns and on their small properties strewn between, probably with houses much like those that are to be seen today. Coimbra and the Mondego and the Tejo shores between Lisbon and Santarém were prosperous and attractive, but by and large Portugal continued to fill her role of the country cousin.

[23] *Ibid.*, p. 18.

CHAPTER 11

The Reconquest of Iberia

PELAYO AND GOTHIC RESURGENCE

EGIÇA, one of the last kings of the Goths, had tried to establish a dynasty with hereditary rights in place of the system of election which had obtained previously. He set up a sort of vice-royalty for his son, Vitiza, in approximately the territory of the former Swabian kingdom.[1] The device proved to be effective, for Vitiza succeeded his father on the Visigothic throne in Toledo. The next link in the dynastic chain would normally have been the assumption of authority by Akhila, the son of Vitiza, but events did not duplicate those of the previous accession. Visigothic nobles rejected Akhila and in his place elected Rodrigo, the Duke of Córdoba, who assumed his throne "tumultuously,"[2] in face of the opposition and plotting of the family of Akhila.

Rodrigo was not to have his position for long, however. The treachery of the family of Akhila furthered the Moslem con-

[1] This was in 698–702. Ramón Menéndez Pidal, *Historia de España,* III, li.

[2] Manuel Torres, "Las Invasiones y los Reinos Germánicos de España (Años 409–711)," *Historia de España,* III, 135.

quest, and after the death of Rodrigo in 711, in the battle which opened the peninsula to the Moslems, their services were rewarded. Akhila was established as surrogate for the Moslem rulers. Isidore of Beja, the first chronicler of the time, does not end the list of Visigothic monarchs with Rodrigo, but continues with Akhila and then Ardobast.[3] In view of this fact, it may be said that the official Goths were Moslem allies. Actually, however, not all Christians accepted this relationship, and many dissidents took refuge in the north and northwest of the peninsula.[4] One of these refugees, Pelayo, is given credit for the origins of the Christian resurgence.

Traditionally, the reconquest of Iberia from the Moslems began with Pelayo "the Goth" and the battle (c. 721) near Cangas de Onis, below the Peñas de Europa in Asturias. Pelayo was a man of the north, or perhaps the northwest.[5] His father, the *dux* Fáfila, had been killed in Túy by Vitiza,[6] the man who later became king of the Goths. It is obvious that Pelayo had no reason to feel affection for the house of Vitiza. From the outset he was opposed to both the complacent heirs of Vitiza and to the Moslems with whom they had become associated. He seems to have been involved in the early revolts in the northwest, for he was taken as hostage by Abde Alazis in the year 716 to assure the obedient submission of the dissidents there. He was taken to Córdoba in the same year, but promptly escaped.[7]

For the period after his escape there is a hiatus of several

[3] Francisco José Velozo, "As Origens Nacionais de Portugal e de Espanha e o domínio Islâmico na península," Reprint from the journal *Gil Vicente* (1951), p. 5.

[4] *Ibid.*, p. 27.

[5] Francisco José Velozo, "Ainda a contribüiçâo Luso-Galaica para a reconquista. A primeira invasão de Entre-Douro-e-Minho pelos Arabes," *Braga, Boletim do Arquivo Municipal*, I, No. 12 (Aug., 1949), 324–328.

[6] Menéndez Pidal, *Historia de España*, III, li.

[7] Velozo, "Ainda a contribüiçâo Luso-Galaica para a reconquista," *Braga, Boletim do Arquivo Municipal*, I, No. 12 (Aug., 1949), 324; "As Origens Nacionais de Portugal e de Espanha," Reprint from the journal *Gil Vicente* (1951), p. 31; "Contribüiçâo Luso-Galaica para a reconquista," *Minia*, I, No. 3 (Dec., 1946), 228.

years in our knowledge of his actions and affairs. He is an obscure figure and the record is far from clear. One Portuguese scholar advances an interesting argument with regard to the lost years. He suggests that Pelayo spent this time in the northwest, in the Portuguese Minho or Galicia, and not in Asturias as commonly believed.[8] There is some reason for such a belief, as Pelayo had formerly lived in the western area. It would have been natural for him to return to the place where he was known and had friends and where Moslem power had never been established. This seems a possibility, particularly in view of the fact that Asturias, the commonly accepted place of his refuge, was held during those years by the Berber, Munuça, who had his headquarters at Gijón [9] in Asturias. Furthermore, the Arab historian, Ibne Idari, referred to the refuge of Pelayo and his small group of supporters as being in the mountains of Galicia, and the chronicle of Alfonso III attests that the conquest of Asturias was made by men from the west and that the counts from the west and their men were mostly Swabians and not Goths.[10]

Also obscure are the original intentions of Pelayo. The idea, which has been so widely accepted, that he was imbued with the desire to free Iberia from the Moslem yoke is almost certainly manufactured to suit a national mythology, but his re-

[8] Velozo, "Contribüição Luso-Galaica para a reconquista," Minia, I, No. 3 (Dec., 1946), 235.

[9] Velozo, "As Origens Nacionais de Portugal e de Espanha," Reprint from the journal Gil Vicente (1951), p. 36.

[10] Velozo, "Contribüição Luso-Galaica para a reconquista," Minia, I, No. 3 (Dec., 1946), 235. The Arab historian Almacari speaks definitely of the invasion of Galicia by the Arab Muça in 716 and the conquest of Viseu in present Portugal. Velozo, "Contribüição Luso-Galaica para a reconquista," Minia, I, No. 2 (May, 1945), 110–111. Muça also conquered Lugo in middle Galicia and ordered "explorations that arrived at the Penha de Pelayo." Velozo thinks that the Penha de Pelayo can be located not far from Lugo, within the triangle Cape Finisterre, Padron (ancient Iria Flavia), and La Coruña, that is, in the extreme northwest area of the peninsula, bordering the Atlantic. Velozo, "As Origens Nacionais de Portugal e de Espanha," Reprint from the journal Gil Vicente (1951), p. 26.

sentment against the Moslems, and the Vitizana dynasty allied with them, can hardly be doubted. It is possible that simply this resentment led him to stubborn and perhaps planless opposition. Or he may have envisaged a re-establishment of the political unit he had known in the northwest under Vitiza, essentially the territory of the Swabian kingdom. Whatever may have been his reasons, they had less to do with his success and that of subsequent Christian monarchs than did the opportunities offered by the Moslems themselves, opportunities too obviously favorable to be overlooked.

The pristine Moslem enthusiasm for their cause was greatly diminished in the early years following the conquest. The Berbers, especially, were dissatisfied with Arab rule. Munuça, of Gijón, was one of the dissidents, as was shown by his ultimate willingness to make bargains with the Christians against the interests of the Arabs. That he was not alone in his feelings was shown by other revolts. If it had not been for this sentiment, the forces of Pelayo might not have been able to win the skirmish in Asturias.[11]

THE BATTLE OF COVADONGA

The whereabouts of Pelayo became a matter of record again at the time of the so-called battle of Covadonga which took place near Cangas de Onis in present Asturias. Although this affair has been greatly romanticized since its occurrence and perhaps should not be termed a battle at all, there was a skirmish, sometime between the years 721 and 725,[12] and Pelayo's group may have included as many as three hundred men.[13] His forces are said to have emerged victorious, although perhaps the Moslems would not have concurred in this judgment. It seems that Pelayo used the hit-and-run tactics common to the Portuguese area and especially notable under the Lusi-

[11] *Ibid.*, p. 38.
[12] Damião Peres, "A Reconquista Cristã," *História de Portugal*, I, 436.
[13] Velozo, "As Origens Nacionais de Portugal e de Espanha," Reprint from the journal *Gil Vicente* (1951), pp. 22, 55.

tanians. His forces damaged the Moslem contingent and then took refuge in the hills. The Moslems may well have taken this to be a retreat and credited themselves with the victory.

Subsequent to this fracas little is known of Pelayo, and his successor, Fáfila,[14] was obscure. It was the third in this line who most distinguished himself as a conqueror. This was Pelayo's son-in-law, who became known to history as Alfonso I (739–757)[15] and who is famous for his great extension of Christian control. His successes, however, like those of his father-in-law, are to be credited only partly to his valor and to that of his followers. Several events of importance, contributory to his success, had taken place in the early years of his reign. First, Berbers in Africa had revolted against Arab domination, and this action had inspired the restive Berbers of northern Iberia to do the same. They marched south against Córdoba in 739 and left the northern territory largely undefended.[16]

The historical record for the period has many blank pages. We know that there was a famine and plague which may have been caused by warfare. However, as there has never been a large food surplus in this area and living has been successful only through frugality, it might be expected that difficulties would ensue through the Moslem conquest. Disruption would have been caused by the most understanding of conquerors, and the Berbers were hardly this. Their home environment, diametrically different from that of northern Iberia, gave them little grasp of the local economy and requirements.

THE CONQUESTS OF ALFONSO I AND THE "DESERT ZONE"

Between 751 and 754, Alfonso I took Chaves, Braga, Porto, Viseu and other settlements and castles.[17] Then he continued his conquest by taking Astorga, León, Zamora, Salamanca,

[14] Pierre David, *Etudes historiques sur la Galice et le Portugal du VIe au XIIIe siècle,* p. 32.

[15] Peres, "A Reconquista Cristã," *História de Portugal,* I, 436.

[16] Torquato de Sousa Soares, "O Repovoamento do Norte de Portugal no século IX," *Congresso do Mundo Português,* II (1940), 396.

[17] *Loc. cit.*

Simancas, Avila, and Miranda de Ebro.[18] To accomplish these victories, he had made thrusts through most of the northern *meseta,* and such a conquest was too rapid to be permanent. Alfonso realized this fact, and to protect the weak frontier he decided to strengthen the Asturian nucleus. To do so he created a politically impotent zone south of Asturias extending to the Duero River. The *Chronicon Sebastiani* says that he killed the Arabs of the cities and that he removed the Christians, taking them back to Asturias with him.[19] The *Chronicon Albedense* reports that he desolated the lands down to the Duero River.[20] The view that a desert waste was literally created was accepted by Herculano, and thus until recently found almost universal acceptance in Iberia. It is still defended by many historians. For example, Sánchez Albornoz [21] brilliantly catalogues the breakdown of civil and religious authority and institutions, and his proof is beyond cavil. However, his assumption that this collapse indicates desertion of the land by the self-sufficient small peasant farmers is in no way demonstrated. His contention [22] that a great band of desert was created from the Atlantic to the Ebro and that depopulation was complete cannot be accepted. The statements to this effect by early chroniclers, upon which he depends, were obviously hyperbole. Nor can his later statement,[23] that the interruption of life on the *meseta* was absolute, be accepted, although the desertion of lands on the *meseta* of present Spain was undoubtedly far greater than that in the mountainous Portuguese north.[24]

[18] Peres, "A Reconquista Cristã," *História de Portugal,* I, 436.
[19] Soares, "O Repovoamento do Norte de Portugal," *Congresso do Mundo Português,* II (1940), 396.
[20] Peres, "A Reconquista Cristã," *História de Portugal,* I, 436.
[21] Claudio Sánchez Albornoz y Menduiña, *Ruina y extinción del municipio romano en España e instituciones que le reemplazan,* p. 120.
[22] *Ibid.,* p. 120.
[23] *Ibid.,* p. 124.
[24] Sánchez Albornoz is not alone in these beliefs. See, for example, Amando Melón y Ruiz de Gordejuela, *Geografía histórica española,* I, 223–225. António Jorge Dias, in his *Rio de Onor,* Chap. I, Note 52, p. 40, has a useful summary of the various positions taken in this argument by various scholars.

The opponents of such a literal acceptance of the early chronicles base their opinions upon facts which the proponents do not take into consideration (or at least do not mention). Alberto Sampaio [25] pointed out that the Christians of the zone of "desert" could not have been taken back to Asturias. It would have been impossible to move that many people into Asturias and to support them there. Undoubtedly individuals followed the king back to the north, including, perhaps, all of the Christian city dwellers, but the great majority must have remained. [26] These would have been the country people, most of them isolated from the main routes.

The terms "desert" and "uninhabited land" can be accepted in only a limited sense. The statement of the *Chronicon* that Alfonso eliminated the cities is reasonable. This would have been a logical procedure, for they were not only nodal points of communication but forts as well. But the suggestion that the individual farmers, scattered across the hilly countryside of North Portugal, could have been eliminated completely strains credulity. The area has always been one of country people rather than one of town dwellers. Armies do not scatter over the land. They march along roads and fight for key points—cities. As both cities and roads were few in North Portugal, the "desolation" was more strategic and political than human.

David describes the conditions of a later period when peasants in France, similarly circumstanced, remained on the land. [27] That the same thing occurred in the Minho is indicated by the typical peasant practices of the area which have their roots in ancient times, long predating the period of the so-called desolation. Undoubtedly contributing to the continuity was the remembrance of the church and of holy places. Even though many churches and monasteries were in ruins, the evidence is plain that they remained places of veneration, for with the re-establishment of the institutional framework, the rebuilt

[25] Alberto Sampaio, "As Vilas do Norte de Portugal," *Estudos históricos e económicos*, I, Pt. 1, 54.

[26] A. A. Mendes Corrêa, *Raízes de Portugal*, pp. 16–18, 80–81.

[27] David, *Etudes historiques*, p. 171.

churches were given their saints' names of the Roman period. New settlers were taken into the old religious framework of the primitive parishes, marked by the church and the cemetery.[28] In terms of politics, however, it was an empty land. Cities, the political nerve centers, were eliminated. So, in the struggle for power, the politically unimportant area of small farmers was a "desert" in the eyes of ambitious men. This condition of political "desolation" between the Minho and Douro rivers in Portugal lasted for about a century.[29]

RESETTLEMENT OF TOWNS OF PRESENT NORTH PORTUGAL

Alfonso II asked for and received aid from Charlemagne in 795. The aid of the Franks made possible Alfonso's advance into Middle Portugal, which reached at least as far as Lisbon. Relieved of the Moslem threat on the south, urban life began to take form again in the Douro-to-Minho region. In 840 the king met with a council of counts and bishops in Guimarães to promote the settlement of these "desolated" lands. From Guimarães they went to Braga to consider its restoration. Nothing was done immediately, for a document of 841 mentions the "great decay of the place," [30] and the Metropolitan of Braga fulfilled the obligations of his office in Lugo.[31] Perhaps their intentions to resettle were thwarted by the considerable difficulties of the decade 840–850, with its internal revolts in the northwest and Norman attacks on the coasts.[32]

Temporarily the trend toward the re-establishment of cities languished, but during the reign of Alfonso's successor, Ordoño I (850–860), another start was made. It was during this period that Túy, on the lower Minho River, was re-established.[33] Al-

[28] Pierre David, "Les Saints Patrons d'églises entre Minho et Mondego jusqu'à la fin du XIᵉ siècle," *Revista Portuguesa de História*, II (1943), 250–251.
[29] Damião Peres, *Como nasceu Portugal*, p. 38.
[30] Peres, "A Reconquista Cristã," *História de Portugal*, I, 441.
[31] David, *Etudes historiques*, pp. 123–124, 128.
[32] Peres, "A Reconquista Cristã," *História de Portugal*, I, 441.
[33] Peres, *Como nasceu Portugal*, p. 38.

fonso III (866–910) continued the policy of resettlement with even more vigor than that of his predecessors.[34] He ordered the re-establishment of Porto,[35] which was done in 868, largely by refugees from Coimbra. After this event the area to the north was repopulated.[36] That this re-establishment was accomplished out of Coimbra and Porto is of fundamental importance for the later Portuguese national state.

THE SPECIAL CHARACTER OF THE AREA OF SETTLEMENT

The resettlement of the north was made in the "desert" zone, which had had no political affiliation for over a century and had severed its economic ties with Galicia and León. Politically and economically, this zone started afresh with new alignments, whereas Galicia had had an unbroken tradition of adherence to the Leonese kingdom of the Iberian plateau. The cultural

[34] Peres, "A Reconquista Cristã," História de Portugal, I, 441.
[35] David, Etudes historiques, p. 159. Porto is the ancient Portus Cale on the Douro River. Calem was probably a Lusitanian citânia that later was used by the Romans as a place of embarkation, hence the prefix portus. See J. Augusto Ferreira, Memórias Archaeológico-históricas da Cidade do Porto, I, 11. The Itinerary of Antoninus placed it on the left bank of the river, in the approximate location of the present Vila Nova de Gaia. H. Lautensach, "Portugal: Auf Grund eigener Reisen und der Literatur." I. "Das Land als Ganzes," Petermann's Mitteilungen, No. 213 (1932), 1. Leite de Vasconcellos thought that it was probably on the right bank, in the approximate place of the present Porto. J. Leite de Vasconcellos, "Delimitação da fronteira Portuguesa," Boletim da Classe de Letras, XIII (1918–1919), 1279. The Swabian parochiale seems to place Roman Portucale to the south of the Douro, Portucale on the north being Swabian. David, Etudes historiques, p. 79. During the period of Swabian rule, the bishop Idatius distinguished the unfortified Portucale locum on the right bank from castrum on the south bank, which was a fortified place on an eminence. Ferreira, Memórias Archaeológico-históricas da Cidade do Porto, I, 11. In the twelfth century there seems to have been a settlement on the left bank. Charles Wendell David, De Expugnatione Lyxbonensi, p. 67. This, of course, does not rule out the probability of the complementary settlement on the other side of the river. Anciently and persistently there has been a tendency for the development of settlements facing each other across the Douro. The position on the river, as a crossing place, has had enduring importance.
[36] "Repopulated" here means the re-establishment of cities and communications.

similarity between Galicia and the north of Portugal remained, but there was a new economic focus and a consciousness of difference, beginning at the north border of the formerly "deserted" zone, the line of the lower Minho River. In a Guimarães document of 841 there is reference to the "Provincia Portucalense," tacitly underlining the special character of the area south of the Minho River, the southern section of the former Swabian realm, the germ of the future Portugal.[37] Thus the present province of the Minho, plus extensions southward, was recognized as a place apart, one with distinct personality. In a document of Alfonso III, of 883, the name "Portugal" was used to identify the Minho-to-Douro lands. The term "Galicia" was restricted to the area to the north of the Minho River.[38] Another document, of 938, uses the term "Portugal" in this precise sense. One of 959 describes Galicia as being only to the north of the Minho River.[39] In the middle of the following century, documents refer to Portugal as one of the parts of the kingdom of León, but as being distinct from Galicia. It seems quite clear that for people of that period the area of present northwest Portugal was distinct from the area of present Galicia, to the north of the Minho River. This is not surprising in view of the fact that the "desert" of Alfonso existed still in part of the present Portuguese lands, making an economic separation between the organized area of Galicia and the area being organized out of the south.

The resettlement of the region of the present province of Minho was not accomplished suddenly. As late as the eleventh century the term Portugal usually referred to the lands between the Mondego and Lima rivers, including the cities of Coimbra, Porto, Braga, Guimarães, and Barcelos.[40] It must be remembered that the resettlement of the "desert" started with the re-establishment of Porto by men from Coimbra. Out of Porto

[37] Alberto Sampaio, quoted by Damião Peres, "Origens da nacionalidade," Congresso do Mundo Português, II, 33.

[38] Ibid., p. 15.

[39] Peres, "Origens da nacionalidade," Congresso do Mundo Português, II, 16.

[40] David, Etudes historiques, p. 332.

the settlement of the cities to the north was effected. As late as the early part of the eleventh century the northern part of present Portugal, the territory lying between the Lima and Minho rivers, had not been effectively resettled. Nor had the present province of Trás-os-Montes become a part of the north-western nucleus. It remained remote from the martial and political events affecting the lowland area to the west and the *meseta* to the east. Even in the early twelfth century it was politically outside of the incipient Portuguese state, although its south and west sections were within the orbit of Portuguese economic affairs. But by the middle of the following century all of the province had become an integral part of Portuguese territory.[41]

REVOLTS IN THE NORTHWEST

The northwest, which had lived with a large degree of isolation and self-sufficiency, had problems of its own that it was forced to meet in its own way. Norman [42] attacks which began in the ninth century were repeated and became especially troublesome during the tenth and early eleventh centuries. In 968 there was a great raid, and in 1016 [43] an especially vicious attack destroyed Túy completely. Against these attacks the problem of defense was local, for the Leonese king and his forces were too remote, and usually too occupied, to offer aid. The local barons had to maintain themselves, and the self-sufficiency engendered by such demands upon their courage and resourcefulness added to the ideas of rebellion common to the times.

Even before the devastation and weakening of León by al-Mansur in the last of the tenth century, attempts had been made by local barons of Galicia to throw off Leonese control. In the last half of the tenth century they rebelled against

[41] Conde de São Payo (D. António), "Esboço da carta histórica de Província de Trás-os-Montes (séculos XIII a XIX)," *Congresso do Mundo Português*, II, 421–433.

[42] That is, "northmen," including various Scandinavians.

[43] Ramón Menéndez Pidal, *La España del Cid*, p. 68.

Ordoño III,[44] and in 1031 other revolts in Galicia against the king of León were aided by the king of Navarra.[45] By the end of the eleventh century the sense of independence had grown so lustily that in 1071 the barons of Entre-Douro-e-Minho (Minho Province) revolted against King García of the ephemeral kingdom of Galicia.[46] This revolt was a precursor of the one of 1128 when Affonso (or Afonso) Henriques took the successful step toward Portuguese independence. The barons might well have advanced the day of Portuguese independence by three generations had it not been for the opposition of Sesnando, Count of Coimbra. Because of his opposition, the barons were squeezed between two forces and defeated.[47]

The remote, increasingly self-sufficient northwest was an obvious candidate for separatism. If means had not been found to avoid it in Galicia, that section of Iberia would almost surely have been lost to Spain, as Portugal was ultimately lost. A device that probably can be credited with maintaining the bonds between Galicia and the *meseta* kingdoms was suggested, perhaps quite fortuitously, by the church. This was the establishment and development of the pilgrimage to Santiago de Compostela along the route from France across north Spain.

THE PILGRIMAGE TO SANTIAGO

The rebelliousness of the northwest had been not only political but also religious. This part of Iberia had long been restless and independently disposed toward Rome (note earlier references to the Priscillianist and Manichaean heresies in Chapter 9). This sense of detachment from the remainder of Iberia was largely dissipated in Galicia by the development of the pilgrimage to the supposed Iberian resting place of the remains of

[44] Peres, "A Reconquista Cristã," *História de Portugal*, I, 454.
[45] Menéndez Pidal, *La España del Cid*, p. 68.
[46] Peres, "A Reconquista Cristã," *História de Portugal*, I, 366.
[47] Sesnando was the son of a wealthy *mozarabe* who became vizier to the Emir of Seville. He transferred his allegiance to Ferdinand the Great and was rewarded by territory south of the Douro River. Alexandre Herculano, *História de Portugal* (7th ed.), p. 10.

St. James, the first reference to which was made in the ninth century.[48]

Although the pilgrimage was started only in the ninth century, by the end of that century it was well known in Iberia. Alfonso III (the Great) came with all of his family. In the tenth century pilgrims came from as far as Egypt and Nubia. By the eleventh century the great movement was thoroughly established.[49] In the twelfth century further efforts were made by the monks of Cluny and by Diego Gelmirez, Archbishop of Santiago, and the pilgrimage became one of the most famous tourist enterprises of all time.[50]

The intermingling of religious and political purposes is indicated by the relations of the leading figures to each other. Calixtus II was a member of a noble Burgundian family, and was chosen Pope at Cluny. As Pope, with support from Cluny, at that time the chief center of religious influence throughout Western Europe, his support of the pilgrimage was an important factor. His decisions may have been influenced by the fact that Raymond, Count of Galicia, had been his brother,[51] as well as the son-in-law of Alfonso VI (see below).

AFFAIRS OF LEÓN DURING THE PERIOD OF THE RESETTLEMENT OF THE NORTHWEST

The rebellious northwest was an obvious and great problem for the king, but it was not his only problem. Conditions in the remainder of the peninsula had been growing worse for León during the centuries. These tangled affairs of the peninsula in general had a decisive bearing upon the achievement of Portuguese independence.

Along the Duero River, in present Spain, where Alfonso I had created the strategic "defensive desert" between the Caliphate and the kingdom of Asturias, the desolation of the open

[48] Georgiana G. King, *The Way of Saint James*, I, 48–49, 58–59, 62, 93.
[49] *Ibid.*, p. 99.
[50] Marques de la Vega Inclan, *Guía del Viaje a Santiago*, V, 7.
[51] *Ibid.*, p. 11.

meseta lands was undoubtedly far greater than that of North and Middle Portugal. In the broken terrain of Portugal it was not difficult for individual farmers to remain; the case was otherwise in the open plateau. Even in prehistoric times the destruction of forests had been largely accomplished on the *meseta*.[52] During the period of the reconquest the advancing Christians, for strategic reasons, eliminated most of the remaining trees and woody growth. It was not a useful refuge area.[53]

RESETTLEMENT OF THE *Meseta*

During the last half of the ninth and the early tenth centuries, resettlement was begun on the *meseta*. The southern part of the province of León was repopulated mostly by Galician and Asturian colonists.[54] This fact, undoubtedly, had an influence upon the later alliance of Galicia with the *meseta* kingdoms. North Portugal, as was pointed out above, was resettled out of the south. This is an important difference and casts more light upon the ultimate separation of Galicia and Portugal.

On the *meseta* the course of resettlement was less smooth than in the remote west. During most of the tenth century Moslem influence was dominant, either by reason of its vigor or because of Christian inefficacy. The Leonese kings seem to have been thoroughly unexceptional. In company with the rulers of Navarra, the counts of the Marca (Catalonia), the great counts of Castile, and even those of Galicia,[55] they were continually found at the court of the Caliphs, both to pay their respects and to receive information about external and even

---

[52] Hermann Lautensach, "Die Iberische Halbinsel als Schauplatz der geschichtlichen Bewegung," *Zeitschrift der Gesellschaft für Erdkunde zu Berlin*, Nos. 3/4 (June, 1948), 104.

[53] Although betokening the tenacity with which peasants cling to their land, it seems probable that even during the long centuries of recurrent disaster it was never completely uninhabited.

[54] Menéndez Pidal, *La España del Cid*, p. 54.

[55] One may safely assume that the northwest, never an area of interest to the Moslems, was less influenced by this political situation than were other Christian areas.

internal affairs of their own domains. The focus of much of Iberia was upon Córdoba,[56] and the Moslems certainly were not interested in Christian resettlement.

That this subservience of the Christians to the Moslems diminished in the last half of the century is made apparent by revolts and the strenuous efforts of al-Mansur to quell them. In a series of thrusts through Iberia, he slashed the countryside through which his armies passed, leveling any cities that resisted. Even the remote northwest was involved, for a revolt there brought him through southwest Spain, up through Coimbra (which he destroyed in 987),[57] Viseu, and to Porto, where he met his fleet, which had sailed from the presently named Alcácer do Sal. From Porto the combined forces marched northward to Galicia. Near Vigo, a few stalwarts set up a brief opposition, but it was a minor incident in the victorious march of al-Mansur. From there they continued to Santiago de Compostela, which was sacked and burned.[58] All along the route destruction was the price of resistance, but the cities of present Portugal, for the most part, chose discretion as the better part of valor and, as they submitted without resistance, were not damaged. The Portuguese counts of the northern province, lying between the Douro and Minho rivers, submitted as allies.[59] In general, by choosing non-resistance, Portugal saved itself from the destruction that was wrought upon the resisters, and especially upon León.

THE DECLINE OF LEÓN AND THE RISE OF CASTILE

León was the strongest opponent of the Moslems and thus the center of their attack in several campaigns. Not only were cities sacked and burned, but the desolation of the farms and

[56] Menéndez Pidal, La España del Cid, p. 36.

[57] It was leveled so completely that for seven years afterward there was no occupation of the site, according to the Chronicon Conimbricense. Quoted in Evariste Lévi-Provençal, Histoire de l'Espagne musulmane, II, 239.

[58] Ibid., p. 249.

[59] Loc. cit.

groves was frightful.[60] Nevertheless, even after these afflictions, León remained the most powerful of the Christian kingdoms in the early eleventh century.[61] But the bell was beginning to toll. The blows of the Moslems had been debilitating [62] and constituted an important reason for its decline. Other reasons for decline are harder to assess but, without doubt, they were of importance. For example, the rigidity of customs and law was such that it was impossible for León to adjust to the changing times. The old Visigothic law, the *Fuero Juzgo*, was grimly applied, even though it failed to fit the conditions of this revolutionary situation. Nor did the Visigothic bequest of unpredictable regal succession help matters.[63] It led to internal tensions and spawned revolts, when unanimity of purpose might have saved the kingdom.

Castile, on the other hand, largely discarded the Visigothic regulations wherever they failed to be suitable, and thus made its whole political structure more resilient and adjustable. Castilian judges, beginning with the early tenth century, began basing their judgments upon local customs, rather than on the *Fuero Juzgo*.[64] This attitude, coupled with the fact that Castile was not the center of Moslem attack and suffered less than León in battle, led to its increasing political importance.

Some relief came to the Christian kingdoms with the death of al-Mansur in 1002, which left a political vacuum in Moslem territory. The disorder that ensued among Moslems did not redound to the benefit of León particularly, although it meant relief from pressure. Castile was the chief beneficiary. During the eleventh century Ferdinand I (1038–1065), king of Castile (and ultimately of Galicia, León, and Navarra), achieved great victories. He reconquered extensive territories from the prince of Badajoz and made incursions into the domains of the king of Saragossa. He made vassals of the kings of Toledo and Se-

[60] *Ibid.*, pp. 234–249.
[61] Menéndez Pidal, *La España del Cid*, p. 40.
[62] *Ibid.*, p. 65.
[63] *Ibid.*, pp. 66–68.
[64] *Ibid.*, p. 55.

ville. By 1054 he had everything from Galicia to the Ebro in his power, and in Portugal he established the south border of Christendom at the Mondego River.[65]

It must have seemed, then, a propitious time for the complete triumph of Christian arms in the peninsula, but such an outcome was still more than four centuries away. The delay was caused by many things, but the immediate reason was that Ferdinand divided his kingdom into three parts and by so doing again set up internal conflict in Christian lands. Although his son, Alfonso VI of León and Asturias, continued the struggle against the Moslems, taking Toledo, virtually controlling Valencia and raiding south of Seville to the sea,[66] he was at odds with the other Christian kingdoms; Castile was against León and Navarra; Aragon was opposed to Catalonia. Moreover, one of the great motivating forces of the reconquest precluded complete victory over the Moslems. This was the desire for quick profit—through loot, ransom for the return of persons or cities, or payment for protection. For centuries, the ordinary way of living was by marauding and pillaging, and Christian armies of the *meseta* (less so in Portugal) often had more interest in winning battles that would involve loot or payment for future protection by Moslem kings than any wish to possess or settle new territory. Christian princes extracted extortionate levies from Moslem kingdoms. Time and again, cities were captured only to be relinquished after they had been sacked or had given promises of payment.[67]

The conquest of Alfonso VI led the Moslems of the south to appeal to the Almorávides of Africa for help. They responded, and in 1086 won a great victory at Zalaca, near Badajoz. After this, the fanatical, well-organized Almorávides controlled a large part of Iberia for over a generation before power began to slip from their grasp. In 1120 they were badly beaten by

---

[65] J. Leite de Vasconcellos, "Delimitação da fronteira Portuguesa," *Boletim da Classe de Letras,* XIII (1918–1919), p. 1276.

[66] This was the period of Rodrigo de Vivar, El Cid Campeador, d. 1099.

[67] Louis Bertrand, *The History of Spain,* p. 159; Peres, "A Reconquista Cristã," *História de Portugal,* I, 451.

Alfonso of Aragon, *el Batallador*. But they were not the last of the Africans to invade Iberia. Later in the century they were followed by the Almohades, who, although never as effective as the Almorávides had been in the first years of their power, established control over the southern part of the peninsula. Moslem pressure from the south remained a serious problem for the Christians until 1212, when the Almohades were decisively beaten at Navas de Tolosa.

The twelfth century as a whole was one of disruption and devastation for the area of present New Castile with the alternating advances and withdrawals of Christians and Moslems, each in turn scorching the land as they passed through it. The inhabitants of the south *meseta*, trying to eke out a living, found that it was useless to plant trees. Such long-term plans were profitless in face of the planned destruction of the countryside. Grain was less a gamble, as it required only a few months' wait before the harvest. Best of all, however, were mobile flocks of animals which could be moved out of harm's way. Moslems complained to the Emperor in Morocco that they could not live isolated on the *meseta* to fall prey to marauders.[68] That Christians were in the same predicament is borne out by Edrisi's twelfth-century report, in which he said that the function of Medellín, Trujillo, and Cáceres was to serve as forts from which raids could be made to devastate and sack Christian places.[69] Loot seems to have been a large part of the motivation.

A change in attitude may be first observed in the mid-eleventh century, when Castile began to exhibit greater interest in the permanent expansion of its borders, rather than the immediate profit to be squeezed from Moslems either for protection or for the recession of conquered territories.[70] This did not represent a complete change in Castilian policy. The predilection for raiding and loot was too strongly ingrained to be

[68] António Dominguez Ortiz, "La Población española a lo largo de nuestra historia," *Boletín de la Real Sociedad Geográfica*, LXXXVI, Nos. 4–6 (Apr.–June, 1950), 273–274.
[69] Abu-Abd-Alla-Mohamed-al-Edrisi, *Descripción de España*, p. 25.
[70] Menéndez Pidal, *La España del Cid*, pp. 42–43.

eliminated quickly. It continued to have importance until Granada fell. The change in attitude was sufficient, however, to give Castile an advantage over León where the preoccupation with loot continued unabated.

THE SHIFT IN POWER AND ITS EFFECT
UPON PORTUGUESE INDEPENDENCE

Of the three distinct centers or nuclei of the north of Iberia, León had been the most powerful and was the object of Moslem attack. Leonese strength in this case was its disadvantage and it suffered under repeated and devastating attacks. Castile, on the east, was less in the Moslem focus and continued to grow in power and to form itself as a political unit. On the other side was the area of present North Portugal, considerably isolated by topography. It was a wet, green country in a blind-alley position and had little to recommend it to either the Moslems or the *meseta* Spaniards. León had its hands full with insuperable problems without being concerned about a remote, somewhat strange and unattractive land. Even less would that part of the peninsula have come into the ken of Castile, so far away and so involved in the great social and military changes that eventuated in its becoming the supreme power of Spain. The emergence of Castile as dominant over León was all to the good for Portugal. It left the latter a free choice of remaining largely aloof, or of taking part in the affairs of the rest of the peninsula. When its interests were served it could take part in the conflict, but otherwise there was little compulsion. When Portugal struck for its freedom, León was well along the road of its decline, but Castile had not yet succeeded in consolidating its power over the more important areas in the east and the south.

The political advantages of the offside position of Portugal are obvious but there was another advantage to this avoidance of involvement in the martial affairs of the peninsula. It allowed the Portuguese farmers, who were more strongly rooted in the land than their *meseta* relatives, an opportunity to continue to improve their agriculture. At the time of the raids and counter-raids on the *meseta*, where potential agricultural land was converted by reasons of necessity into sheep runs, the Portuguese farmers continued their agriculture without disruption. On the Spanish side, the herder, always strong, was strengthened further, whereas on the Portuguese side if there was change it was in favor of the farmer.

CHAPTER 12

Final Steps toward Portuguese Independence

THE BURGUNDIANS IN THE NORTHWEST

DURING the eleventh century, Pope Alexander II encouraged Europeans to go to Spain to fight Moslems. Of the many French who heeded the call and became permanent settlers in Iberia [1] two are particularly to be noted. The first, Raymond, son of the Count of Burgundy, arrived before the end of the century. He married Urraca, the only legitimate daughter of Alfonso. As Galicia was a troubled place, Alfonso decided to put this newly acquired member of his family in authority there, as a sort of viceroy.[2] The second figure of importance was Henry, cousin of Raymond and grandson of Robert, Duke of Burgundy. By 1095 he was married to Theresa (or Tarasia or Tareja), an illegitimate daughter of

---

[1] Several settlements were established or influenced by the French. J. Leite de Vasconcellos, *Origem histórica e formação do povo Português*, pp. 8–13.

[2] Alexandre Herculano, *História de Portugal* (7th ed.), pp. 14–15; Damião Peres, *Como nasceu Portugal*, p. 48.

Alfonso.[3] Henry was also given territory, that of present North Portugal. In the first year he may have been subject to the authority of Raymond,[4] although this is not certain. He may never have been answerable to anyone but Alfonso from the year 1095, when he was first given authority in the region south of the Minho River.[5]

Documents of the period make a clear distinction between this territory and that of Raymond, to the north of the Minho.[6] Henry held his territory with sovereign rights, which were also rights of inheritance. This fact was demonstrated by the reversion of the territory without question, first to his widow and then to his son, Affonso Henriques. Nevertheless, it was not autonomy; Henry was the vassal of the Spanish king.[7] His situation was altered in the early years of the twelfth century when fundamental changes took place, brought about in the first instance by the death of the principal contenders for power. Raymond, who had laid plans to succeed his father-in-law, Alfonso, died in 1107. Alfonso's son, Sancho, the heir, died in 1108. Alfonso himself died the next year. From these deaths came the various problems of succession and inheritance. Urraca, daughter of Alfonso and widow of Raymond of Galicia, was the legitimate heir to the Leonese throne; but when she assumed authority over the whole kingdom, Henry in Portugal felt that he had been bilked of his due. His anger was a promise of trouble to come.[8]

Urraca added to her difficulties by marrying Alfonso of Aragon, known to history as *"el Batallador."* This union created antagonism among the clergy, who were vocal in their opposition. Her newly acquired husband took umbrage at these ecclesiastics and marched against them into Galicia, thereby

[3] Herculano, *História de Portugal*, pp. 16–17.
[4] *Ibid.*, p. 17.
[5] Damião Peres, "A Reconquista Cristã," *História de Portugal*, I, 477.
[6] Damião Peres, "Origens da nacionalidade," *Congresso do Mundo Português*, II, 20.
[7] *Ibid.*, p. 21.
[8] Herculano, *História de Portugal*, p. 32.

causing further antagonism,[9] not only with them, but even with his bride. Also, he occasionally beat her in public. She alternately opposed or joined her Aragonese husband, depending upon strategic expediency.

To add further confusion to the disrupted political affairs of the time, the Galician barons formed a nucleus around Urraca's son, Alfonso Raimundez, to the end of establishing him in power in the northwest.[10]

DISRUPTION IN SPAIN, AN OPPORTUNITY FOR PORTUGAL

Spanish disruption was great, and neither of the Spanish rivals had clear superiority of power. The balance held by Henry gave him a wonderful bargaining position. Never, it seems, was Portugal considered valuable enough to invade and conquer for itself. But the support that it could give to one or the other of the contestants was to be sought. The distress of León made Portuguese opportunity and Henry played both sides to his own advantage, changing quickly from one to the other and back again, according to the price offered for his aid.[11] He was never punished for his perfidy, but rewarded each time that he changed sides. The result was increased strength for Henry and Portugal, and exhaustion for León and, in part, for Galicia. Henry reduced his dependence upon the king of León to virtually nothing.[12]

Henry died, probably in 1112. His widow, Theresa, assumed power without any questions being raised as to her hereditary rights over the territory. At first she gave a nominal allegiance to the queen of León, but at the same time she was making secret plans with dissident groups in Galicia.[13] She established a

[9] *Ibid.*, p. 36.
[10] They claimed that Alfonso, prior to his death, stipulated that Alfonso Raimundez should inherit Galicia in the event that Urraca married again. Whether or not this was true, it became their shibboleth.
[11] Peres, *Como nasceu Portugal*, pp. 90–91.
[12] *Loc. cit.*
[13] Peres, "Origens da nacionalidade," *Congresso do Mundo Português,* II, 27.

union, perhaps a marriage, with Fernando Peres of Galicia, which did not endear her to the local barons of the lands south of the Minho, for Peres was given lands there, in addition to authority.[14]

That Theresa's independent strength was considerable at this time is shown by the fact that in 1117, when Urraca was at war with her husband, Galicians, Leonese, Castilians, and Asturians all fought with her, while Theresa took no part.[15] As far as can be determined she was in no way penalized for her lack of submission to the Spanish queen. In 1116 Theresa took a part of Galicia and in 1119 Túy and Orense,[16] which, however, she held but temporarily.

As the barons of Galicia had formed around Alfonso Raimundez, so did the barons of the territory south of the Minho River gather around Theresa's son, Affonso Henriques, forming a party of revolt against his mother. In 1128 the land to the north of the Douro was in the hands of this group, while Theresa and Peres were in control to the south. In the same year, at the Battle of São Mamede near Guimarães, Theresa and Peres were beaten and expelled from Portugal.[17]

INDEPENDENT PORTUGAL

From this time forward, the area was under the control of local persons, exclusively occupied with what has become recognized as Portuguese and conscious of their determination to maintain an independent unit in present North Portugal. Their intentions as to the south were as yet unformed, insofar as we have evidence. Supposedly, the centuries-old habit of fighting Moslems on the south border was not lost to sight. Affonso Henriques successfully fought alternately the Moslems on the south and Alfonso VII on the east and north. In 1139 or 1140

[14] Peres, *Como nasceu Portugal*, pp. 96–100.
[15] *Ibid.*, p. 92.
[16] J. Leite de Vasconcellos, "Delimitação da fronteira Portuguesa," *Boletim da Classe de Letras*, XIII (1918–1919), 1281.
[17] Peres, "Origens da nacionalidade," *Congresso do Mundo Português*, II, 32.

THE INDIVIDUALITY OF PORTUGAL

he assumed the title of king [18] and proclaimed the official independence of Portugal. Pope Alexander III underwrote this claim in 1179.[19]

The particular opportunity offered to Count Henry and his son, Affonso Henriques, was a result of Spanish politics, but it was no accident of history that the independence of Portugal was achieved. The basis of an independent western nation in the Iberian peninsula had existed through all known time. It should be remembered that Portugal took form in the area with a persistent core of independent character, in the northwest of the peninsula.[20]

Portugal is named fittingly. The name suggests historical reality, as "Lusitania," a literary creation of the sixteenth century, does not.[21] This statement in no sense is meant to contradict Leite de Vasconcellos [22] and Mendes Corrêa,[23] who insist

[18] Carl Erdmann, "A Adapção do título de Rei por D. Afonso Henriques" (trans. Rodolfo Frederico Knapic), *Congresso do Mundo Português*, II, 65.

[19] Amando Melón y Ruiz de Gordejuela, *Geografía histórica española*, I, 257.

[20] Herculano rejected the historical and ethnic background of the Portuguese state. He did so on the grounds that the Lusitanian territory and the Lusitanians themselves could not be equated with the area within present Portuguese boundaries. This is a straw man that he pushes over. Common to his period was an unwarranted, romantic belief in the exclusively Lusitanian background of Portugal. Reasonably, he found this to be erroneous. However, to reject the ethnic and historical continuity of the nuclear area in North Portugal is another matter. See A. A. Mendes Corrêa, *Raízes de Portugal* (2nd ed.), especially pp. 117–118.
Another factor, the importance of which it is impossible to gauge, is that indicated by physical anthropology. Although there is no doubt as to the close cultural relation between the two areas, the striking variance shown by physical anthropology between Galicia and present North Portugal may indicate deep-seated differences that may have conduced to political separation of the areas. Eastern Galicia with northern Asturias shows the greatest brachycephaly of Iberia, whereas to the south, in the mountains of North Portugal, there is the greatest dolichocephaly of the peninsula. Mendes Corrêa, *Raízes de Portugal*, pp. 90–91.

[21] Pierre David, *Etudes historiques sur la Galice et le Portugal du VIᵉ au XIIIᵉ siècle*, p. xix.

[22] J. Leite de Vasconcellos, *Religiões da Lusitânia*, I, xxv–xxvi.

[23] A. A. Mendes Corrêa, "A Lusitânia pré-romana," *História de Portugal*, I, 185.

that the Lusitanians were clearly an important part of the Portuguese admixture. But that they were an important part of the blend of peoples who ultimately achieved independence does not imply that it was in their territory that the movement started or, indeed, that in that area there was the psychological basis of such a movement. For this one must look to northwest Portugal.

THE BASIS OF SEPARATION OF PORTUGAL AND GALICIA

It would seem more difficult to explain why Galicia, which had always been an integral part of the northwest culture region, remained separate from the Portuguese state. However, the reasons may not be difficult to find. One of them, obviously, is the fact that the re-establishment of political control of the province of the Minho came from Porto in the south and not from Galicia. León, on the other hand, was resettled out of the north, with Galicians making up part of the group of settlers. For the Portuguese area a new political and economic orientation had been established. Nuclear Portugal (the Minho Province) had a degree of isolation not possessed by Galicia. The only good entryway into the north of Portugal is along the western seacoast. Another entryway, from Verín along the Tâmega River Valley through Chaves and then, over a slight rise, into the valley of the Corgo River and finally into that of the Douro, is of local economic and of limited strategic importance.[24] A third possible entryway is that along the high plain of northeastern Portugal leading into Spain in the neighborhood of the town of Alcañices. This, however, is even more inaccessible than that of Verín-Chaves.[25] On the east there is none until south of the latitude of Salamanca where, after the twelfth century, a connection was made between Ciudad Rod-

[24] Even though it is the entryway used by Soult in Napoleonic times, the fault valley of the Tâmega belongs essentially to Portugal and not to Galicia. Not far north of the Portuguese border is a highland which effectively separates the valley of the Tâmega from the Galician basin of the Miño River in Spain.
[25] Mendes Corrêa, *Raízes de Portugal*, p. 42.

170

rigo [26] in Spain and the Portuguese city of Guarda, settled in 1197.[27] The Romans had used a route across this middle country, but it ran somewhat to the south of the Ciudad Rodrigo-Guarda road.[28]

Galicia itself is readily entered from the east, along the north coast or from the *meseta* directly, through the city of León to Astorga, and from there to Lugo. This is the old Roman road which was established in keeping with topography. Nowhere does it present great problems of slope. The same is true of the road leading from Lugo to the *ria* harbors of the west. This facility of entry is lacking in the mountain and canyon borderland separating Spain from most of the north and northeast of Portugal.

Perhaps an even more important reason for the separation of Galicia from nuclear Portugal concerns the establishment of Santiago de Compostela as a great religious and pilgrimage center. The road to Santiago across the north of Spain was a famous and important route, linking Spain with Galicia physically and emotionally. There was no such link between Portugal and Spain. On the contrary, the Portuguese church had been a relatively independent institution. The Bishop and later Metropolitan in Braga had independent rights. If, as was once hoped, the Metropolitan of Braga had become the Iberian Primate, Portuguese history might have been different, but this did not occur and his authority became localized.

There is no single, simple reason for Portuguese independence. Individual judgments, institutional decisions, historical backgrounds, and the position and nature of the land all contributed to the result.

[26] Repopulated in 1161. Júlio Gonzalez, "Repoblación de la 'Extremadura' leonesa," *Hispania*, XI, 226.

[27] Hermann Lautensach, "Portugal. Auf Grund eigener Reisen und der Literatur." 2. "Die portugiesischen Landschaften" (Gotha, *Petermann's Mitteilungen*, No. 230, 1937), 31.

[28] A. de Amorim Girão, *Geografia de Portugal*, facing p. 366.

CHAPTER 13

Completion of the Portuguese State

SOUTHWARD EXPANSION

THE NUCLEUS area has been fundamental to Portuguese existence. After the independence of the north, the problem ceased to be that of the establishment of the Portuguese nation, but became a matter of its extension. The lands later added had not been exclusively Portuguese, culturally and historically, nor did they, through much of their extent, belong physically more to an Atlantic fringe than to the central *meseta*.

The extension of Portuguese control from the nuclear area is, to some degree at least, a matter of politics and opportunism. The inclusion of the Alentejo and the Algarve may be largely, although not entirely, credited to the determination of ambitious Portuguese kings and nobles, and to the preoccupation of Spanish kings and nobles with affairs elsewhere in the peninsula. Conquest was achieved against a weakening resistance and a diminishing base of Moslem action. Everywhere south of the Mondego the extension of political control was simplified for the Christians by dissension among the Moslem Taifa kingdoms, and their willingness, often indeed their desire, to give ground to the Christians, who presented a lesser evil than that of their co-religionists, the Almorávides and Almohades. To a considerable extent the task of conquest, control, and re-settlement was assigned to the military orders [1] which, in re-turn, received great grants of land in the Alentejo, where the problem was mostly one of establishing a population and arranging means for its support, rather than that of conquest.

For the first time this territory became exclusively Portu-guese. However, that it was not merely an historical accident— the chance decisions of kings and nobles—that made the area Portuguese, is indicated by the boundaries of the Roman Con-ventus Iuridicus as well as the boundaries of the church, neither of which differed greatly from those of present southern Portu-gal.[2] As has been said above, the Romans were not unconscious of local cultural differences, and their placement of boundaries was not capricious. Rather, it was based upon local loyalties, wherever possible. Certainly this seems to have been the fact in the north, where the persistence of the Minho and Douro River boundaries is striking. The conditions in the Alentejo were in some degree comparable. Here, however, the differ-ences were considerable, for the Alentejo was thinly populated and strongly influenced by herding peoples during Moslem, Visigoth, Roman, and pre-Roman times. This was very different from the conditions in the north, where the strongly rooted farming populations always thought of themselves in relation to one piece of land with fixed boundaries.

The Portuguese Algarve is a case apart. It had been an iso-lated and individualized territory through most of its existence until the fifteenth and sixteenth centuries, the Age of Discover-ies. The serras of Monchique and Caldeirão separated it effec-tively from the Alentejo on the north, and the open coastal areas to the east of the Guadiana River generally isolated it on

---

[1] H. V. Livermore, A History of Portugal, pp. 98, 135; Edgar Prestage, "The Chivalry of Portugal," Chivalry, pp. 150–151.

[2] António García y Bellido, La Península Ibérica en los comienzos de su historia, p. 393.

that side. In the earliest records, the local people were recognized as being distinct from their neighbors. The influence of Tartessós had reached into it, but without submerging it. Later, Celtic influences were felt, but still the area remained distinct. The Carthaginians fished and evaporated salt in nearly a dozen places along the coast, but changed the ways of life little, if any. The Greeks had less interest than did the Carthaginians. The Romans fitted the Algarve into their Conventus Iuridicus, which included a larger territory to the north and east. This obviously was procrustean, but expedient to administration. However, there is no evidence to the effect that the area was drawn culturally closer to the territories with which it was politically associated. Under the Arabs the association with Andalusia was greater than it had previously been, an obviously reasonable arrangement in view of the similarities of climate, vegetation, and exploitation. Nevertheless, the immemorially old zone of separation, the sterile coastal lands to either side of Huelva, was again determinative when, at the time of the break-up of the Moslem Caliphate, one of the little Taifa kingdoms established its eastern boundary along the Guadiana River.

At the time of the reconquest the Algarve was neither clearly Spanish nor Portuguese. Its inclusion in the Portuguese state had nothing at all to do with historical cultural affinity. It was a matter of political opportunism.

IMPORTANCE OF ATLANTIC POSITION
IN THE PORTUGUESE RECONQUEST

Atlantic position served Portugal well during her period of southward expansion. Maritime aid shortened the schedule of the reconquest and perhaps without it Portugal would not have maintained her independence. When seventy vessels of crusaders dropped anchor in the mouth of the Douro at Porto they were greeted effusively by Affonso Henriques and persuaded to join in an attack upon Lisbon. They sailed southward, while he marched overland to meet them. Between the two forces the countryside was devastated, but Lisbon held out.[3] Seven years later, however, another group of crusaders made up of several nationalities, including English, Flemings, Germans, and French, were enlisted by the rallying call to restore Lisbon to Christian hands, and also by Affonso's promise of all of the loot and ransom of the city, as well as donations of lands to be taken from the Moslems.[4] Lisbon fell after seventeen weeks of siege.[5] Directly after this, Sintra was taken, and Palmela was found to have been abandoned, as hopeless of defense, when the Christians arrived.[6] Silves, in the Algarve, was temporarily subjugated with the aid of crusaders in 1189.[7] Alvôr was taken temporarily as well,[8] and in 1217 crusaders took part in the conquest of Alcácer do Sal.[9]

BOUNDARIES

In the quick southern expansion of both the Portuguese and Castilian-Leonese states the problem of delimitation of their respective areas could have been the source of disastrous conflict. That it was not was largely a matter of enlightened cupidity. In all of Iberia, the drives against the Moslems were aimed southward or southeastward against the centers of wealth.[10] While the Portuguese were driving south, pointed toward the Algarve, a small area of prosperity, the Leonese had their eyes upon Seville and Andalusia, the great Moslem center of wealth, which under all conquerors had been considered a premium area.

During the reign of Affonso Henriques, the northern bound-

[3] Charles Wendell David (ed. and trans.), *De Expugnatione Lyxbonensi*, pp. 16–17.
[4] *Ibid.*, pp. 111, 113.
[5] *Ibid.*, p. 14.
[6] *Ibid.*, p. 179.
[7] João Baptista da Silva Lopes, *Relação da derrota, naval, façanhas, e successos dos cruzados que parti rão do escalda para a Terra Santa no Anno de 1189*, p. 12.
[8] Prestage, *Chivalry*, p. 151.
[9] *Loc. cit.*
[10] See Chapter 11 of this book.

ary of Portugal had been established as almost precisely that of the present.[11] During his life, the northern section of the east boundary was probably also established approximately along the line of the present boundary of eastern Trás-os-Montes.[12] South of this province, the Spanish-Portuguese boundary between the Douro and Tejo rivers then ran along the Côa River, somewhat to the west of the present boundary. Below the Tejo River, the problem was more complex, as there were fewer of the physical characteristics useful for boundary lines. This area was largely bounded through agreements. Due to its lack of attractions through much of its extent, the precise lines had little importance. It was at this time that Affonso Henriques of Portugal and Ferdinand II of León, recognizing that they stood to profit more from Moslem lands than they could from trying to take land from each other, agreed in the Treaty of Celanova, probably in 1160, to respect a certain line of division to separate the lands yet to be conquered toward the south.[13]

The Portuguese took Evora in the Alentejo permanently from the Moslems in 1166. It never again fell into Moslem hands, even in the great Almohad drive of 1191, which captured virtually everything up to the Tejo. With the conquest of Alcácer do Sal in 1217, the Christians controlled the strong points of Alcácer and Evora and the territory between them. To the east of Evora, Moslem control extended north, probably to Marvão, but during the reign of Sancho II (1223–1248) this salient was eliminated by taking Elvas and Juromenho. The southern

[11] J. Leite de Vasconcellos, "Delimitação da fronteira Portuguesa," *Boletim da Classe de Letras*, XIII (1918–1919), 1282. Not that it would have seemed stable at the time, for Affonso Henriques had pushed beyond it as did his successors. They, like Affonso, were ultimately obliged to renounce their claims.

[12] Leite de Vasconcellos believed this to be so. *Ibid.*, p. 1282. However this may be, the Portuguese culture region had not filled out the territory that far eastward. See Vasconcellos, reference above, note, p. 160 and citation of Conde de São Payo.

[13] Hermann Lautensach, "A Individualidade geográfica de Portugal no conjunto da Península Ibérica," *Boletim da Sociedade de Geografia de Lisboa*, XLIV (1931), 386; Amando Melón y Ruiz de Gordejeula, *Geografía histórica española*, I, 258.

The Old Fortress City of Elvas in the Alentejo

boundary was thereby somewhat straightened, so that it ran in a gentle arc across Portugal from Alcácer do Sal to Evora to Elvas.[14] With these strongholds in Portuguese hands, the end of Moslem occupation of Portugal was in sight.

The exact terms of the Treaty of Celanova are not known, but it seems probable that the boundary on the south was the line of the lower Guadiana River. If this was the decision it was reasonable, as it re-established an immemorially old boundary that had been serviceable throughout millennia. The Castilian-Leonese conquest of Seville was completed in 1248, after first piercing southeastward to Málaga and then following the coast westward. This was just prior to the conquest of Silves (1249–1250) in the Algarve by the Portuguese,[15] which virtually established the form of present Portugal.

Only minor adjustments followed. For example, there was a short period of tension and rivalry for the borderlands along the Guadiana River. Ayamonte, to the east of the river, was in Portuguese hands in 1255, and other small territories, now Spanish, were held by Portugal until 1267.[16] The Castilian-Leonese crossed the Guadiana River near its mouth, apparently contrary to the agreement of Celanova, and occupied some Algarvian towns. Alfonso X believed that he had a proper claim to the territory, as he had purchased it from the local Moslem ruler while he (Alfonso) was Infante.[17] In any case, this problem was settled in 1267, when the Castilian-Leonese king renounced all claim to territory in the Algarve while Portugal relinquished its castles in present Spain. Later in the century, in 1281, Serpa, now of the Portuguese Alentejo, was still under Spanish control,[18] as were the territories north of the Tejo, west

[14] Leite de Vasconcellos, "Delimitação da fronteira Portuguesa," *Boletim da Classe de Letras,* XIII, 1283–1284.

[15] *Ibid.,* p. 1284.

[16] *Loc. cit.*

[17] Amando Melón y Ruiz de Gordejuela, *Geografía histórica española,* I, 257–258.

[18] Leite de Vasconcellos, "Delimitação da fronteira Portuguesa," *Boletim da Classe de Letras,* XIII, 1285.

178

to the Côa River. It was in 1295 that King Diniz of Portugal essentially established the present eastern boundaries of Portugal, with one exception. He acquired the areas of the Côa River basin, Castelo Rodrigo, Sabugal, Campo Maior, and Monforte in the north, and Serpa, Moura, and Mourão in the south.[19] The only change of importance in Portuguese boundaries since that time is that of the region of Olivença, which was Portuguese, except for the two-year interim (1657–1658), until the Spanish took it in 1801. This matter is discussed below.

THE INTEGRATION OF THE SOUTHERN TERRITORIES

By the end of the thirteenth century the question of boundaries was no longer a major problem to the national state of Portugal. The problem had become one of assimilation of the newly acquired southern territories. The lands south of the Tejo River were effectively made Portuguese during the fourteenth and fifteenth centuries. Prior to this time, on the basis of their physical constitution, climate, vegetation, economic exploitation, or cultural development, they could have become Spanish as well as Portuguese.

During these centuries the Castilian conquest of Iberia stagnated against the kingdom of Granada, not because of Moslem strength, but because of the internal quarrels between Castile and Aragon and the remnant of the immemorially old attitude of Spanish leaders to derive profit from raiding, looting, and ransom, which at times took precedence over the permanent conquest of territory.[20] This situation redounded to the benefit of Portugal, which was left generally in peace. This Atlantic fringe, not greatly desired at any time by the Spanish, only occasionally fell within the focus of their interest. Disturbances that occurred were minor and quickly settled. Portugal was given the opportunity of consolidating its territory under the leadership of the court at Lisbon, which became the center of political balance in the country. Here the various economic and

[19] *Loc. cit.*
[20] Louis Bertrand, *The History of Spain*, p. 197.

political lines of the state were drawn together and effectively tied.[21]

INTERNAL ECONOMIC DEVELOPMENT

After completing the reconquest of its territory from the Moslems, Portugal promptly set about establishing the economic life of the nation. An interesting comparison can be made between the attitudes and methods of Portugal of that time and those of neighboring Spain. Differences were clearly marked in the opposed attitudes toward the exploitation of land, partly, but only partly, induced by climate. Portugal established a well-rooted and ultimately prosperous agriculture in the southern lands taken from the Moslems. The record is clear as to the intention of the Portuguese kings. Numerous laws set up provisions under which families settled on the land for the purpose of planting and harvesting crops. The primary concern of the Portuguese governments, for long generations, was to establish a settled peasantry.[22] Unoccupied land was given to families with the express intention of establishing permanent cultivation. Uncultivated land reverted to the crown to be redistributed. One of the most famous of Portuguese kings, Diniz (or Deniz), was especially active in this,[23] and because of his contribution to the well-being of his country he is gratefully known to history as "the Farmer King" (o Rei Lavrador). He publicly proclaimed that "no baron would lose caste by dedi-

[21] Affonso III moved the capital from the north—Coimbra and Guimarães had both served—to Lisbon, in 1248, just prior to the completion of the Portuguese reconquest. Livermore, *A History of Portugal*, p. 134. A. de Amorim Girão speaks of Lisbon, centering upon the sea, as being the polarizing element bringing diverse parts together. See his *Condicões geográficas e históricas da autonomia política de Portugal*, p. 21, and "Origines de l'état Portugais," *Revue Géographique des Pyrénées et du Sud-Ouest*, XI, Nos. 3–4 (1940), 158. His concept is somewhat mystical but has the basis of reality in it.

[22] Virginia Rau, *Sesmarias medievais portuguesas*, pp. 42 (especially), 54 *et seq.*, 68–71.

[23] Damião Peres, "A Actividade agrícola em Portugal nos séculos XII a XIV, *Congresso do Mundo Português*, II, 469, 471, 472.

180

THE INDIVIDUALITY OF PORTUGAL

cating himself to the soil" [24] and thus helped to avoid one of the great Spanish plagues, the distaste for labor. The results of the efforts of Diniz and others was that at the end of the fourteenth and the beginning of the fifteenth century, when it entered into the great period of "discoveries," Portugal had a prosperous agriculture.[25] It had little need for imports or for exports to obtain foreign currency. Fruits and wine had been exported prior to this time,[26] and by the end of the fourteenth century olive oil—earlier of little importance—entered the export lists. It appears that home consumption of the olive was then negligible and that the tree had been planted and cultivated chiefly to provide an export product for cash.[27]

Development of Economy on the Spanish *Meseta*

Affairs in Spain were taking a very different course. Political control was in the hands of nobles of the *meseta* whose interest had been in pastoral industries long before the territory had been fully conquered from the Moslems, an interest that had been furthered by the exigencies of the centuries of siege. During the years of the reconquest, tax exemptions were given to sheepherders along the routes of migrations, in exchange for loyalty to and support of the crown. Klein reports dozens of such exceptions in the documents of the period, 970–1273.[28] These, in turn, apparently harked back to Visigothic regulations of the *Fuero Juzgo*, which favored sheepmen in the semiannual migrations with their flocks.[29] The Visigothic regulations, we

[24] Livermore, A History of Portugal, p. 152.
[25] Peres, "A Actividade agrícola em Portugal," Congresso do Mundo Português, II, 478.
[26] Ibid., p. 466.
[27] In the north of Portugal olive oil began gradually to replace butter in the sixteenth century. See Orlando Ribeiro, "Cultura do Milho, economía agrária e povoamento," Biblos, XVII, No. 2 (Coimbra, 1941), 645–663.
[28] Julius Klein, The Mesta, A Study in Spanish Economic History, 1273–1836, p. 162.
[29] Ibid., p. 301.

may assume, were based on attitudes present in the peninsula prior to the arrival of the Visigoths. In all probability they were merely codifications made in the sixth or seventh centuries of ancient Visigothic and local practices.

Under the *Mesta* (the sheepowners' organization) the sheep industry of Spain developed in a fashion somewhat comparable to that of England. In both cases the industry satisfied the king's need for cash. Wool, high-priced, compact, readily preserved, and with a large world demand, made a good export item. It became so important to the Spanish kings that they imported wheat from Aragon to feed Castile, so that there should be no inducement for farmers to plant grain on pasture lands.[30] In the fourteenth century Castile had the largest pastoral industry in Western Europe and a growing foreign trade. By the mid-sixteenth century the *Mesta*, greatly favored by the crown, was so powerful and arrogant that it took over town commons and town pastures and other special enclosures for its flocks. Every device of the government was used to support sheep raising,[31] obviously to the detriment of planting. Toward the end of the sixteenth century *corregidores* sent out by the central government almost unanimously reported that the sparsity and poverty of agricultural population was due to the emphasis on sheep raising.[32] The extent to which this was true is indicated by the law passed under Ferdinand and Isabel by which a *Mesta* member had permanent tenancy of a given field, either at a rent paid under his earliest lease or, if his flocks occupied these fields for a season or even a few months without being discovered by the landowner, for nothing at all.[33]

How very different this was from the attitude in Portugal, where, for the most part, the cultivator was supported against the herder.[34]

[30] *Ibid.*, p. 314.   [31] *Ibid.*, p. 318.
[32] *Ibid.*, p. 94.   [33] *Ibid.*, p. 328.
[34] The Alentejo is the most Spanish of the Portuguese provinces. Physically there is no sharp distinction to be made between it and Spanish Extremadura. Historically the two regions have had somewhat parallel experiences; both were given into the hands of the religious-military

Clearly such a striking economic difference, with all that it entails with regard to social attitudes, could contribute to a separation of the peoples involved and likewise to the ultimate political division.

---

orders. The Alentejo is now noted for its great estates and owners, whose titles, in many cases, come down from the period of the reconquest. As in Spanish Extremadura, grazing is important, but the farmer was not sacrificed to the herder. In the Alentejo, now as at the time of Diniz, there is a blend of pastoralism and agriculture.

CHAPTER 14

Development of Portuguese International Relations

FOREIGN TRADE AND BRITISH ALLIANCES

HE AID GIVEN by north Europeans to Portugal in the conquest of Moslem cities during the time of the Crusades was clear demonstration to Portugal of the strategic importance of its position. Location on the Atlantic Ocean continued to have strategic importance militarily during the fourteenth century, but, more than this, it became a source of economic advantage. Portuguese commerce grew and its fishing industry expanded.[1] The first commercial treaty of Portuguese history was made in 1294 with England. A half century later, in 1353, another treaty was signed with England, allowing the Portuguese to fish off British shores. Internally, industry and mining were encouraged and commerce expanded as the government supported the development of commercial fairs throughout the country.[2] Commercial connec-

---

[1] Hermann Lautensach, "A Individualidade geográfica de Portugal no conjunto da Península Ibérica," *Boletim da Sociedade de Geografia de Lisboa*, XLIX (1931), 390.

[2] Mario Gonçalves Viana, *Rei D. Deniz*, pp. 80–85.

184

tions with England developed into a military alliance in 1381.[3] It is a much-argued question among Portuguese today whether the commercial connections established during this period, and continued ever since by various treaties and agreements, were beneficial or detrimental to Portugal. The same may be said for the military alliance. At first the latter yielded nothing but trouble, as Portugal was drawn into conflict with Spain over matters in which it had little interest. Involved were the affairs of John of Gaunt, who had married the daughter of Pedro the Cruel of Spain. Later, as Duke of Lancaster, John laid claim to the Spanish throne and tried to take it by force. His invasions of Spain were fiascos, and Portugal as an ally, having been forced to support him, paid the penalty. Nevertheless, it should not be forgotten that it was archers from England who swung the balance for a numerically inferior Portuguese army in the defeat of the heavily armored, mounted Spaniards at Aljubar-rota in 1385.[4] This victory ended the major threat of the period to Portuguese independence, and, incidentally, sounded the knell of the importance of such cavalry.

The commercial agreements of the later fourteenth century had followed upon a period of increasing exchange of goods, the profit from which was available to Portugal during her Age of Discoveries. It was during the fifteenth century that the Portuguese kingdom, through her overseas exploration and expansion, first became consolidated, in spirit as well as in economy. This was the century of the settlement of Maderia [5] and the Azores, and of the explorations directed by Prince Henry the Navigator along the African coast, which ultimately skirted the Cape of Good Hope to reach India.

[3] P. E. Russell, "João Fernandes Andeiro at the Court of John of Lancaster," *Revista da Universidade de Coimbra*, XIV (1940), 20.

[4] H. V. Livermore, *A History of Portugal*, p. 175.

[5] The islands were known in the fourteenth century but occupied only after 1425. Orlando Ribeiro, *L'Ile de Madère*, p. 6. Settlement probably took place five years earlier than stated by Ribeiro, or so one of the earliest documents relating to the fact reports. See Jerónimo Dias Leite, *Descobrimento da Ilha da Madeira*, pp. 15–25.

CONSOLIDATION OF PORTUGAL

A stirring period of Portuguese history this was, and it effectively tied the south—particularly the Algarve, which otherwise might have remained apart in spirit—into the Portuguese nation. Algarvians played an important part in the explorations, and they took an important part in the conquest of Ceuta, and other expeditions to follow. It is perhaps more important to Portuguese consolidation that Algarvians took part in these exploits than the fact that the romantic, inspiring, and profitable fifteenth-century achievements were common also to Trasmontanos, Minhotos, Beirões and Alentejanos. All of them shared and took pride in the national achievement, and this pride was focused upon the great port of the lower Tejo River.

The importance of Lisbon is no accident. This is one of the great natural harbors of the world. Once the western part of Iberia was established as a national unit, it was mandatory that Lisbon should become the center of control. Not only is it the finest harbor of the country, but behind it lies one of Portugal's most productive areas, one that was prized by both Romans and Moslems. With the Atlantic orientation emphasized by the Age of Discoveries, it goes without saying that Lisbon would inevitably be of supreme importance. It was through Lisbon, and only secondarily through Porto and lesser ports, that contact was maintained with Africa and the Portuguese possessions in Asia, with the Azores, Madeira, the Guiné colonies, and perhaps more importantly, with England.

By the end of the fifteenth century, when Castile had finished her conquest of Moslem territory in the peninsula and might have turned her ideas of conquest westward to "fill out the peninsula," Portugal was firmly glued together with a common pride, common purpose, and common loyalties. In unity the various, disparate parts were prospering commercially, and all was based on a thriving agriculture. By this time it was patently impossible for any part of present Portugal to be dismembered from the whole without deep and pervading resentment.[6]

[6] A case in point is the still festering sore of Olivença. See further in this chapter.

186

THE SPANISH CAPTIVITY

In the sixteenth century, Spain, under Philip II, took Portugal, with some political justification, and held it for the period known as the Spanish Captivity, from 1580 to 1640. The Spanish king had a legitimate claim to the throne. Whether or not it was the best claim may still be argued.[7] He had strong Portuguese adherents at the time of union among the Portuguese nobles and the higher authorities of the church. The people of lesser political category and the lower clergy, plus the general populace, were said to be in opposition,[8] but as their opposition was not politically effective, union became a fact.

Under Philip II, the promises that he originally made were fulfilled.[9] Portugal remained effectively autonomous. Portuguese citizens held the important positions, indeed, virtually all positions, within Portugal. The laws of Portugal were essentially unchanged. Taxes were not raised to benefit Spain at the expense of Portugal. Unfortunately, this condition began to change under the administration of Philip III, and under Philip IV the policy was completely altered, greatly contrary to Portuguese interest.[10]

This was a period of inclement political weather for Spain in Europe. Lack of funds led the king to raise revenues where he could. Portugal was obviously an untapped source. His associates swarmed into the places of preferment there. This would have been enough to convert even the formerly Hispanophile Portuguese nobles into enemies. But added to this was the disastrous effect upon Portuguese colonial holdings and Portuguese world trade. The English, the Dutch, and other Western European nations used the Spanish connection as a pretext for stripping Portugal of valuable foreign possessions. Lisbon de-

[7] See his letter of 1579. "Carta de S.M. para los estados de Portugal, condoliéndose de la muerte del Rey D. Sebastián y avisando del derecho que tiene a la sucesión de aquel reino, 14 de Marzo de 1579," *Colección de documentos inéditos para la historia de España*, XL, 230–232.

[8] Rafael Altamira y Crevea, *Historia de España*, III (3rd ed.), 96–97.

[9] *Ibid.*, p. 151.

[10] Charles E. Nowell, *A History of Portugal*, pp. 142–144.

clined as a commercial center by reason of competition with the harbors of England and Holland and, what was felt to be especially grievous, by the competition of Spanish Cádiz. Notwithstanding all of this, Portugal, once within the grasp of the Spanish, could not have hoped for independence if Spain had not been in dire straits. Spanish troubles were both external and internal. Externally, her traditional enemies were pressing her. Internally, separatist movements were of serious proportions. The most important of these was that of Catalonia, where the first large-scale revolt broke out. The Duke of Bragança and other Portuguese were ordered to aid in quelling the Catalans.[11] This obviously was a Portuguese opportunity, as Spanish distress has ever been. Now even the higher members of the Portuguese nobility and church rebelled against Spain and succeeded with a minimum effort. The Duke of Bragança, whose forbear had knelt smilingly to kiss the hand of Philip II at the beginning of the "captivity," [12] was drafted to become the leader of the revolt. He certainly was not an inspired leader and had to be pressed into taking the position. Notwithstanding this, Portuguese success made him the first of a new dynasty when the decisive victory was won at Vila Viçosa, in 1665, and the final peace treaty was signed in 1668.

Since the period of the "captivity" the changes in the Spanish-Portuguese border have been minor, with the exception of the territory of Olivença. This area, lying to the south of Elvas, was accepted as being Portuguese in the Treaty of Alcañices, made between Dom Diniz of Portugal and Ferdinand IV of Castile, at the end of the fourteenth century. In the war of restoration following the "captivity," it was temporarily held by Spain, but was returned to Portugal in the treaty of 1668.[13]

---

[11] *Ibid.*, pp. 144, 148.
[12] "Relación de la entrada del duque de Braganza y del de Barcelos su hijo en esta corte á besar las manos á S.M. en 17 de enero 1581," *Colección de documentos inéditos para la historia de España*, XL, 383. This document describes their joy and their affection for Philip II.
[13] J. M. de Queiroz Velloso, *Como perdemos Olivença*, p. 8.

THE QUESTION OF OLIVENÇA

The question of the Olivença territory is difficult to understand because of the slight value of the area in question by any standards other than sentimental. The matters of international politics which resulted in its being dismembered from Portugal were in no way concerned with such a minor territory, and its international transfer is quite coincidental to them.

Portugal's treaty with England was troublesome to Napoleon. It was a leak in the dike of his European policy. Through the Spanish-French "offensive and defensive alliance" an agreement was struck in 1801 for the invasion of Portugal, to compel her to break her English connections.[14] As a requisite to peace, Godoy, the close friend of the King of Spain and a closer friend of the Queen, insisted upon the retention of the Olivença territory. It is difficult to understand his determination, as the Spanish king did not insist upon it,[15] and Godoy earlier had described it contemptuously as a "child of smugglers." Perhaps its propinquity to his birthplace may have induced him to take and cling to the territory, for Godoy was born in Badajoz, just to the northeast of the Olivença area. Or, more likely, its retention gave him the little prestige which otherwise was lacking to him in the whole endeavor.

The treaty of the Congress of Vienna awarded the territory to Portugal. Spain protested this, on no very reasonable grounds, but finally signed the treaty [16] in 1817. However, this had no effect upon possession, for Spain continued to hold the territory. Such unimportant territory surely would have been restored, had animosities and tension of the time not been involved. In the year 1817 Brazil occupied Montevideo and feeling in Spain was strong against Portugal. Portugal tried to exchange Montevideo for Olivença.[17] Representations about Olivença were continued by Portugal to Spain until 1841. After this, little was done officially, but the feeling within Portugal has not changed. "The Group of the Friends of Olivença" still meets

14 *Ibid.*, p. 37. 15 *Ibid.*, p. 85.
16 *Ibid.*, pp. 118, 121. 17 *Ibid.*, pp. 128, 130–133.

in Lisbon and hopes for the restitution of this "Portuguese territory." On the other hand, the Spanish either have lost interest,
or having possession, feel that it is safer not to mention the
matter. The name is not even listed in the accumulated index
of the *Boletín de la Real Academia de la Historia.*[18]

Aside from the Olivença territory, certain small areas have
been amicably passed back and forth between Spain and Portugal as marriage portions: Sabugal, Segura, Alburquerque, etc.,
up to the eighteenth century.[19] In the nineteenth century, subsequent to the Olivença imbroglio, an increasing attempt was
made by peaceful means to correct the confusion caused by the
marriage dots. In 1864–1866 the Spanish and Portuguese governments acted to adjust the matter of the *Contenda de Moura,*
involving territory south-southwest of the Olivença lands.[20] In
1893 this matter was completed amicably and another adjustment made in the same manner in 1926.[21]

With a growing foreign trade, and in a period of exploration,
expansion, and achievement, Portugal developed a new national
self-consciousness. An increasing feeling of unity in common
purposes, loyalties, and national pride hastened the settling of
boundary disputes and gave Portugal definitive borders.

[18] 1877–1944. Vicente Castañeda Alcover.
[19] Hermann Lautensach, "Geopolitisches von der Spanisch-Portugiesischen Grenze," *Zeitschrift für Geopolitik,* V (1928), 371–372.
[20] J. Leite de Vasconcellos, "Delimitação da fronteira Portuguesa,"
Boletim da Classe de Letras, XIII (1918–1919), 1289.
[21] Lautensach,"Geopolitisches von der Spanisch-Portugiesischen Grenze,"
Zeitschrift für Geopolitik, V (1928), 372.

CHAPTER 15

The Geography of
Portuguese-Spanish Boundaries

THROUGHOUT this book there are occasional references to boundaries, considered sometimes historically and sometimes, implicitly at least, as natural phenomena. As they are always potentially important, and sometimes crucially so, a few pages may be taken profitably to consider them.

BOUNDARIES THROUGH AREAS OF LITTLE ATTRACTION

In Iberia international boundary lines have been drawn, for the most part, through zones of limited desirability. Roughly nine-tenths of the Spanish-Portuguese border is located in such areas, and the reflection of this fact is to be seen in the sparseness of population nearly everywhere along the frontier (Fig. 13).[1] The one important exception is the area of the lower

---

[1] Figure 13 is taken from Figure 4 of Luis de Hoyos Sáinz, *La Densidad de población y el acrecentamiento en España.* The statistics used by Hoyos Sáinz were those of the 1940 census. Unfortunately the statistics from the 1950 census are not available in such form as to be used for a

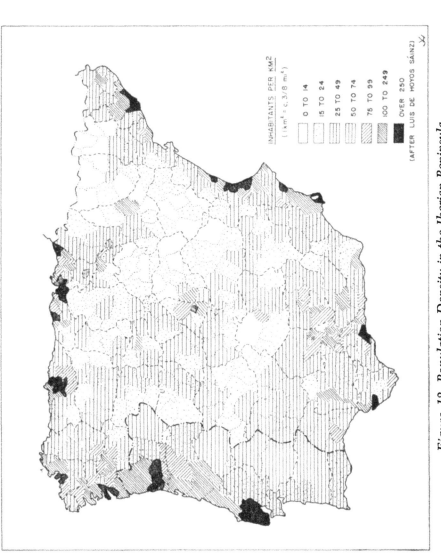

Figure 13. Population Density in the Iberian Peninsula

Minho River, which is certainly not a region characterized by undesirability.[2]

It should be remembered that the lower Minho River was the northern limit of the "desolation" of Alfonso I. Cities to the south had been eliminated. The filling-in of the routes of communications and the restoration of cities up to that line was accomplished by a southern group working northward from Porto. In the area of the lower Minho River a group of settlers that was oriented politically and economically toward the south met one of Galicia, where ancient connections eastward toward Spain had never been broken for more than short periods of time.[3]

Less than fifty miles upstream from the mouth of the Minho River the boundary turns sharply southward, and the population density falls off rapidly as the boundary rises along the slopes up to the high, winter-cold Serra de Laboreiro. After crossing the sharp, deep gorge of the Lima River, the border turns eastward again, following near the crests of other high mountains, the *serras* of Gerez and Larouco. To the east of Larouco is another exception to the general unattractiveness of locale along the border. This is the upper valley of the Tâmega River, between the Portuguese city of Chaves and the Galician

new map. However, a comparison of the 1950 statistics for the sparsely settled border region of Spain where it touches eastern Portugal with those used by Hoyos Sáinz shows that there has been no material change in the situation in the decade. That border area is still, as it was in 1940, a land of slight attraction for population.

For a discussion of the distribution of population along the international boundary, see Artur de Magalhães Basto, "A Fronteira Hispano-Portuguesa," *O Instituto*, LXX (1923), 62–63.

[2] This fact is made manifest also by the Hoyos Sáinz map of population, but the end map of J. Dantin Cereceda, *Distribución geográfica de la población en Galicia*, makes it even more obvious. Compare this with the map of *Distribüição da população de Portugal* based on the 1940 census, published by the Centro de Estudos Geográficos of Lisbon under the direction of Orlando Ribeiro. Both of the latter references are more detailed than the work of Hoyos Sáinz, but unfortunately they are concerned with limited areas and do not serve for a comparison with the rest of Iberia.

[3] Although the river splits a population cluster, it has served usefully as an administrative boundary as far back as prehistory.

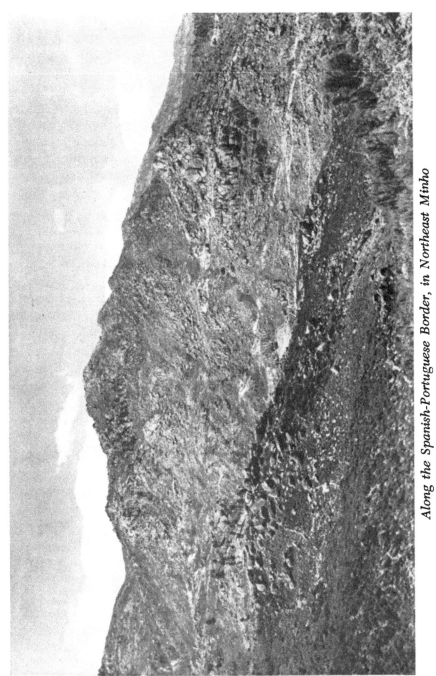

Along the Spanish-Portuguese Border, in Northeast Minho

town of Verín. A fertile valley, protected from the worst of the winter cold by uplands to the west, north, and east, it supports a modest cluster of population, and there is no break between settlement on the Portuguese side and in Galicia. In addition, the mountains, virtually encircling Verín, separate it clearly from the rest of Galicia. Its normal associations should be with Chaves and southward into Portugal, and one would have expected the boundary line to have been established along the barren uplands lying between the upper Limia (Lima) and the middle Miño (Minho) rivers, thus putting Verín into Portugal. However, another factor was more important than geography in the matter. Verín lies on the early pilgrimage road from Zamora to Orense, which skirts the north border of Portugal, and from there leads into Santiago de Compostela.[4] At Orense, this road is joined by that from León. The importance of Santiago as a religious and pilgrimage center after the ninth century was a sufficient reason for Verín to have remained under Spanish control. The area was remote from the center of authority of either León or Portugal. It is a relatively unimportant area to either state. An arbitrary political decision, although seemingly in violation of local economics, could have been enforced without difficulty, for actually political boundaries had, and have, very little effect upon such distant and self-sufficient communities. A Portuguese author recently referring to the area of Soajo, in the northeast of the Minho Province near the Spanish border, described the inhabitants thus: "Soajeiros are very independent. They are not irritated by the laws. They just do not pay much attention to them. Their 'leading men' are the authorities recognized by the people. Their customs are their laws . . ."[5] No doubt life in Verín continued much in the same way that it would have done had the border been drawn elsewhere.

Beyond the valley of the Tâmega River the northern boundary line is again to be found at sufficient elevation so that the

[4] António López Ferreiro, *Historia de la Santa A. M. Iglesia de Santiago de Compostela*, V, p. 91.

[5] Basto, "A Fronteira Hispano-Portuguesa," *O Instituto*, LXX, 104.

Trás-os-Montes: a Tin Mine

factor of undesirability is marked. This is the higher, more mountainous part of the province of Trás-os-Montes, where the limitation of population is imposed, not only by slope, but by duration of winter cold.

The east boundary of Trás-os-Montes is drawn through an extension of the Leonese plateau, high and sufficiently exposed to the winter cold of interior Iberia to inhibit agriculture. For all of Trás-os-Montes another fact is of importance. The province lies in the lee of the mountains that separate it from the "green Minho." The orographic barrier causes a rainshadow condition. Drought thus adds another factor to the impoverishment of cultivation.[6] All of this "explains the relative isolation and the tenuous social and economic relations between the human groups on the two sides of the frontier. This isolation is particularly marked along the Leonese frontier. In almost all

[6] Vergilio Taborda, *Alto Trás-os-Montes*, p. 9. Also see Jorge Dias, *Rio de Onor*, especially pp. 79–85. The village of Rio de Onor, which Dias describes, straddles the international boundary at the extreme northeast of Trás-os-Montes. It is a small oasis of fertility in an otherwise barren land.

Trás-os-Montes: Threshing Rye

of the territory between the Macãs and the lands of Vinhais, the character of the frontier is much like that of a *marca* (a remote frontier province), so slight is the human occupation. He who goes from Bragança to Puebla de Senabria [*sic*] has the bleak sensation of travelling in 'Terra nullius domini' . . . ," so spoke a geographer born and raised in the region.[7]

The physical conditions of eastern Trás-os-Montes extend beyond the Douro until south of the Serra das Mesas, a Portuguese continuation of the great central mountain system of Spain. Both elevation and rainshadow continue to limit productivity along the boundary zone. South of this, the lack of rainfall and the winter cold continue to be the obstacles to a more productive use of the land, but the causes are somewhat different. Although elevation decreases, outbreaks of cold from the Iberian *meseta* are a threat to crops through the winter. The growing season is longer than that of Trás-os-Montes, but so is the period of summer drought and, unfortunately, in a land of little rain, the evaporation rate is high during the spring and fall when there is maximum precipitation.[8]

There are minor areas of increased population near the eastern border of Middle Portugal, those of Sabugal, Portalegre, and Elvas. In each case there is a higher rainfall, due to somewhat greater elevation. In no case, however, could the population be called dense.[9] Beyond Elvas, toward the south, the

[7] Taborda, *Alto Trás-os-Montes* (author's translation), p. 21.

[8] The sparseness of population of the Alentejo has been attributed to the system of *latifundia*, the great estates. This may be accurate but one cannot be sure. We do not know that exploitation of a territory so limited by physical factors could be effectively accomplished in small units. Absentee ownership, also typical of the area, is, of course, another matter.

[9] The equation of increased population and rainfall is obvious in a comparison of the rainfall in H. Amorim Ferreira, *Carta Pluviométrica de Portugal* of 1943, with population density as shown on the Ribeiro map (see Note 2 of this chapter). One anomaly should be noted. The population density of the Spanish province facing the Sabugal area is virtually as low as any in Spain, although rainfall there, as in Sabugal, is a little higher than in the adjacent areas in Spain. This condition, in part at least, may be ascribed to the effects of the *Mesta* and the discouragement of agriculture in favor of sheep herding.

An Estate of the Lower Alentejo

obvious lack of appeal of the boundary zone continues to be shown in the sparseness of population. The length of the summer season and the evaporation rate both increase as total rainfall remains low down to the area of the lower slopes of the Serra do Caldeirão, which separates the Alentejo Province from the Algarve. Rainfall is higher here, but this advantage is more than offset by the nature of the soil materials. These schists do not allow an easy penetration of water. Rainfall mostly drains off by surface flow, and in these now deforested mountains each winter season sees the removal of another sheet of surface. Two generations ago, directly following upon the clearing of the natural vegetation, the harvests were copious. Now after years of erosion, the yield is but a fraction of that of the early years. Only at the extreme southeast is there a slight increase in the population of the border zone, but this is limited to the Portuguese side. There are two reasons for it: first, the mine of Sto. Domingos, producing copper and sulphur, supports several thousand people gathered immediately around it; [10] and second, the recently developed area of early vegetable production near Vila Real de Santo António at the mouth of the Guadiana River supports another concentration of population. Truck gardens here supply Lisbon with early vegetables. This phenomenon developed during recent generations as a result of improved transport. This population area, like that of Sto. Domingos, appears as merely a spot against the border, for it is limited to the coastal sands and does not follow the Guadiana upstream. Across the Guadiana, the Spanish area lacks the economic advantage of Vila Real. Spanish growers would not be able to compete in the Lisbon market due to import restrictions, and there is no nearby home market to support such an enterprise.

[10] This cluster appears on the Ribeiro map as a spot of settlement in an otherwise meagerly inhabited area. Such an agglomeration of population probably exists also in the area near the mines of Rio Tinto, which are geologically akin to those of Sto. Domingos and represent the Spanish counterpart. Unfortunately there is no Spanish map of sufficient detail available to substantiate such an assumption.

RIVERS AS BOUNDARIES

National states require more than a frontier zone. They require a boundary line. This line in Iberia, more often than not, is a river; such is the case for over 60 per cent of the Portuguese land boundaries and for over 70 per cent of the eastern border. Along the eastern border, rivers are signally useful, for they not only traverse land of little attraction, but have carved deep, steep-sided canyons into the plateau surface, which effectively cut communications. Fifty-four per cent of the eastern border is along such canyons. A striking example is that of the international Douro between Paradela and Barca d'Alva, where the river flows through a canyon, at times with vertical walls several hundred feet high, for over 76 miles, falling 1600 feet in the distance. The great descent takes place through a series of falls and rapids, making navigation impossible.[11] A left-bank tributary of the Douro, the Agueda River, and farther south its affluent, the Tourões, both act as boundaries. The Agueda cuts a deep canyon; the Tourões does so in part of its course.

South of the Tourões, in the relatively high country between Ciudad Rodrigo and Guarda, the boundary does not follow rivers but is drawn across the headwaters of several small streams. It follows approximately the divide between the drainage of the Agueda and Côa rivers. Beyond this area, in the Tejo drainage, streams again are used to mark the boundary line; the Torto and the Erges both run well below the surface of the country on either side of them. Where the Erges meets the Tejo, the boundary line turns sharply west, to follow the larger stream in a deep canyon to its juncture with the Sever. Here it again turns sharply, in an acute angle, to follow the canyon of the latter almost to its source in the Serra de S. Mamede. South of the Serra there is another stretch of boundary that is erratic and oblivious of hydrography. This is part of the territory passed back and forth in the marriage portions of the

---

[11] None of the Portuguese boundary streams are navigable for useful distances except at the lower extremities.

Mértola on the Guadiana River

seventeenth and eighteenth centuries whose ultimate possession was decided arbitrarily, although in amity, and largely in
disregard of physical factors.

A water course again becomes the boundary along the lower
Caia River just before it joins the Guadiana. The boundary
follows this river and the Guadiana almost to the latitude of
Mourão, where there are other lands of frequent exchange between the Iberian monarchs. These too were finally apportioned
amicably, although arbitrarily in terms of physical factors. The
boundary of Portugal here runs well to the east of the Guadiana.
At the latitude of Serpa the boundary meets and follows the
Chança (Chanza) River to its juncture with the Guadiana, and
then again follows the Guadiana. This is the ultimate stretch
of the international boundary southward to the ocean.

In Iberia, particularly, another fact makes rivers useful as
boundaries. This is the great difference between flood and low
water, and the resulting economic uselessness, which makes
them barriers rather than means of communication. The bare,
deforested Iberian *meseta* has a quick run-off, and the floods
of the rainy season are sudden and devastating wherever the
streams are not incased between high canyon walls. This factor
makes the use of the streams difficult for virtually any purpose.[12]

Rivers have served Portugal and Spain as boundaries as far
back in time as we have knowledge of the peninsula. For Rome
it was standard practice to use them, and this was especially
notable in Iberia. As stated above, it was the Roman intent,
for reasons beneficial to herself in the matter of control, to follow custom where possible, and her choice commonly mirrored
the established habits of the local peoples. It should not be surprising that later boundary makers and present governments
have found rivers to be equally serviceable.

[12] The Guadiana at Mértola increases over eighty feet (25 meters)
above low water during flood. The Tajo at Alcántara increases up to
nearly one hundred feet (30 meters). Hermann Lautensach, "Lebensraumfragen der Iberischen Völker," *Lebensraumfragen Europäischer
Völker, I: Europa,* p. 505; Pedro M. González Quijano, *Mapa pluviométrico de España,* pp. 277 et seq.

Nevertheless, no matter how useful the rivers have been as political boundaries, the most important factor in the political separation of the Iberian countries is the distribution of population. Some of the distribution is, no doubt, induced by the fact of the boundary, but it is clearly obvious that the physical nature of the land has limited population density along the line of the present frontier.

CHAPTER 16

Environment and Culture

OVER THE HABITABLE world there have been repeated migrations. With negligible exceptions, even the most undesirable regions have had repeated contacts with outsiders and have experienced changes brought about by the transfer of culture entailed in such movements of peoples. As both sedentary and migrating groups of farmers are tenacious of their culture traits, usually there is not an elimination of those of either (unless one population is obliterated as were many tribes of American Indians), but only a partial elimination and an amalgamation of the residues.

The process of amalgamation is ordinarily not difficult, for migrating farming groups do not bring entirely different attitudes to the areas of their choice. As they do not wander aimlessly and choose casually, but rather select areas to their taste, the ideas and techniques that they bring with them are fitting to the situation. Unless forced, such migrants choose regions that are environmentally satisfactory to their knowledge, equipment, and techniques. Thus one might expect that cultivated areas would exhibit few radical changes in the fundamental

Tajo River in Cáceres Province, Spain

forms of land use throughout their historical development, and that their inhabitants would likewise show few radical differences in attitudes toward the exploitation of the land from those people who preceded them. This conclusion seems to be borne out in Iberia.

PERSISTENCE OF CULTURE REGIONS OF THE PENINSULA

The relative importance of Iberian areas seems to have changed but little through all of the time of their development. Through history and the periods of time illuminated for us by archaeology, the peripheries have been prized and the interior has been an area of little appeal, except for the centuries of Visigothic control. These Romanized herders preferred the grazing lands of the bleak *meseta* to the productive agricultural lands of the fringes. On the peripheries the Mediterranean coasts have been consistently underlined, since the first Neolithic farmers arrived there, as the premium area of all of the peninsula. The area of the northern mountains, while not so heralded as the Mediterranean zone, has supported a relatively dense population throughout all time for which there is information. The Romans found large numbers of people who had been long rooted there, and even the recent industrialization of parts of this zone, which has made dramatic social and economic changes, has not brought about an important shift in the balance of population of the peninsula. The west coast has consistently had less appeal for migrants—perhaps because it lies farther from the source of immigration—but the population density has been surprisingly high, at least in the northwest, since the late Neolithic period.

On the other hand, the historical zones of disinterest remain unattractive for habitation. The *meseta* has always been an area of sparse settlement, an area of the import of ideas and technical improvements from the peripheries, where contact with other cultures has begotten political and military ferment but hardly cultural originality. Even the reconquest, although

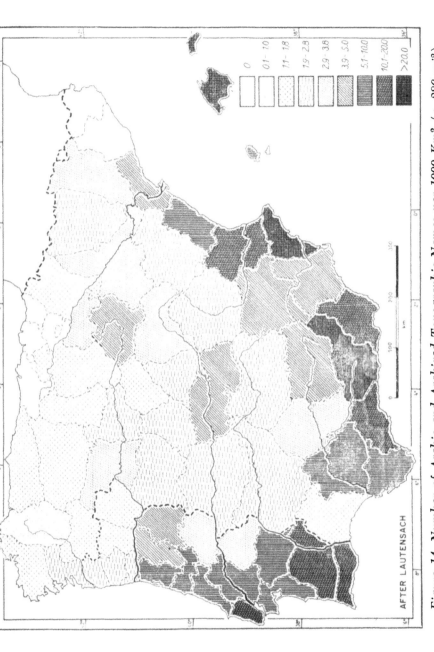

Figure 14. Number of Arabic and Arabized Topographic Names per 1000 Km² (c. 386 mi²)
(Without River Names)

AFTER LAUTENSACH

208

chiefly the achievement of *meseta* kingdoms, was given its first impulse in the northern periphery by men of the north or possibly the northwest;[1] it was aimed at the profit to be had from the southern peripheries. It has been, and is, an area of strong local cultural character, not because of its own ferment, but because it is an area in which the contrasting ideas of disparate peripheries can be blended. Aside from simple geography, this fact is the basis of its political importance.

Whatever knowledge we have of the historical and prehistorical backgrounds of the peninsula indicates that changes have been "more of the same." Migrations and cultural introductions have come from comparable environments, and the areas chosen by immigrants have been elected in terms of environmental preference. Changes have been mostly of degree, not of kind. The developments of culture and techniques have increased earlier capacities of the areas involved, but have not changed their relative importance. Humid Iberia has been dominantly Central European in the basis of its culture for as far back as we have knowledge. This equates with the facts of climate, soils, and vegetation, which are closely similar to those of Central and northern Europe. The same can be said for the south. The Iberian Mediterranean bears the same relation to the eastern Mediterranean in its physical nature and in its cultural development.

The population pattern of the present is approximately that of all earlier time, insofar as we know it, with unimportant exceptions. For example, during the "desolation" of Alfonso I and the succeeding centuries, in parts of the *meseta* the population was reduced. This change, however, merely accentuated the normal condition, sparsity in the *meseta* as opposed to the well-populated peripheries. Today the areas of slowest increase in population are *meseta* provinces, which have a history of the lowest population densities of the peninsula.[2] Even Madrid

---

[1] See above, Chap. 11.

[2] Luis de Hoyos Sáinz, *La Densidad de población y el acrecentamiento en España*, pp. 178–179.

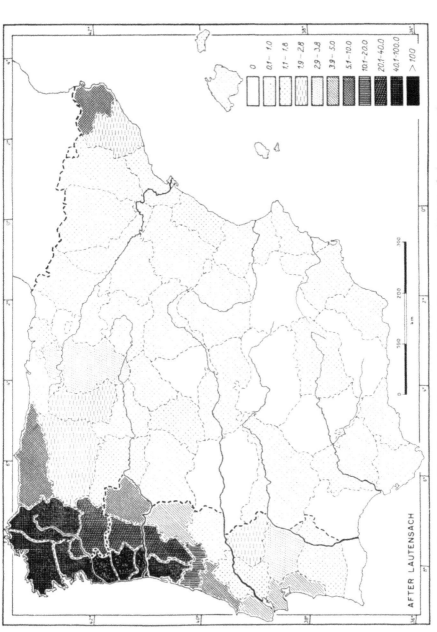

Figure 15. Number of Germanic Place Names per 1000 Km² (c. 386 mi²)

0
0.1 – 1.0
1.1 – 1.8
1.9 – 2.8
2.9 – 3.8
3.9 – 5.0
5.1 – 10.0
10.1 – 20.0
20.1 – 40.0
40.1 – 100.0
> 100

AFTER LAUTENSACH

does not bring about an exception to the general historical situation. Its growth, comparable to the recent world-wide urban growth and the growth of political capitals, has been great. If the figures for the present city are added to those of the *meseta,* the relation between *meseta* and periphery is somewhat altered, but insufficiently to shift the balance. The areas of greatest increase are the historical and prehistorical zones of attraction along the fringes.

The same conclusion may be bolstered more specifically in the case of Portugal. For example, the interest of the Mediterraneans became attenuated with the decrease northward of the summer dry period. The Carthaginians limited their activities almost entirely to the south and southwest coasts. The Greeks may have traded with the north, but the last of the Greek *-oussa* names toward the north was that near Lisbon, at the beginning of the transition from Mediterranean to north European climate. The Mediterranean Romans showed an avid interest in Galicia at the outset,[3] but after the gold sands were worked out they paid scant attention to any of the north except for purposes of strategic control. The same lack of interest was true of the Visigoths, and the Moslem distaste for the rainy lands was obvious. They could not have been evicted so quickly had they wanted to hold the north.

On the contrary, the Central Europeans made their strongest mark in the north country that was similar to their homeland in Central Europe. Not only did they like it but they needed the forests for their animals,[4] whereas the Mediterraneans, with their more casual interest in the care of animals, had no such point of view. This forestland exploitation was a feature of the life of the pre-Indo-European immigrants as well as that of the Celts and of the Swabians.

The middle region of Portugal, between the Tejo and Douro

[3] Juan Maluquer de Motes, "Los Pueblos de la España céltica," *Historia de España,* Tomo I, Vol. III, Pt. 1, 9, 79.

[4] Grahame Clarke, "Farmers and Forests in Neolithic Europe," *Antiquity,* XIX, No. 74 (June, 1945), 67, 70.

rivers, is transitional geomorphologically, in climate, soils, and vegetation. Culturally it shows a mixture of traits, derived from the north on the one hand and from the south on the other. This is clearly indicated in the maps taken from Lautensach's study of Arabic and Germanic topographic names.[5]

A review of the history of land-use in the peninsula indicates a considerable conservatism for all major areas.

[5] Hermann Lautensach, "Uber die topographischen Namen arabischen Ursprungs in Spanien und Portugal," *Die Erde,* Nos. 3–4 (March–April, 1954), pp. 219–243.

CHAPTER 17

The Geographical Basis of Portuguese Political Independence: A Summation

WHILE THIS WORK is primarily concerned with Portugal, the evidence considered in it has been drawn widely from areas throughout the peninsula. In conclusion it will be well to focus especially upon Portugal, in a summation of the factors that have conduced to its separateness and to its independence. I shall discuss them in what seems to me to be the order of their importance.

In the first place, and of crucial importance, are the immemorially old cultural differences between the humid periphery of the peninsula and the *meseta*. These are basically associated with the physical differences of the areas involved. Thus all of the north and northwest is set apart from the remainder of the peninsula. In the second place, the present international border, throughout most of its extent, runs through zones of disinterest, imposed by physical conditions. These zones have isolated Portugal, especially in the north, the cradle area of Portuguese independence. Thirdly, there was the political isolation of present northwest Portugal during parts of the eighth and ninth centuries, following the creation of the so-called "desert" lands by Alfonso I. During this period an early line of cultural subdivision was made more pronounced, and economic ties were re-oriented in such fashion that Galicia and Portugal were drawn apart. Fourthly, there were the troubles of the *meseta* kingdoms prior to and at the time of Affonso Henriques. Although this fact was of lesser importance than the factors outlined above, it had great immediate importance. The Portuguese had freedom of action that would have been impossible had they been opposed by the full power of the kings of León. The above factors are salient, for they were crucial to the establishment of freedom in the germ cell of the Portuguese state, whereas the extensions southward from that region were partly a result of political opportunism, after the northern nucleus had been established as an independent unit.

Aside from the factors enumerated above, there were others less important, yet contributing to Portuguese independence. For example, even after the time of Affonso Henriques, Spain continued to be beset with internal difficulties which occupied her attention. Even more important than this was the Spanish concern with the loot to be gained from the Moslem kingdoms to the south. These Spanish preoccupations offered Portugal relative freedom from threats to her independence. Particularly after 1267, peace offered the opportunity to assimilate the southern lands, the Alentejo and the Algarve, which had become integral parts of the Portuguese state by the time that Spain had ended its Moslem conquest in 1492.

Much has been written and said about Portuguese position relative to the Atlantic. Part of it has been sheer mysticism. But after that element has been discarded, there is merit in the idea that this position has contributed to Portuguese independence. In the first place, due to partial isolation, it offered Portugal the opportunity to turn her back upon Iberian turmoil, just as Holland was able to ignore Germany.[1]

[1] For this comparison see Otto Jessen, "Politisch-geographische Betrachtungen über die Iberische Halbinsel," *Freie Wege Vergleichender Erdkunde*, pp. 118–139, especially pp. 131–134.

Yet no freedom of action would have served, had Portugal not been equipped to take advantage of it. Here again good fortune was a factor. Few countries have a harbor of the quality of that of Lisbon, and the harbors of Porto, Setúbal, and others along the west and south coasts serve most parts of the country. They are an obvious invitation to the sea. Not the smallest item in Portugal's luck is the fact that none of the international rivers is navigable into Spain, so that there has been no tendency for either country to follow the stream beyond the border. However, as ports may be valuable even without further inland navigation, the Portuguese harbors might have tempted Spain had she needed them. Luckily for Portugal there is no part of Spain, except for the very sparsely populated section in the province of Cáceres and a part of the middle Tajo River valley, that is closer to Lisbon than to one of the Spanish ports. The *ria*, or river-mouth, harbors of Galicia are infinitely superior to the harbor of Porto, as that of Cádiz is to those of the Algarve.

The association with England was mutually advantageous. Both countries profited by the trade that was established. Portugal also received much-needed support on several occasions when otherwise it might well have lost its independence.

Portuguese independence and the reconquest of her territories from the Moslems came concurrently with improved techniques in navigation, and when Portugal was in a position to take advantage of them. These techniques were to be credited partly to the Arabs, who also offered specific knowledge as to the areas of Africa, and within Portugal there were men suitable to the opportunities available. Under such conditions opened the great Age of Discoveries, commonly associated with the name of Prince Henry, the Navigator. The Age of Discoveries created a sense of common experience, common pride, and a community of interest for all parts of the country, welding it together as perhaps nothing else could have done.

The division between modern Portugal and Galicia cannot be satisfactorily explained by age-old differences, even by those that have existed since prehistoric time—notably the physical differences between the two peoples involved, and the suggestive fact of the Roman division along the Minho River—because modern Galicia is closely allied to Portugal in its language and customs. The separation of the two areas, politically, results partly from the fact that Galician physical connections with Spain are better than those between Spain and Portugal. It results also, again in part only, from the fact that its emotional ties with Spain have been strong ever since the time of the establishment of the great peregrination to Santiago de Compostela, which bound the area to Spain in a very positive sense. There is also the important fact, albeit negative, that Galicia did not take part with Portugal in the Age of Discoveries. The sense of common experience in this achievement which is felt by all Portuguese is lacking to Galicians. On the contrary, through the centuries that have elapsed since Galicia was separated from the culturally similar Minho, its economy has become closely geared into that of Spain. Its harbors and pastoral industry have become essential to Spanish economy. Through time, the political boundary, somewhat arbitrary at first, has become culturally satisfactory, if not perfect.

THE OFFSIDE POSITION OF PORTUGAL

Through the history and prehistory of the area of present Portugal, there seems to have been a general lack of interest in the region. The area was offside and apparently little exploited throughout most of prehistory. There is almost no evidence of Upper Paleolithic occupation nor of settlement during most of the Neolithic, much of the Bronze Age, and considerable parts of the Iron Age. The Tartessians had but slight interest even in the Algarve, an area physically similar to their own. To the conquerors of Iberia, Portugal has always been a largely unwanted, but sometimes troublesome land, which had to be taken under control to secure the places of greater profit elsewhere in the peninsula. Phoenicians and Carthaginians were little attracted, except to small areas of the south. Greek interest was even less than that of the Punic peoples. To the Romans only limited areas were attractive; the remainder was

occupied and controlled only because its occupants presented
a threat to their use of desirable territories, especially that of
the lower Guadalquivir River. Within Portugal proper the only
areas of primary importance for the Romans were those of the
lower Tejo River, Beja, Evora, the Algarve in part, and a few
others of lesser importance. For the most part Roman interest
was attracted elsewhere. The Visigoths had even less interest
than did the Romans but assumed control for essentially the
same reasons that had prompted Rome. It was Swabian in-
transigence that prompted the Visigoths to end the independence of the Swabian kingdom in the late sixth century. Moslem
interest, like that of the other Mediterranean conquerors, was
mostly confined to areas that are climatically Mediterranean.

The exceptions to the above statements apply to the north.
To the unidentified prehistoric Central European farmers, and
to the Celts and the Swabians, the humid northwest of the
peninsula was attractive in itself, and the early fundamentals
of Portuguese culture are largely to be traced to these peoples.

Spain at times has wanted to "fill out the peninsula," but with
no more than this vague and ultimately profitless mystique on
the one hand and the meagreness of Portuguese territory on
the other, she has made little consistent effort. Actually, Spain
needs very little that now appertains to Portugal. The economy
of Portugal, like that of Spain, is based on agriculture and stock
raising, and the chief products of one country duplicate those
of the other. Furthermore, Spain has already in her possession
nearly all of the good irrigable lowlands near the border, those
of the Guadiana, the Alagón, the Salor, and the Tajo around
Alcántara. To the west of these there are large areas of little
promise, for the most part, before the fertile coastal regions are
reached. The only good reason for Spanish desire to control
Portugal now—aside from the megalomaniac drive for prestige
through size which afflicts most national states—would be
based upon a matter of defense strategy.

Portugal is an excellent land for a frugal, self-sufficient agriculture. The proof of this can be seen in the number and variety
of things that can be cultivated there. But it does not offer

A SUMMATION

surpluses for absentee owners nor does it lend itself to large ownership.[2] It offers no prize for conquest, but only satisfaction to humble farmers on the land. The values of Portugal are fundamental but unappropriable. They can be realized only by people with the age-old traditions and techniques of frugality, such as those of the Portuguese farmers.

[2] The Alentejo, of course, is to be excluded from the above two statements. It is an area of large estates and of absentee ownership. The great bulk of the population of Portugal is not there, however, but in areas for which the above statements are valid.

Bibliography

Albright, W. F. *The Archaeology of Palestine.* Pelican Books, Harmondsworth, 1949.

Almagro, Martín. "La Invasión Céltica en España" (*Historia de España,* ed. Ramón Menéndez Pidal). Madrid, Espasa Calpe, S.A., 1952. Tomo I, Vol. II, 3–278.

Alt, E. *Klimakunde von Mittel-und-Südeuropa* (*Handbuch der Klimatologie,* ed. W. Köppen and R. Geiger). Berlin, Borntraeger, 1932. Vol. III, Pt. M.

Altamira y Crevea, Rafael. *Historia de España* (3rd ed.) Barcelona, Edit. Hered. de Juan Gili, 1913. Vol. III.

Bang, Martin. "Expansion of the Teutons (to A.D. 378)" (*Cambridge Medieval History*). Cambridge, The University Press, 1911. Vol. I, Chap. VII.

Basto, Artur de Magalhães. "A Fronteira Hispano-Portuguesa," *O Instituto,* LXX (1923), 57–69, 103–117.

Bertrand, Louis. *The History of Spain.* New York, D. Appleton–Century Co., 1934.

Birot, Pierre. *Le Portugal.* Paris, Librairie Armand Colin, 1950.

Bloch, Raymond, and René Joffroy. "L'Alphabet du Cratère de Vix," *Revue de Philologie,* XXVII, No. 11 (1953), 175–191.

Bosch Gimpera, Pedro. *Etnología de la Península Ibérica.* Barcelona, Editorial Alpha, 1932.

———. "Los Iberos," *Cuadernos de Historia de España.* Buenos Aires, 1948. IX, 5–93.

———. "Two Celtic Waves in Spain" (Sir John Rhŷs Memorial Lecture of November 8, 1939), *Proceedings of the British Academy,* XXVI (1940), 25–148.

220

BIBLIOGRAPHY

——— and Pedro Aguado Bleye. "La Conquista de España por Roma (218 a 19 a. de J. C.)" (*Historia de España*, ed. R. Menéndez Pidal). Madrid, Espasa Calpe, S.A., 1935. II, 3–283.

Bramão, Luis (ed.). *Carta dos Solos de Portugal*. Lisboa, Estação Agronómica Nacional, 1949.

Cardozo, Mário. *Citânia e Sabroso*. Guimarães, Instituto para a Alta Cultura, 1948.

Caro Baroja, Júlio. "Los Arados españoles, sus tipos y repartición," *Revista de Dialectología y Tradiciones populares*, V (Madrid, 1949), No. 1.

———. *Los Pueblos de España*. Barcelona, Editorial Barna, S.A., 1946.

———. *Los Pueblos del Norte de la Península Ibérica*. Madrid, Consejo Superior de investigaciones científicas, 1943.

———. "La Vida agraria tradicional reflejada en el arte Español," *Estudios de Historia Social de España*, I (Madrid, 1949), 44–138.

Carpenter, Rhys. *The Greeks in Spain*. London and New York, Longmans, Green and Co., 1925.

"Carta de S.M. para los estados de Portugal condoliéndose de la muerte del Rey D. Sebastián y avisando del derecho que tiene a la sucesión de aquel reino . . . 14 de Marzo de 1579" (*Colección de documentos inéditos para la historia de España*). Madrid, Impr. de la viuda de Calero, 1862. XL, 230–232.

Castañeda Alcover, Vicente. [Accumulated Index], *Boletín de la Real Academia de la Historia*. Madrid, 1947.

Clark, J. G. D. *Prehistoric Europe, the Economic Basis*. London, Methuen, 1952.

Clarke, Grahame. "Farmers and Forests in Neolithic Europe," *Antiquity*, XIX, No. 74 (June, 1945), 57–71.

O Clima de Portugal. Observatório do Infante D. Luiz (Later, Serviço Meteorológico Nacional). Lisboa. Pts. I–V (1942–1946); Pts. VI–VII (1950–1952).

Coon, Carleton S. *The Races of Europe*. New York, Macmillan, 1939.

Corrêa, A. A. Mendes. "Celtas na Beira," *Boletim da Casa das Beiras*, X, No. 6 (Lisboa, 1943), 5–11.

———. *A Geografia da pré-história*. Porto, 1929.

———. "A Lusitânia pré-romana" (*História de Portugal*). Barcelos, Portucalense Editora, 1928. Vol. I.

———. *Os Povos Primitivos da Lusitânia*. Porto, 1924.

———. *Raízes de Portugal* (2nd ed.). Lisboa, Revista "Occidente," 1944.

Correia, Vergílio. "O Domínio Romana," *História de Portugal*. Barcelos, Portucalense Editora, 1928. Vol. I.

BIBLIOGRAPHY

Costa, J. Carríngton da. "Evolução do meio geográfico na Pré–história de Portugal" (*Congresso do Mundo Português*). Lisboa, Comissão executiva dos centenários, 1940. I, 11–58.

Cutting, Charles L. *Fish Saving*. London, L. Hill, 1955.

Dantin Cereceda, J. *Distribución geográfica de la población en Galicia*. Madrid, Centro de Estudios Históricos, 1925.

Daveau, J. "Géographie botanique du Portugal: 1. La Flore littorale du Portugal," *Boletim da Sociedade Broteriana*, XIV (1897), 3–54; 2. "La Flore des plaines et collines voisines du littoral," XIX (1902), 3–140; 3. "Les stations de la zone des plaines et collines," XXI (1904–05), 16–85.

David, Charles Wendell (ed. and trans.). *De Expugnatione Lyxbonensi*. New York, Columbia University Press, 1936.

David, Pierre. *Etudes historiques sur la Galice et le Portugal du VIe au XIIIe siècle*. Lisbon and Paris, Livraria Portugalia, 1947.

———. "Les Saints Patrons d'églises entre Minho et Mondego jusqu'à la fin du XIe siècle," *Revista Portuguesa de História*, II (1943), 221–254.

Del Castillo, Alberto. "El Neoeneolítico" (*Historia de España*, ed. Ramón Menéndez Pidal). Madrid, Espasa Calpe, S. A., 1947. Tomo I, Vol. I, Pt. 4, 489–714.

Del Villar, Emilio H. *Los Suelos de la Península Luso-Ibérica*. English text by G. W. Robinson. Madrid, 1937.

Dias, Jorge (António Jorge Dias). *Aparelhos de elevar a Agua de Rega*. Porto, Junta de Província do Douro-Litoral, 1953.

———. *Os Arados Portugueses e as suas prováveis origens*. Porto, Instituto para a Alta Cultura, 1948.

———. "Las Construcciones circulares del Noroeste de la Península Ibérica y las citánias," *Cuadernos de Estudios Gallegos*, VI (1946), 173–194.

———. *Rio de Onor*. Porto, Instituto de Alta Cultura, 1953.

———. *Vilarinho da Furna*. Porto, Instituto para a Alta Cultura, 1948.

Dixon, Pierson. *The Iberians of Spain and Their Relations with the Aegean World*. London, Oxford University Press, 1940.

Dominguez Ortiz, António. "La Población española a lo largo de nuestra historia," *Boletín de la Real Sociedad Geográfica*, LXXXVI, Nos. 4–6 (April–June, 1950), 250–285.

Dunbabin, T. J. *The Western Greeks*. Oxford, Clarendon Press, 1948.

Edrisi, Abu-Abd-Alla-Mohamed-al. *Descripción de España*. Madrid, 1901.

Erdmann, Carl. "A Adapção do título de Rei por D. Afonso Henriques" (*Congresso do Mundo Português*, trans. Rodolfo Frederico

BIBLIOGRAPHY

Knapic). Lisboa, Comissão executiva dos centenários, 1940–1942. II, 55–72.

Feio, Mariano. *A Evolução do relevo do baixo Alentejo e Algarve.* Lisboa, 1952.

Ferreira, H. Amorim. *Distribuição da chuva no território do continente Português* and *Carta Pluviométrica de Portugal.* Lisboa, Observatório do Infante D. Luiz, 1943.

Ferreira, J. Augusto. *Memórias Archaeológico-históricas da Cidade do Porto.* Braga, 1923. Vol. I.

García y Bellido, António. *Hispania Graeca.* 3 vols. Barcelona, Instituto Español de Estudios Mediterráneos, 1948.

——. *La Península Ibérica en los comienzos de su historia.* Madrid, Consejo Superior de Investigaciones Científicas, 1953.

——. "Protohistoria," "Colonización Púnica," and "La Colonización Griega" (*Historia de España*, ed. R. Menéndez Pidal). Madrid, Espasa Calpe, S.A., 1952. Tomo I, Vol. II, 281–310, 311–494, 495–680.

García Mercadal, J. (trans. and ed.). *Viajes de extranjeros por España y Portugal.* Madrid, Aguilar, S.A., 1952.

Gaussen, H. "Le Milieu physique et la forêt au Portugal," *Revue Géographique des Pyrénées et du Sud-Ouest,* XI, Nos. 3–4 (Toulouse, 1940), 219–267.

Girão, Aristides de Amorim. *Condicões geográficas e históricas da autonomia política de Portugal.* Coimbra, Coimbra Editora L^(da), 1935.

——. *Geografia de Portugal.* Porto, Portucalense Editora, 1949–1951.

——. "Imposibilidade de sustentar pela geografia a separação política entre Portugal e Espanha," *Biblos,* V (1929), 304–314.

——. "Origines de l'état Portugais," *Revue Géographique des Pyrénées et du Sud-Ouest,* XI (1940), Nos. 3–4 (Toulouse, 1941), 155–158.

Gonzales, Júlio. "Repoblación de la 'Extremadura' leonesa," *Hispania, Revista española de historia,* XI, 202–264.

González Quijano, Pedro M. *Mapa pluviométrico de España* (text and map of nine sheets). Madrid, Consejo Superior de Investigaciones Científicas, 1946.

"Le Grand Cratère de Vix: produit de l'Italia meridionale ou 'vase etrusque'? Quelques théories à ne pas prendre 'à la lettre.'" *Revue Archéologique,* Ser. 6, XLIII (Jan.–March, 1954). No author given.

Guiart, Jules. "Anthropologie des populations dolichocéphales de l'Europe Méridionale et de l'Afrique Septentrionale" (*Congresso*

do Mundo Português). Lisboa, Comissão executiva dos cen-
tenários, 1940. XVII, 365–386.
Hawks, Christopher, and Jacquetta Hawks. Prehistoric Britain.
Pelican Books, Harmondsworth, 1949.
Herculano, Alexandre. História de Portugal (7th ed.). Paris and
Lisboa, 1914–1916.
Hessinger, Eduardo. "La Distribución estacional de las precipi-
taciones en la península Ibérica y sus causas," Estudios Geográficos,
X, No. 34 (Feb., 1949), 59–128. Trans. Valentín Masachs Ala-
vedra. Madrid, Instituto Juan Sebastian Elcano, 1949.
Hoyos Sáinz, Luis de. La Densidad de población y el acrecenta-
miento en España. Madrid, Instituto Juan Sebastian Elcano,
1952.
————— and Nieves de Hoyos Sancho. Manual de Folklore. Madrid,
Revista de Occidente, 1947.
Jessen, Otto. "Politisch-geographische Betrachtungen über die
Iberische Halbinsel," Freie Wege Vergleichender Erdkunde,
München and Berlin, 1925. pp. 118–139.
King, Georgiana G. The Way of Saint James. 3 vols. New York
and London, G. P. Putnam's Sons, 1920.
Klein, Julius. The Mesta, a Study in Spanish Economic History,
1273–1836. Cambridge, Harvard University Press, 1920.
Krüger, Fritz. El Léxico rural del noroeste Ibérico. (Trans.)
Madrid, 1947.
Lautensach, Hermann. "Die diluviale Umwelt des Menschen in
Portugal" (Congresso do Mundo Português). Lisboa, Comissão
executiva dos centenários, 1940. XVIII, 706–756.
—————. "Geopolitisches von der Spanisch-Portugiesischen Grenze,"
Zeitschrift für Geopolitik, V (1928), 371–374.
—————. "Die Iberische Halbinsel als Schauplatz der geschichtlichen
Bewegung," Zeitschrift der Gesellschaft für Erdkunde zu Berlin,
Nos. 3/4 (June, 1948), 101–123.
—————. "A Individualidade geográfica de Portugal no conjunto da
Península Ibérica," Boletim da Sociedade de Geografia de Lisboa,
XLIX (1931), 362–409. Originally published, in a somewhat
shorter form, in Jahrbuch der geographischen Gesellschaft zu
Hannover, 1928, pp. 215–248.
—————. "Lebensraumfragen der Iberischen Völker," Europa (Le-
bensraumfragen Europäischer Völker). Leipzig, Quelle & Meyer,
1941. I, 493–536.
—————. "Der politische Dualismus der Iberischen Halbinsel," Zeit-
schrift für Geopolitik, VI, No. 2 (1929), 782–788.
—————. "Portugal: Auf Grund eigener Reisen und der Literatur."

224

BIBLIOGRAPHY

1. "Das Land als Ganzes," *Petermann's Mitteilungen*, No. 213 (Gotha, 1932); 2. "Die portugiesischen Landschaften," *ibid.*, No. 230 (Gotha, 1937).

———. "Über die topographischen Namen arabischen Ursprungs in Spanien und Portugal," *Die Erde*, Nos. 3–4 (1954), pp. 219–243.

Leite, Jerónimo Dias. *Descobrimento da Ilha da Madeira.* Barcelos, 1947.

Lévi-Provençal, Evariste. *Histoire de l'Espagne musulmane.* 3 vols. Paris and Leiden, 1950–1953.

Livermore, H. V. *A History of Portugal.* Cambridge, University Press, 1947.

Lopes, David. "O Domínio Arabe," *História de Portugal.* Barcelos, Portucalense Editoria, 1928. I, 391–432.

Lopes, João Baptista da Silva. *Relação da derrota naval, façanhas e successos dos cruzados que parti rão do escalda para a terra santa no anno de 1189.* Lisboa, 1844.

López Cuevillas, Florentino y Joaquín Lorenzo Fernández. "Las Habitaciones de los Castros," *Cuadernos de Estudios Gallegos,* No. 5, Tomo II (Santiago de Compostela, 1946–1947), 5–74.

López Ferreiro, António. *Historia de la Santa A. M. Iglesia de Santiago de Compostela,* Santiago de Compostela, Imp. del Seminário conciliar central, 1902. Vol. V.

Lutz, H. F. *Viticulture and Brewing in the Ancient Orient.* Leipzig, J. C. Hinrichs, 1922.

Macalister, R. A. S. *Tara, a Pagan Sanctuary of Ancient Ireland.* New York and London, C. Scribner's Sons, 1931.

Macedo, F. Newton de. "O Domínio Germânico" (*História de Portugal*). Barcelos, Portucalense Editora, 1928. I, 298–388.

Maluquer de Motes, Juan. "Los Pueblos de la España céltica" (*Historia de España*, ed. R. Menéndez Pidal). Madrid, Espasa Calpe, S.A., 1954. Tomo I, Vol. III, Pt. 1, 5–194.

———. "Pueblos Ibéricos," (*Historia de España*, ed. R. Menéndez Pidal). Madrid, Espasa Calpe, S.A., 1954. Tomo I, Vol. III, Pt. 2, 305–370.

Martínez Santa-Olalla, Júlio. *Esquema paletnológico de la Península Hispánica* (2nd ed.). Madrid, 1946.

Melón y Ruiz de Gordejuela, Amando. *Geografía histórica española.* Madrid, Editorial Voluntad, 1928. Vol. I.

Menéndez Pidal, Ramón. *La España del Cid.* Buenos Aires and Mexico, 1939.

———. "El Imperio romano y su provincia" (*Historia de España,* ed. R. Menéndez Pidal). Madrid, Espasa Calpe, S.A., 1935. II, ix–xl.

———. "Introduction," *España Visigoda* (*Historia de España*, ed. R. Menéndez Pidal). Madrid, Espasa Calpe, S.A., 1940. III, vii–lv.

Merino, Abelardo. "El Regionalismo peninsular y la geografía histórica," *Boletín de la Real Sociedad Geográfica*, LVIII (1916), 280–318.

"Le Mobilier Funéraire de la Tombe de Vix," *La Revue des Arts*, No. 4 (1953), pp. 99–202. No author given.

Nowell, Charles E. *A History of Portugal.* New York, Van Nostrand, 1952.

Obermaier, Hugo, and António García y Bellido. *El Hombre prehistórico y los orígenes de la humanidad* (2nd ed.). Madrid, Revista de Occidente, 1941.

Peres, Damião. "A Actividade agrícola em Portugal nos séculos XII a XIV" (*Congresso do Mundo Português*). Lisboa, Comissão executiva dos centenários, 1940. II, 465–480.

———. *Como nasceu Portugal.* Porto, Portucalense Editora, 1946.

———. "Origens da nacionalidade" (*Congresso do Mundo Português*). Lisboa, Comissão executiva dos centenários, 1940. II, 13–33.

———. "A Reconquista Cristã" (*História de Portugal*). Barcelos, Portucalense Editora, 1928. I, 433–480.

Pericot García, Luis. *La España primitiva.* Barcelona, Editorial Barna, S.A., 1950.

———. *Las Raices de España.* Madrid, Consejo Superior de Investigaciones Científicas, 1952.

Piel, Joseph M. *Os Nomes germânicos na toponímia portuguesa.* 2 vols. in 1. Lisboa, Impr. Nacional, 1936.

Pinto, Sergio Silva. "O Bispo de Braga, Balcónio, e a primeira conversão dos Suevos," *Braga, Boletim do Arquivo Municipal*, I, No. 13 (Dec., 1949), 407–416.

Prestage, Edgar. "The Chivalry of Portugal," *Chivalry*, ed. E. Prestage. New York, A. A. Knopf, 1928. pp. 141–165.

Ramon, José and Fernández Oxea. "Toponímias agrícolas gallegas," *Cuadernos de Estudios Gallegos*, V, No. 16 (1950), 221–240.

Rau, Virginia. *Sesmarias medievais portuguesas.* Lisboa, 1946.

"Relación de la entrada del duque de Braganza y del de Barcelos su hijo en esta corte á besar las manos á S.M. en 17 de enero 1581," *Colección de documentos inéditos para la historia de España.* Madrid, Impr. de la viuda de Calero, 1862. XL, 383.

Ribeiro, Orlando. "Cultura do Milho, economía agrária e povoamento," *Biblos*, XVII. No. 2 (Coimbra, 1941), 645–663.

———. (ed.). *Distribüição da população de Portugal.* Lisboa,

BIBLIOGRAPHY

Instituto para a Alta Cultura, Centro de Estudos Geográficos, 1946.
———. *L'Ile de Madère.* Lisboa, Congrès Internationale de Géographie, 1949.
———. *Portugal (Geografía de España y Portugal,* ed. Manuel de Terán). Barcelona, Montaner y Simón, S.A., 1955. Vol V.
———. *Portugal, o mediterráneo e o atlántico.* Coimbra, Coimbra Editora Limitada, 1945.
———. "Villages et communautés rurales au Portugal," *Biblos,* XVI, No. II (Coimbra, 1940), 411–425.
Russell, P. E. "João Fernandes Andeiro at the Court of John of Lancaster," *Revista da Universidade de Coimbra,* XIV (1940), 20–30.
Sampaio, Alberto. "As Vilas do Norte de Portugal," *Estudos históricos e económicos.* Paris–Lisboa, Livraria Chardron, 1923. I, Pt. 1.
Sánchez Albornoz y Menduiña, Claudio. "Divisiones tribales y administrativas del solar del reino de Asturias en la época romana," *Boletín de la Real Academia de la Historia,* XCV, No. 1 (July–Sept., 1929), 315–395.
———. *La España Musulmana.* Buenos Aires, El Ateneo, 1946. Vol. I.
———. "Itinerário de la conquista por los musulmanes," *Cuadernos de Historia de España.* Buenos Aires, 1948. Vol. X.
———. *Ruina y extinción del municipio romano en España e instituciones que le reemplazan.* Buenos Aires, Facultad de filosofía y letras, 1943.
São Payo, D. A. Conde de (D. António). "Esboço da carta histórica de Província de Trás-os-Montes (séculos XIII a XIX)" *(Congresso do Mundo Português).* Lisboa, Comissão executiva dos centenários, 1940. II, 421–433.
Schmidt, Ludwig. "Teutonic Kingdoms in Gaul" *(Cambridge Medieval History).* Cambridge, The University Press, 1911. I, Chaps. 1, 10.
Schulten, Adolfo. *Historia de Numancia.* Barcelona, 1945.
Semmelhack, Wilhelm. "Beiträge zur Klimatographie von Nordspanien und Portugal," "Die Niederschlagsverhältnisse," *Archiv der Deutschen Seewarte,* XXXIII, No. 2 (Hamburg, 1910), 1–90.
———. "Niederschlagskarte der Iberischen Halbinsel," *Annalen der Hydrographie,* LX (1932), 28–32, and map.
———. "Temperaturkarten der Iberischen Halbinsel," *Annalen der Hydrographie,* LX (1932), 327–333.
Smith, H. R. W. Review of *Hispania Graeca,* bv António García y Bellido. *American Journal of Archaeology,* LVII, No. 1 (Jan., 1953), 31–36.

BIBLIOGRAPHY

Soares, Torquato de Sousa. "O Repovoamento de Norte de Portugal no século IX" (*Congresso do Mundo Português*). Lisboa, Comissão executiva dos centenários, 1940. II, 395–415.

Soils and Men, Yearbook of the United States Department of Agriculture. 1938.

Solé Sabarís, L., and Llopis Lladó. *España, Geografía física* (*Geografía de España y Portugal*, ed. Manuel de Terán). Barcelona, Montaner y Simón, S.A., 1952. Vol. I.

Stremme, H. (chairman). *General Map of the Soils of Europe*, by the Sub-Commission for the European Soil Map of the Fifth Commission of the International Society of Soil Science. German text published in Danzig, 1927. Trans. by Dr. W. G. Ogg, 1929.

Taboada, Jesus. "La Cultura de los verracos en el noroeste hispánico," *Cuadernos de Estudios Gallegos*, IV, No 12 (1949), 5–26.

Taborda, Vergilio. *Alto Trás-os-Montes.* Coimbra, Impr. da Universidade, 1932.

Torres, Casimiro. "Las Kassitérides," *Cuadernos de Estudios Gallegos*, IV (1945), 621–632.

———. "Límites geográficos de Galicia en los siglos IV y V," *Cuadernos de Estudios Gallegos*, IV, No. 14 (1949), 367–384.

Torres, Manuel. "Las Invasiones y los Reinos Germánicos de España (Años 409–711)" (*Historia de España*, ed. R. Menéndez Pidal). Madrid, Espasa Calpe, S.A., 1940. III, 1–140.

———. "La Península hispánica, província romana (218 a de J.C.–409 de J.C.)," *Historia de España*, ed. R. Menéndez Pidal. Madrid, Espasa Calpe, S.A., 1935. II, 287–519.

Torres Rodríguez, C. "La Venida de los Griegos a Galicia," *Cuadernos de Estudios Gallegos*, VI (1946), 195–222.

Troll, Karl. "Ozeanische Züge im Pflanzenkleid Mitteleuropas," *Freie Wege Vergleichender Erdkunde*, München and Berlin, R. Oldenbourg, 1925. pp. 307–335.

Varro, M. T. *M. T. Varro on Farming*, trans. Lloyd Storr-Best. London, G. Bell & Sons, Ltd., 1912.

Vasconcellos, J. Leite de. "Delimitação da fronteira Portuguesa," *Boletim da Classe de Letras*, XIII (1918–1919), Academia das sciencias de Lisboa, 1921, pp. 1275–1292.

———. *Origem histórica e formação do povo Português*, Mémoires publiés par la Société portugaise de Sciences Naturelles, série anthropologique et archéologique, No. 2. Lisboa, 1923.

———. *Religiões da Lusitânia.* 3 vols. Lisboa, Imprensa Nacional, 1897, 1905, and 1913.

Vega Inclan, Marques de la. *Guía del Viaje a Santiago* (Libro V del Codice Calixtino), Real Academia de la Historia. Madrid, 1927.

228

BIBLIOGRAPHY

Velloso, J. M. de Queiroz. *Como perdemos Olivença.* Lisboa, 1932.
Velozo, Francisco José. "Ainda a contribüição Luso-Galaica para a reconquista. A primeira invasão de Entre-Douro-e-Minho pelos Arabes," *Braga, Boletim do Arquivo Municipal,* I, No. 12 (Aug., 1949), 313–328.

————. "Contribüição Luso-Galaica para a reconquista," *Minia,* I, No. 2 (May, 1945), 100–112; No. 3 (Dec., 1946), 223–237.

————. "A Lusitânia Suevico-Bizantina," *Bracara Augusta,* II, No. 2 (July, 1950), 115–154; II, No. 3 (Oct., 1950), 221–256; II, No. 4 (Feb., 1951), 389–402; IV, Nos. 1–3 (Dec., 1952), 46–69.

————. *Oestrymnis.* Braga, Associação Luso-Britânica do Minho, 1956.

————. "As Origens Nacionais de Portugal e de Espanha e o domínio Islâmico na península." Reprint from the journal *Gil Vicente.* Guimarães, 1951.

Viana, Abel. "Os Problemas do Asturiense Português" (*Congresso do Mundo Português*). Lisboa, Comissão dos centenários, 1940. V, 169–194.

Viana, Mario Gonçalves. *Rei D. Deniz.* Porto, Editora Educação Nacional, 1937.

Willkomm, M. *Grundzüge der Pflanzenverbreitung auf der Iberischen Halbinsel (Die Vegetation der Erde,* ed. A. Engler and O. Drude). Leipzig, O. Spamer, 1896. Trans. for the *Boletim da Sociedade Broteriana* of Coimbra as "As Regiões botánicas de Portugal." See V, No. 17 (1900), 89–154.

Index

Acid-humic soil: areas of, 47

Acorns: Celtic dependence upon, 78

Affonso Henriques: revolts of, against Theresa, 167; proclaims independence of Portugal, 168; reign of, 174, 175, 213; mentioned, 155, 165, 173, 174

Afonso Henriques. See Affonso Henriques

Africa: Germanic tribes move to, 127

Agadir. See Gadir

Agriculture: affected by rivers, 19; effect of, upon soils, 48; of Neolithic people, 64–65; of Megalithic people, 66; early Portuguese lag in advancement of, 68; of the Celts, 73, 75–78, 84–85; as women's work, 75–76; of Tartessians, 92; in the Algarve, 106; in southern Portugal, 117; along humid fringe, 108–109; introduction of draft animals into, 119; affected by plow, 119; varying attitudes of Germans toward, 122–123; as factor in migration, 129; in the Algarve, 141; and irrigation by Moslems, 141, 142; in Tejo Valley, 142; affected by war, 158–159, 160, 161; affected by isolation of Portugal, 162–163; in relation to love of the land, 172; Portuguese, encouraged by kings, 179–180; and use of the land, 179–182; as base of Portuguese economy, 185, 216; on Leonese plateau, 195; at mouth of Guadiana River, 199; effect of soil on, 199; rich lands for, 206; and contribution of farmers to Portuguese culture, 216

Agropedic soil: areas of, 48

Agueda River: as boundary, 200; mentioned, 21, 22

Akhila: allied with Moslems, 144–145

Akragas: 98 n. 42

Alagón River: irrigable lands of, 216

Alalia: founding of, 96; mentioned, 99

Alalia: battle of, 114

Alans: entry of into Iberia, 124–125; location of in Iberia, 125; move of to Africa, 127; mentioned, 122

Alava, province of: Celts in, 72

Alazis, Abde (Moslem leader): 139, 145

Albuquerque: 189

Alcácer do Sal: Moslem conquest of, 139; under the Moslems, 142, 143; falls to crusaders, 174, 175; mentioned, 89 n. 4, 91, 158

Alcalá: site of, 67

Alcalar dolmen: development of, 67

Alcañices: 169

236

Raymond as viceroy, 164; part taken by Theresa, 167; physical anthropology of, 168 n. 20; entryways into, 170; Tâmega River Valley as border of, 194; Roman interest in, 210; *ria* harbors of, 214; cultural similarity to Portugal, 214–215; mentioned, 12, 19, 157; separation from Portugal, 214–215

García (Galician king): revolt against, 155

Gates of Hercules: 101

Gathering: as form of economy, 78

Gelmierez, Diego (Archbishop): 156

Geologic history: in creation of landforms, 3–10 *passim*, 11–31 *passim*

Geology. *See* Geologic history; Topography

Gerez Mountains: *serras* of, 192; mentioned, 11, 12. *See also as Montanhas*

Germans. *See* Immigrants to Iberia: Germans

Gijón: 146

Glacial Period: 61, 63

Godoy: insists Olivença kept by Spain, 188

Goidelic Celts: 71, 84

Gold: as trade article of Tartessians, 92

Grain: in Tejo Valley, 142

Granada: fall of, 162; mentioned, 178

Granite formations: of Minho province, 12, 14; of Serra da Estrêla, 24; soils developed from, 46

Grape cultivation: of North Portugal, 55; introduction of, 98 n. 42; 117

Greeks. *See* Immigrants to Iberia: Greeks

Group of Friends of Olivença: 188

Guadalajara province: 61

Guadalquiver River: agriculturists of, 66; Tartessians in, 91; metal traffic in, 92, 93; silver mines near, 102; Moslems in, 143; Romans in area of, 216; mentioned, 9

Guadiana River: Celts living near, 82; flood plain settled by Arabs, 142; as boundary, 177, 202; lands of, 216; mentioned, 30, 172, 173, 199, 202 n. 12

Guarda: settled in 1197, 170; mentioned, 12, 22, 200

Guarda Gate: 22, 23

Guimarães: document of 841 from, 153; battle near, 167; mentioned, 151, 153, 179 n. 21

Guipúzcoa, province of: 72

Hallstatt culture: 80 n. 49

Hallstatt techniques: of Goidelic Celts, 83

Hannibal: army of, 103, 104

Helvetians (Celts): 122

Henry (Prince) the Navigator: 184, 214

Henry of North Portugal: marriage to Theresa, 164; increases strength, 166; death of, 166

Herculano: cited, 149, 168 n. 20

Herding: of Megalithic men, 66; of the Celts, 73–75, 75, 78, 84–85; at Gadir, 94; along humid fringe, 108–109; reduced by introduction of plow, 119; varying attitudes of Germans toward, 122–123; as factor in migration, 127–129; effect of military raids on, 163; in Alentejo, 172; and use of land, 180–182; attitude of Visigoths toward, 180–181; as Spanish industry, 180–181; by Visigoths, 206; as base of Portuguese economy, 216

Hermos (Gediz) River: 96

Herodotus: 82, 95

Hesiod: cited, 91

Hiram of Tyre: 93

Holland: soil of, 48

Holly Region: vegetation of, 54; mentioned, 52

Homen River: 14

Homo Sapiens: appearance of in Iberia, 60

Horsts: of Marão and Padrela, 14

Huelva: area of, 91, 173

Huelva helmet: 94 n. 24

Humid Iberia: vegetation of, 53–56; subdivision of, 54–56; dominantly Central European in culture, 208

Humid siallitic soil: area of, 47

Hunting: by Paleolithic men, 60, 61; affected by climate, 63; by Celts, 75, 76 n. 29

242

www.ingramcontent.com/pod-product-compliance
Ingram Content Group UK Ltd.
Pitfield, Milton Keynes, MK11 3LW, UK
UKHW041005050325
455862UK00002B/130